AI Explained

A Guide for Non-Technical Readers

Pete Rai
Dame Wendy Hall

WILEY

Published by John Wiley & Sons, Inc., Hoboken, New Jersey.

Library of Congress Cataloging-in-Publication Data has been applied for:

Print ISBN: 9781394431144
ePDF ISBN: 9781394431168
ePub ISBN: 9781394431151
oBook ISBN: 9781394431175

Cover Design: Wiley

SKY10163251_072226

To my wonderful family—Mandy, Kiran, and Callum—for their love and support.

—Pete

To my wonderful husband Peter, who says I always have a lot of explaining to do.

—Wendy

Contents

About the Author

Pete Rai is an independent AI researcher and principal engineer with experience across a range of technology companies. Working at the frontier of applied AI in enterprise contexts, he holds more than two dozen patents and is active in responsible AI initiatives. He brings a practitioner's perspective on how AI is built, deployed, operated, and governed in real-world settings.

Dame Wendy Hall, DBE, FRS, FREng is Regius Professor of Computer Science and Director of the Web Science Institute at the University of Southampton. She became a Dame Commander of the British Empire in the 2009 UK New Year's Honours list and is a Fellow of the Royal Society, the Royal Academy of Engineering, the ACM, the BCS, and the IET. Dame Wendy was co-Chair of the UK government's AI Review, which was published in October 2017, and is a member of the AI Council. In 2023 she was appointed to the United Nations high-level advisory body on AI. Her current policy work focuses on global AI governance for the good of society.

Introduction

Two hundred years ago, Mary Shelley published a book that challenged its readers with a profound reflection on the consequences of unchecked scientific and technical hubris. She recounted the story of Dr. Frankenstein, a young and ambitious scientist who believed he could overcome the limitations of the human condition and conquer death itself. But the creature he created was not the one he had dreamed of—it became a monster of his nightmares.

Over the years, Shelley's book has become the seminal work of Gothic horror and a staple of analysis for English Literature students. Two important themes emerge from its pages: *the dangers of overreaching ambition* and *the responsibility and consequences of innovation.*

Her book is part of a rich tradition of stories exploring such ideas—one that stretches back as far as human history. For centuries, authors and philosophers have used these themes to question the limits of humanity and ask what it means to be human.

These musings, once thought to be abstract thought experiments, have now become some of the most pressing and immediate questions of our time. Science fiction has melded with reality. We now stand on the threshold of creating entities that *give the appearance*, at least, of thinking and behaving like us.

Behind the Curtain

In a world where technology has become an integral part of daily life, it's easy to find ourselves caught in a whirlwind of acronyms, buzzwords, and jargon. Every day seems to bring new concepts and phrases—each more confusing than the last. At the same time, the capabilities of technology are evolving at a breakneck pace. Features roll out rapidly, achieving ever more sophisticated and beneficial outcomes.

Trying to understand the world of artificial intelligence (AI) can feel like a journey through a confusing and mystifying landscape. But coming to grips with this technology is both important and necessary, as it will soon come to influence many aspects of our lives. In the coming years, AIs will become a vital part of law, medicine, art, transport, finance—and just about every other domain of daily life.

For most non-technical people, it can be hard to understand the mechanisms driving this process. While many can grasp the workings of physical machinery, the realm of abstract machines can feel other-worldly and difficult to fathom. It's hardly surprising that people often remark that "it's all magic"—an expression used to convey something that lies beyond immediate understanding.

But technology is not magic; it's a giant, intricate symphony of otherwise simple concepts and ideas. By revealing the secrets "behind the curtain," users of AI can gain a clearer and more confident understanding of what it is—and a deeper appreciation of its advantages and limitations.

Who Is This Book For?

This book is for anyone who wants to understand what artificial intelligence really is—beyond the buzzwords, headlines, and hype. You don't need a technical background and you won't find equations or programming tutorials here. What you *will* find is a clear and engaging guide to the ideas, implications, and realities of AI.

It's written for the curious and the thoughtful—people who want to make sense of a fast-changing world. That could include journalists, teachers, business leaders, policymakers, and professionals in industries likely to be reshaped by AI. It's also for readers who simply want to understand the technology that's becoming part of their everyday lives.

This is not a "how to build AI" book—nor is it a "how to best use AI" guide. Both types of books have value, but this is not the type of book we are presenting here. Instead, this book is for people who look at AI outcomes and ask, "How on Earth can this be happening?"—or, more precisely, "What underlying processes can achieve these outputs?" In a confusing world of technological advance, our hope is that this book gives you something to hold on to—a way to begin making sense of it all.

While those working within the computer and AI industries may find much of this material familiar, *this book is not written for engineers.* It is intended for intelligent, curious nonspecialists who want to think more clearly, critically, and confidently about the systems that are increasingly shaping our lives and our future.

To make this possible, we occasionally simplify, reorganise, or generalise concepts in ways that may feel imprecise or even unsatisfying to a technically trained reader. This is intentional. Our aim is to offer newcomers an accessible introduction and a gentle glide into a subject that can otherwise feel dense, fragmented, or intimidating.

If you are an expert reader already, then we ask for your indulgence. The framing used here is designed to open the door rather than to close it—removing unnecessary barriers so that more people can participate meaningfully in the conversations, decisions, and debates surrounding artificial intelligence.

So if you are curious but not confident, informed but not technical, or simply trying to make sense of the rapid changes around you—if you've ever felt like AI is something happening *to* you rather than something you can actively engage with—then this book is for you.

Demystifying AI

This book is a guide to help navigate the changes that are about to sweep over us all. Using simple, accessible language, it aims to chart a path through the labyrinthine world of AI—equipping readers with a clearer understanding and a deeper appreciation of its mechanisms, advantages, and limitations.

In **Chapter 1, "The Evolution of AI,"** the book begins with a concise chronicle of AI's evolution, tracing its historical roots and the key milestones that have shaped the landscape we see today.

From there, the book moves into a structured exploration of AI, dividing it into five distinct segments or realms. Each one reveals a different aspect of the technology—its core characteristics and its broader implications.

Chapter 2: Symbolic AI *Symbolic AI* is the traditional form of AI, built on predefined symbols, rules, and logic. It works like a computer programme that makes decisions based on explicit instructions—a model well suited to situations where predictability and consistency are essential. This chapter explores how symbolic systems formed the foundation of early AI, and why they remain relevant in many applications today.

Chapter 3: Statistical AI *Statistical AI* focuses on learning and making predictions from data. It uses statistical methods to identify patterns in large datasets, allowing it to make informed guesses or decisions. This chapter explores how this approach has revolutionised AI, driving major advances in areas such as language processing, image recognition, and predictive analytics.

Chapter 4: Connected AI *Connected AI*, which includes neural networks, is inspired by the human brain's ability to learn and recognise patterns. This chapter explores how these networks process information, learn from data, and have become fundamental to advances in complex AI tasks such as speech and visual recognition.

Chapter 5: Learning AI *Learning AI*, or *machine learning*, evolves through experience. Unlike rule-based systems, these models improve their performance as they are exposed to more data over time. This chapter explores key machine learning methods and how they have enabled AI to make decisions, solve problems, and even predict future outcomes.

Chapter 6: Generative AI *Generative AI* represents the frontier of AI's ability to produce original content. This chapter explores how these systems not only learn from data but also generate novel outputs—such as art, music, and text—extending AI into domains once thought to belong solely to human creativity.

It's important to recognise that while these categories offer a useful framework for understanding AI, they don't neatly reflect its historical development. In reality, AI has not evolved through separate, sequential phases, but through a complex, overlapping tapestry of ideas—each influencing, and being influenced by, the others. Earlier approaches haven't been discarded; instead, they form the foundation on which later innovations are built.

To support comprehension, each of the five chapters is divided into four parts:

Overview *A concise summary, offering a broad perspective on each AI phase.*

This section is designed to give readers a foundational understanding of each AI phase—highlighting the historical context, core concepts, and central themes, while avoiding overly technical detail.

In-depth *A deeper exploration delving into the nuances and complexities of each AI phase.*

This section offers a more detailed analysis and broader perspective, while maintaining clarity and accessibility for non-technical readers. For each phase of AI, it aims to provide core insights that go beyond surface-level understanding.

Use Cases *Practical applications and real-world examples of each AI phase.*
This section brings the theoretical concepts to life by showing how they are used across industries and everyday situations. It aims to give context to the previous sections by illustrating how the technologies operate in the real world.

Conclusion *A brief reflection on the impact, challenges, and legacy of each phase.*
This section briefly summarises the significance, obstacles, and lasting effects of each phase. It encourages readers to appreciate the broader significance of the outlined technologies and to think critically about the ongoing evolution of AI.

While every chapter of this book is written in accessible, non-technical language, we recognise that the "In-depth" sections explore more detailed aspects of AI that may not align with everyone's immediate interests or needs. If you prefer, you can skip or scan the "In-depth" sections without missing the core ideas. The "Overview," "Use Cases," and "Conclusion" sections are designed to provide a complete and enriching understanding on their own.

As the book concludes, you'll find a speculative Afterword focused on the future of AI. It offers predictions about where the technology may be heading in the years to come. We explore the challenges AI could pose to individuals and societies, and consider how we might coexist with such transformative systems.

The Road Ahead

In the coming months and years, we will see computers performing actions that surprise, delight, and concern us in equal measure. Very soon, they will be capable of things that force us to ask profound questions about what makes us human—and what role AI should play in our lives and in our society.

As we all embark on this complex journey, remember that it need not be a solitary one. The pages that follow are here to serve as your companion and guide.

Whether you're an industry expert, a policymaker, a business leader, an impacted professional, or simply a curious mind, we hope this book will help you unravel the mysteries and confront the uncertainties of this technology—so that you can harness the potential of AI not as a passive observer, but as an active participant.

CHAPTER

1

The Evolution of AI

Artificial intelligence (AI) is a complex field that has evolved continuously over several decades. Its origins trace back to the period just before World War II, when the discipline we now call computer science had yet to take shape.

The journey from those early days to today's AI has been full of twists and turns. At times, external events accelerated its development; at others, progress stalled in long periods of relative stagnation.

But in recent years, a seismic shift has taken place.

Driven by rapid advances in computation, storage, digital data, and global connectivity, the field has undergone a dramatic and sudden expansion. New applications and possibilities are emerging at an astonishing pace. It's now impossible to ignore the conclusion that AI will play a defining role in the future of human development.

Yet, amidst all this promise—and potential peril—it all traces back some 90 years to a conceptual and infinite roll of virtual tape.

The Birth of Electronic Computation

In 1936, screen legend Charlie Chaplin captivated cinema audiences with his latest creation, *Modern Times*. In this film, he reprised his iconic character, the *Little Tramp*, this time confronting the relentless march of industrialisation.

Chaplin's character personified the ordinary person struggling to cope with a rapidly changing world. Over the course of the film, he unwittingly becomes a symbol of resistance against the dehumanising forces of modernisation.

The theme of humans reduced to cogs in the machinery of automation had already been explored a decade earlier in Fritz Lang's cinematic masterpiece, *Metropolis*. There, humans were consumed by machines—pitiless instruments of social inequality.

While mechanical automation had been a source of concern since the Industrial Revolution, audiences in 1936 would not have been thinking about electronic automation. Concepts such as digital systems, programming, and computation had not yet entered mainstream thought—and were far from the minds of ordinary people.

Fortunately for us, in that same year, an extraordinary person was hard at work.

Alan Turing and Computability

In 1936, within the hallowed halls of King's College, Cambridge, a young mathematician was quietly reshaping the course of history. Alan Turing, though unaware of the full extent of his influence at the time, was on the cusp of introducing ideas that would help give birth to our modern world.

Turing's journey began with a profound mathematical question posed by German mathematician David Hilbert: Could one devise an algorithm to determine the truth or falsehood of any mathematical proposition? This question, known as the *Entscheidungsproblem*, intrigued the mathematical community. It was part of a broader goal by Hilbert to establish a solid foundation for all of mathematics using formal logic. But his ambitions would face a formidable challenge from a young, audacious maverick—Kurt Gödel.

Gödel, an unconventional thinker, developed an innovative technique known as Gödel numbering, which he used to prove a groundbreaking concept we now call Gödel's Incompleteness Theorem. In this theorem, he showed that in any formal mathematical system, there exist true statements that cannot be proved from *within* that system. Though initially met with scepticism, his discovery would later shake the very foundations of mathematics.

Inspired by the lingering mystery of the *Entscheidungsproblem* and the challenge posed by Gödel's discoveries, Turing began to explore the nature of computation itself. In the spring of that year, he submitted his findings to the London Mathematical Society in a paper titled *On Computable Numbers, with an Application to the Entscheidungsproblem*.

Within this landmark paper, Turing introduced the concept of a universal machine—later commonly referred to as a Turing machine. This was an abstract computing device capable of executing any mathematical computation expressible as an algorithm. It was one of the first formal descriptions of a theoretical model of computation.

His Turing machine comprised an infinite roll of tape marked with symbols, a read-write head, and a set of rules for symbol manipulation. Turing demonstrated that this deceptively simple yet powerful machine could, in theory, carry out any computation described algorithmically. He also made a startling discovery: Some problems can never be solved by any machine, no matter how powerful. This result—known as the halting problem—defined fundamental limits of algorithmic computation.

Turing's work was instrumental in both introducing and formalising the idea of a universal computing machine—one that could simulate the behaviour of any other computing machine, given the right programme. His work forms the bedrock of the computational theories underpinning today's AI.

Turing would famously go on to play a key role in the team that broke the Nazis' Enigma code and helped to save countless lives. He will return later in our story—for, not content with introducing computation as we know it, he would later light the touchpaper for machine intelligence.

Claude Shannon and Information Theory

As Alan Turing was making waves with his seminal paper, another luminary in the world of computing was quietly beginning his graduate studies in electrical engineering at the Massachusetts Institute of Technology.

Claude Shannon was already excelling as both a mathematician and an electrical engineer. At MIT, he studied mathematics and electrical engineering while working under Vannevar Bush on the Differential Analyser—an early analogue computer. He also explored the logic of George Boole, whose work would later influence many aspects of computing.

During the war, Shannon joined Bell Labs to work—like Turing—on cryptography. While Turing was breaking codes, Shannon was laying the mathematical foundations of modern cryptography, helping prove the security of one-time pad encryption and defining principles for secure communication.

In 1948, he published a groundbreaking article in two parts in the *Bell System Technical Journal*, titled "A Mathematical Theory of Communication." This seminal work laid the foundation for what we now know as *information theory*.

At its core, this theory seeks to quantify and understand the transmission of information across communication channels. Shannon's genius lay in his ability to abstract complex problems into elegant mathematical constructs. He formalised the concept of a *bit* as the fundamental unit of information—a language for measuring data that we still use today.

Shannon also introduced a concept he called *entropy* to measure uncertainty in information. Although inspired by thermodynamics, Shannon's entropy was a novel mathematical framework for quantifying how much information is contained in a message. This insight became pivotal to the design of error-correcting codes—an essential element of modern digital communication.

Despite the abstract nature of his work, Shannon's ideas permeate our daily lives. They underpin the efficient transmission of data over the internet, the design of reliable digital storage, and the compression algorithms that allow us to stream high-definition video with ease.

Claude Shannon is often hailed as the "father of information theory." His work revolutionised digital communication and laid the groundwork for many of the technologies that power the digital age—including AI.

John von Neumann and Stored Programmes

In the immediate aftermath of World War II, the landscape of computing was dominated by machines with fixed, hard-wired programmes. These early computers were built for specific purposes. Changing their function often required rewiring, structural modifications, or even complete redesigns. As demand grew for machines that could tackle a wider range of tasks, the limitations of this rigid architecture became increasingly clear.

Among the brilliant minds involved in the Manhattan Project—the effort to build the first atomic bomb—was a Hungarian-American mathematician, physicist, and polymath named John von Neumann. Faced with the enormous computational demands of the project, von Neumann quickly recognised the impracticality of *reprogramming* machines by hand. This challenge pushed him towards a groundbreaking innovation.

The idea of a stored-programme computer was already taking shape among pioneers like J. Presper Eckert and John Mauchly. But it was von Neumann who, in 1945, formally articulated the concept in a way that would shape the future of computing. His work brought together emerging ideas about memory, logic, and control into a single, coherent framework that would define the architecture of modern computers.

The key insight was that programme instructions could be stored in memory alongside data, allowing computers to be reprogrammed without any physical modification. This became the foundation of what is now known as the *von Neumann architecture*.

At the heart of this model was the idea of *memory* capable of holding both instructions and data. This shift introduced programmatic flexibility—enabling a single machine to perform many tasks simply by changing the software it ran.

Today, the distinction between programme files and data files is so embedded in everyday computing that it's hard to imagine it had a starting point. Yet it did. Von Neumann's architecture laid the foundation for modern computing—making it possible to build the complex software systems that underpin everything from operating systems to artificial intelligence.

A New Science

Emerging from the nightmare of global war, early computer pioneers were driven by the belief that they could create tools essential for rebuilding a shattered world in a fresh and modern way.

The trio of Turing, Shannon, and von Neumann stand as towering figures in this transformative era—but they were far from alone. The landscape of early computing was teeming with visionaries, each contributing to the nascent field in their own distinctive ways—too many to name here. These pioneers worked across university mathematics departments, military institutes like Bletchley Park and ARPA, and renowned research centres and organisations such as Bell Labs, IBM, and the Rand Corporation.

Their collective efforts laid the groundwork for what would later become known as *computer science*—a discipline that blends mathematics, engineering, and logic.

In these academic and industrial crucibles, ideas were exchanged, theories forged, and innovations born. From the fundamental concepts of algorithms and computation to the practical engineering of computing machines, this dynamic community laid the foundation for the digital revolution that was yet to come.

The Dartmouth Conference

In the summer of 1956, Soviet leader Nikita Khrushchev broke with tradition and began openly criticising the regime of his predecessor, Joseph Stalin. A US federal court ruled that racial segregation on Montgomery buses was unconstitutional. A young, upcoming singer named Elvis Presley had just released a new song called *Heartbreak Hotel*. At the cinema, audiences queued to watch the science fiction film *Forbidden Planet*, with its thrilling themes of intelligent robots and out-of-control technology.

A Seminal Conference

Also that same month, at Dartmouth College in New Hampshire, a young and eager computer scientist was preparing rooms for the arrival of colleagues from around the world. They were gathering to discuss a niche and abstract topic: *machine intelligence*.

The college students had left for the summer break, and John McCarthy had seized the opportunity to organise what would later be recognised as a landmark event in the history of technology.

But that wasn't clear to McCarthy in those summer months in New England. At just 28, he had already built a strong reputation as a mathematician, having earned a PhD from Princeton. He had recently become one of the youngest professors on campus and was pressing ahead with cutting-edge research in the emerging field of computer science.

The Infancy of Computing

Computing was still in its infancy and, by modern standards, only a handful of computers existed at all. Those that did were used by research institutions, government agencies, universities, and large corporations. Their use was limited by extremely high costs, vast physical size, and complex, specialised operation.

If you had a spare million dollars in 1956, you could have purchased an IBM 704 with a few tens of kilobytes of memory—capable of processing 40,000 instructions per second. That's many billions of times less capable than a one-dollar computer chip available today.

AI Visionaries

So one might ask—given the state of the art at the time—why was McCarthy organising a conference on such an advanced topic? The answer is that he, like the other attendees, was a visionary.

In those early days of computing, the field generated enormous excitement among researchers. The focus quickly honed in on human-level capabilities—both physical (robotics) and cognitive (machine intelligence). At the time, these areas were seen as intertwined, not separate disciplines. Today, robotics and artificial intelligence are distinct fields, but in the 1950s, they were all part of a thrilling, unified vision of the future.

Earlier that decade, Alan Turing had written a paper titled *Computing Machinery and Intelligence*, where he set the stage for the idea of "thinking machines." Turing explored the possibility of machines exhibiting intelligent behaviour indistinguishable from that of a human. His paper sparked intense debate within the nascent computer science community and lit the fuse on a topic that still resonates today.

That fuse-wire burnt its way right through that sleepy college in New England in the summer of '56.

The Gathering

Turing had already—sadly and tragically—died before the conference began. But many of those who attended would, like Turing, go on to become the rock stars of computer science. In 1956, however, they were more scruffy academics than revered experts.

It's almost tempting not to name individuals, as so many great minds took part. But let's at least acknowledge the principal organisers of the event. Alongside McCarthy, there were: Marvin Minsky (who later founded the MIT AI Lab), Nathaniel Rochester (a key figure in early IBM computer development), Claude Shannon (the father of digital circuit design theory and information theory), and Oliver Selfridge (a pioneer in perception, pattern recognition, and machine learning).

The conference brought together experts from diverse fields, fostering discussions that laid the groundwork for artificial intelligence and helped shape both its early development and long-term direction. It was not a short affair, stretching over several weeks. Roaming the empty maths building, the participants would meet in ad hoc groups to probe various aspects of the problem domain.

Legacy

In hindsight, a great deal of mythology has developed around the conference—much of it deserved, but some rooted in hero worship.

The Dartmouth Conference is often miscredited as the birthplace of AI. In reality, its participants were building on ideas that had been circulating for over a decade. Some attendees were active in the cybernetics movement, which had already laid important groundwork for machine intelligence research.

Two key technical themes emerged from the proceedings: a focus on symbolic methodologies and a contrast between deductive and inductive systems (both of which we explore in later chapters). But perhaps the most enduring outcome of the workshop was the popularisation of the term *artificial intelligence*. This simple, memorable, and powerful phrase has echoed through the decades to the present day.

In the conference proceedings, we find a striking sentence:

> Every aspect of learning, or any other feature of intelligence, can in principle be so precisely described that a machine can be made to simulate it.

Right from the outset, computer scientists planted a marker pointing directly towards a future of intelligent machines. Was this prophetic insight—or hubristic boldness? One thing is clear: This was the beginning of a long tradition of overly optimistic and embellished claims—a pattern that has shadowed the field for decades and still persists today.

The Timeline of AI

The path of artificial intelligence to date has been winding and erratic—marked by moments of great promise, frustrating dead ends, and long periods where progress seemed to stall indefinitely.

Yet with each setback, the AI community persisted, building on the thoughts and achievements of those who came before them. It was an era of great ambiguity, rudimentary technology, and uncertain outcomes. Countless individuals toiled away, driven by a shared vision of machines that could one day think, act, and behave like us.

Their collective efforts—often against the odds—have brought us to where we stand today, reaping the fruits of their labour. Let's now explore the milestones, breakthroughs, and relentless spirit that have shaped the remarkable evolution of artificial intelligence.

It's worth noting that, while we present a timeline of AI here, *there is no single, universally agreed way to capture its genesis and history.*

Early Foundations (1940–1956)

The roots of artificial intelligence can be traced back to the 1940s—a time when the world was engulfed in the terrible events of World War II. Amid the chaos, a group of brilliant minds quietly laid the groundwork for a technological revolution that would one day shape the future of humanity.

At the heart of this foundational period was Alan Turing, whose work in the 1930s and 1940s was instrumental in defining the theoretical underpinnings of computation. His groundbreaking concept of the *Turing machine*—a theoretical model of computation—laid the foundation for modern computing.

At the same time, other trailblazers were making significant contributions in areas such as stored programmes, information theory, and programming languages.

Early artificial intelligence was closely intertwined with *cybernetics*—a field that gained prominence during this period. Coined by Norbert Wiener in 1948, cybernetics explored the relationships between control, communication, and intelligence—both in machines and living organisms.

Many early pioneers of AI were influenced by the emerging ideas of cybernetics. Alan Turing interacted with figures in the British cybernetics community, and Oliver Selfridge—a key figure at the 1956 Dartmouth Summer Research Project on Artificial Intelligence—made notable early contributions to pattern recognition that resonated strongly with cybernetic thinking.

Cybernetics also captured the public imagination. During this period, it featured in newspaper articles, radio programmes, and even popular films. The idea that machines could mimic intelligence and behaviour was already being explored—both in technical research and in cultural discourse.

This was a period marked by optimism, as pioneers set the stage for AI's emergence as a distinct field of study. It was the dawn of a new era—when the quest to replicate human intelligence and create thinking machines truly began.

The Birth of AI (1956–1969)

The 1950s ushered in a remarkable era of exploration as AI began to take shape. Emerging from a period of war and conflict, a mood of optimism fuelled intense research, leading to groundbreaking discoveries.

During this period, the dominant approach was *symbolic AI*—later referred to as "good old-fashioned AI" (GOFAI). Researchers sought to build intelligent systems using symbolic representations and rule-based reasoning. Early achievements included basic decision systems, game-playing programmes, and rudimentary natural language processing—all pioneering efforts to emulate human cognitive abilities.

However, not all researchers agreed on the best path forward. While symbolic AI dominated the era, alternative approaches—such as *connectionism*, which later inspired neural networks, and probabilistic methods rooted in statistical reasoning—were the subject of early research and theoretical debate.

The birth of AI was marked by great enthusiasm and a shared belief that intelligent machines were not only possible but also within reach. Researchers tackled challenges such as problem-solving, reasoning, and knowledge representation, convinced that these systems could soon match human intelligence.

Although early AI systems showed promise, they also revealed fundamental limitations—foreshadowing the challenges that would define AI's development for decades to come. Nevertheless, the stage was set for AI to evolve, advance, and shape the future of human–machine interactions.

The First AI Winter (1970–1980)

The early promise and optimism of AI gave way to a challenging period known as the *first AI winter*, during the 1970s and 1980s. This phase was marked by scepticism, reduced funding, and a decline in AI research activity.

As the 1960s transitioned into the 1970s, the initial excitement surrounding AI began to fade. A major reason for this shift was the growing gap between lofty expectations and the actual progress being made. Early AI systems struggled with complex, real-world problems, exposing the limitations of existing approaches.

These difficulties were compounded by structural constraints—limited computational power, scarce data, and overhyped claims about AI's capabilities. As disillusionment spread, many governments and organisations began to question AI's practical feasibility, and research funding had begun to dry up.

Yet while mainstream enthusiasm faded, important progress continued behind the scenes. Basic rule-based tools for decision-making were beginning to emerge in specific industries. Meanwhile, alternative approaches based on networks of simple, interconnected units (the ancestors of modern neural networks) were quietly researched by a small but dedicated group of researchers.

Although AI had entered a winter, these quiet developments ensured the field would not remain dormant forever.

AI Research Resurgence (1980–1987)

Following the challenges of the first AI winter, the field experienced a revival in the 1980s and early 1990s. This period was marked by renewed enthusiasm, technological progress, and a broader approach to AI research.

A significant development was the growing success of earlier forms of AI such as expert systems, which aimed to encapsulate domain expertise within a computational structure. These began gaining traction in industries like healthcare, finance, and engineering. Although these systems used narrow reasoning based on lists of rules and domain-specific knowledge, they nonetheless delivered some practical value and demonstrated a tangible return on investment.

Another key factor driving this resurgence was a gradual shift in research focus. Symbolic AI, which had dominated earlier decades, began to face growing scrutiny as researchers recognised its limitations. This encouraged exploration of alternative paradigms and more practical approaches suited to real-world constraints.

Further momentum came from the growing availability of computational power and digital data. Advances in hardware, algorithms, and data storage enabled researchers to tackle more complex problems and process larger datasets than ever before.

AI research also became more interdisciplinary, drawing on fields such as cognitive psychology, neuroscience, and linguistics. Researchers aimed to develop systems capable of mimicking human cognitive functions—including natural language understanding, reasoning, and learning.

This resurgence laid the groundwork for AI's diversification into multiple subfields, including machine learning, computer vision, natural language processing, and robotics. It was a pivotal era that restored momentum to AI research and set the stage for the breakthroughs that would define the decades to come.

The Second AI Winter (1987–1997)

The 1990s marked a period of renewed challenges and scepticism, often referred to as the *second AI winter.* Following the resurgence of AI in the 1980s, enthusiasm began to cool and funding declined. Once again, AI was perceived as having overpromised and underdelivered.

Several factors contributed to this downturn. A key issue was the widening gap between AI's theoretical potential and the practical limitations of existing technology. While researchers had made meaningful progress, AI systems still fell short of the ambitious expectations set by funding bodies and industry leaders.

The limitations of these systems in handling uncertainty, context, and real-world complexity became increasingly apparent. Early AI struggled with tasks requiring common-sense reasoning or the interpretation of vague or ambiguous information. These shortcomings reinforced doubts about AI's viability beyond highly specialised applications.

Despite the setbacks, important work continued. Researchers refined existing methods and advanced newer approaches that had begun gaining momentum in the late 1980s, such as probabilistic reasoning and reinforcement learning. These developments strengthened the foundations of modern machine learning and helped prepare the ground for later breakthroughs in neural networks.

In hindsight, the second AI winter served as a critical learning period for the field. It underscored the importance of setting realistic expectations, fostering interdisciplinary collaboration, and committing to sustained innovation—lessons that would ultimately drive AI's transformation in the years to come.

Rise of Machine Learning (1998–2015)

The mid-2000s marked a transformative era in AI research, driven by the resurgence of *machine learning*. This period saw major advancements in algorithms, computing power, and data availability—leading to breakthroughs that would redefine artificial intelligence.

A key factor behind this resurgence was the renewed focus on machine learning, a subfield of AI concerned with building models that learn from data. While machine learning had been part of AI since its earliest days, it gained new prominence as researchers moved beyond handcrafted, rule-based systems and embraced more flexible, data-driven approaches.

This era also saw the expansion of neural networks. Loosely inspired by the structure of the human brain, neural networks began to demonstrate value in tasks such as image recognition, speech processing, and natural language understanding. Their success paved the way for AI systems that could process and interpret information in increasingly human-like ways.

It is also important to clarify the relationship between neural networks and machine learning, as these terms are often confused within the media, but in reality they are closely intertwined. Within the chapters of this book, we treat them distinctly to help non-technical readers understand the concepts more clearly.

However, in practice, the two areas have become deeply integrated. Neural networks are not an alternative to machine learning, but a powerful family within it—one that has become the dominant class of machine-learning techniques. Modern neural nets use machine-learning methods to adjust their internal parameters automatically as they learn from data, enabling them to recognise patterns, make predictions, and generate content with remarkable accuracy.

Progress in machine learning was enabled by two critical developments. First, a substantial increase in computational power—driven by advances in hardware—allowed researchers to use more advanced algorithms, train more complex models, and process larger datasets.

Second, the rise of the internet, social media, and sensor-rich environments produced vast amounts of digital data. This gave researchers access to an unprecedented volume of information with which to train AI systems, enabling models to recognise patterns and make accurate predictions.

The rise of machine learning reinvigorated the AI community and sparked a wave of innovation and investment. Startups and tech giants alike began applying machine learning to a wide range of real-world problems.

During this period, the terms *machine learning* and *artificial intelligence* began to be used interchangeably—though not quite accurately. It was by the end of this era that AI-powered applications started to become a part of daily life, marking the beginning of AI's widespread societal impact.

Renaissance and Commercialisation (2015–Present)

This was an era of unprecedented growth and innovation, marking the renaissance and commercialisation of AI—a shift that continues to shape today's technological landscape. AI has moved from research labs into everyday life, becoming an integral part of both the digital and physical worlds.

This transformation has been driven by the convergence of several key factors. First, advances in machine learning and deep learning have enabled AI systems to achieve remarkable results in pattern recognition, natural language understanding, and decision-making. Deep learning, in particular, has propelled neural networks to the forefront of modern AI, making them the backbone of today's most powerful applications.

Another critical driver has been the availability of massive datasets and powerful computing infrastructure. The rise of the internet, mobile technologies, and data-driven industries has provided researchers with vast amounts of training data. Meanwhile, cloud platforms and specialised AI hardware (such as GPUs and TPUs) have made high-performance computing more accessible, allowing organisations to scale AI initiatives rapidly.

The late 2010s also saw significant investment in AI research and development from tech giants, startups, and governments alike. These investments pushed the boundaries in areas such as computer vision, reinforcement learning, and generative AI.

AI applications have become pervasive across industries—transforming healthcare, finance, manufacturing, and entertainment. AI-powered systems now drive personalised content recommendations, enhance medical diagnostics, optimise supply chains, and support the development of autonomous vehicles.

As AI's influence on society deepens, ethical considerations have taken centre stage. Issues such as bias, transparency, and accountability have led to the creation of ethical AI frameworks, guidelines, and legislation aimed at ensuring these systems are used fairly and responsibly.

The commercialisation of AI has become a powerful force behind its expansion. Businesses increasingly recognise AI's potential to improve operations, boost productivity, and unlock new revenue streams. Today, the AI industry is a thriving global ecosystem of startups, technology providers, and service companies supporting organisations in every sector.

Generative AI and Machine Creativity (2022–Present)

AI has entered a transformative phase, marked by the rise of *generative AI* and machine creativity—pushing the boundaries of what technology can achieve. This period represents a remarkable fusion of art, technology, and innovation, where AI systems are beginning to display creative capabilities once considered uniquely human.

At the heart of this evolution are generative AI models, which have shown astonishing abilities to produce content across a range of domains—including images, music, prose, and interactive media. *Machine creativity* is now a prominent theme, as AI systems are no longer just automating tasks but generating original artistic and intellectual work.

Advances in *natural language processing* have also transformed how machines understand and generate human language. Large-scale language models can now engage in complex conversations, generate human-like text, and utilise context with unprecedented depth. This has fuelled the rise of *conversational AI*, with chatbots, virtual assistants, and AI-powered customer service agents becoming increasingly human-like in their interactions.

Alongside the excitement surrounding generative AI, ethical considerations have taken centre stage. Questions of authorship, originality, bias, misinformation, and the societal implications of AI-generated content are now widely debated. The balance of power between human and machine creativity—once a science fiction scenario—has become a real-world policy issue, shaping conversations on regulation, intellectual property, and the future role of AI in the creative industries.

Summary

What lies ahead for AI is uncertain, but recurring patterns and promising directions are emerging—we will examine these more closely in the closing Afterword chapter.

The journey AI has taken so far stands as a testament to human ingenuity and perseverance. Throughout its history—briefly chronicled in this chapter—AI's evolution has been a tapestry woven with moments of triumph and uncertainty. From the post-war era to the present day, its trajectory has been marked by cycles of hope, disillusionment, and resurgence.

At the heart of this narrative lies a legacy of individuals who embodied innovation, resilience, and an unwavering belief in AI's potential. Armed with rudimentary tools and constrained by the limits of their time, they achieved remarkable feats in environments that would seem inconceivably primitive to today's AI developers.

Through scarce hardware, data limitations, algorithmic uncertainty, unclear use cases, and funding gaps, these pioneers persisted. Their unshakable faith in machine intelligence propelled them forward, laying the foundations for today's breakthroughs.

Now, we stand at the dawn of a new AI era—one in which AI has broken through into many facets of society. It is a time when its capabilities increasingly rival those of its human creators, reshaping how we live, work, and interact with the world.

As you engage with AI—whether seeking travel recommendations, refining an email, enhancing an image, or exploring creative tools—take a moment to reflect on the visionary minds who made this technology possible.

Let us thank them for leaving an indelible mark on our modern world—a legacy that will continue to shape our future for decades to come.

CHAPTER

2

Symbolic AI

In the aftermath of World War II, there was a significant shift in how societies perceived the role of experts and centralised planning. Emerging from the chaos of global war, many nations placed growing trust in expert-led systems built on logic, rationality, and formal rules.

Even in countries not rooted in socialist principles, there was a widespread belief that expert insights—grounded in structured, logical thinking—were key to solving the complex problems of rebuilding, stabilisation, and growth. Technocratic institutions run by specialists began to emerge in fields as varied as economics, infrastructure planning, defence strategy, and healthcare. This mindset, along with its broader themes and long-term effects, is often commonly referred to by contemporary historians as *the post-war consensus*.

The shift was mirrored in many areas and found expression within computer science through the emergence of various forms of *symbolic AI*—a traditional approach to AI based on symbols, rules, and logic. This early form of machine intelligence reflected a growing belief in the power of organisation, formal reasoning, and structured knowledge.

Overview

Before exploring the details of symbolic AI, we will begin with a concise overview of the key ideas, techniques, and motivations behind it. We start by introducing how symbolic approaches represent knowledge, apply rules, and support reasoning, giving you a clear sense of what symbolic AI is and why it matters, without getting into the detailed mechanisms.

Enabling Machine Understanding

Early, pioneering symbolic AI systems aimed to directly encapsulate the knowledge and reasoning of domain experts in ways that could be processed and applied by machines. The idea of constructing "an expert in silicon" was a direct and obvious route towards achieving the goals set out at the Dartmouth Conference. Many revered ancient philosophers had presented clear arguments in favour of logic and rationality, and Enlightenment thinkers had carried these ideas forward through their work on empiricism and rationalism.

In tandem, researchers were developing fields like *modern linguistics*, the formal study of human language—and *semiotics*, the study of signs and symbols and how humans perceive and interpret them. Given the historical backdrop and the prevailing trends, it's unsurprising that, in the early days of AI, all roads appeared to lead to structured symbolic systems.

But how could a machine made up of circuits and wires "understand" anything at all? How could it even begin to mirror the processes that happen effortlessly in a human mind? In these early stages of AI, the key technique was to reduce the domain being modelled into formal systems—to fully describe it in ways that are mathematical and logical. To this extent, early AI researchers were building out from the basic blocks of computers towards the space of human thought. They started with primitives that machines could easily model.

At its core, symbolic AI is made up of three fundamental elements:

- **Symbols:** Abstract representations of concepts or objects.
- **Rules:** Logical relationships that connect symbols.
- **Processes:** Operations that act *on* symbols *based on* the rules.

Early on, researchers recognised that the volume of symbols and rules required to model a domain would likely be vast. Capturing domain expertise in a machine-processable form would require significant investment. But once encoded, this knowledge could be applied and scaled far beyond the capacity of any individual human expert.

Implicitly, early AI systems worked in narrow domains—use cases were restricted to problems with neat boundaries, such as chess, tax calculations, or medical diagnosis. The idea of open-ended machine intelligence, while still a dream, was not a targeted goal. Instead, systems worked towards more practical outcomes, where some measure of success could be achieved and demonstrated to stakeholders and funders.

Symbolic AI caused a great deal of excitement in the early days of AI. It is a canonical example of a *deductive system*—characterised by the use of symbolic representations, formal logic, and reasoning from general

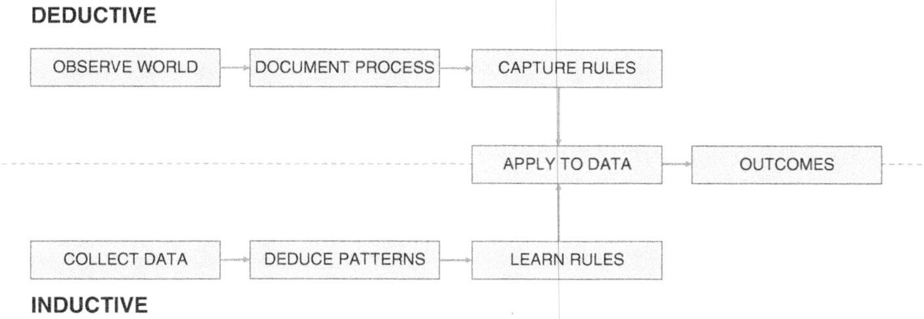

Figure 2.1: Deductive vs. inductive approaches

principles to specific conclusions. This can be contrasted with *inductive systems*, where systems infer general rules from observed data—learning patterns and associations from examples rather than applying prewritten rules.

As can be seen in Figure 2.1, in general terms, deductive systems start with structure and place data *within* it, whereas inductive systems start with data and derive structure *from* it. The focus on structure over data is not surprising when we remember that when early AI was being developed, digital data was in short supply. Data-led approaches, which are commonplace today, implicitly benefit from the explosion of digital data that has taken place over the last decade. Early researchers worked with what they had, and that was not large amounts of data.

Two Dartmouth attendees, Herbert Simon and Allen Newell, were instrumental in the development of symbolic AI. Their early research laid the groundwork for rule-based reasoning, problem-solving, and expert systems. The methods forged in those early days are so commonplace today, it's hard to remember they had a genesis at all. These early symbolic AI pioneers were not just developing methodologies; they were establishing the foundations of a new scientific discipline.

The work of early AI researchers introduced several key concepts. Principal among these was the idea of problem-solving through symbolic manipulation. Before symbolic AI, computers were mostly limited to rote mathematical tasks—processing payrolls, calculating missile trajectories, or predicting orbital paths. Simon, Newell, and their peers opened the door to more open-ended questions: "Find me the shortest route to …" "Is it correct to say …" "What proof exists that …"—dramatically expanding the perceived potential of what computers could do.

Symbolic AI laid a foundation of techniques and methods which still underpin the grand cathedrals of today's AI. While the zeitgeist has moved to data-driven approaches, these still sit atop the approaches and methods built during this time of structure and formality.

Core Concepts and Mechanisms

Symbolic AI comprises several key approaches that collectively define its systematic approach, rooted in symbolic representation, rule-based processing, and formal logic. Here we will outline a handful of these approaches in broad terms, to give you a working sense of the toolkit and where each method fits.

note **Each of these concepts—along with several others—is covered in much more detail in the upcoming "In-depth" section.**

To process information, computers must translate text, images, and sounds into numbers—a process known as *encoding*. Encoding is the essential step that transforms the rich variety of real-world data into a digital format that machines can understand and manipulate. By converting everything into numbers, encoding allows computers to treat all kinds of information in a consistent, computable way.

To represent knowledge, computers use *symbolic representation*—the process of encoding ideas, objects, and rules as symbols that machines can store and manipulate. This approach brings order and clarity, making it possible to interpret, combine, and reason about information. However, symbolic systems can be rigid when faced with ambiguity or incomplete data, so modern AI often blends symbolic and other methods to overcome such limits.

To process information, computers rely on *rules*—explicit instructions that tell them how to act on data. In symbolic AI, rules provide the structure for machine reasoning, ranging from step-by-step procedures (*imperative*) to statements of desired outcomes (*declarative*). Rules can also be *conditional*, following the familiar "if this, then that" pattern, and may address specific domains, time, uncertainty, or relationships between items.

Rather than existing in isolation, rules are usually organised into *rule sets*—collections that work together to solve problems or manage tasks. This organisation allows symbolic systems to handle complex decision-making, but also means that the quality and flexibility of the system depend on how well rules are designed and maintained.

Logic provides the formal structure for rules in symbolic AI, allowing computers to reason about truth, relationships, and conditions. Using *logical operators* like AND, OR, and NOT, machines can combine and evaluate statements, while more advanced forms like *predicate logic* enable rules to apply across sets of data. This logical foundation is essential for translating human expertise into a form that computers can process and use for decision-making.

Reasoning is where symbolic AI's true power emerges. By combining symbols, rules, and logic, computers can draw conclusions, make decisions, and infer new information from what they already know. An important process, called *inference,* allows machines to "connect the dots" and uncover knowledge that isn't explicitly stated—sometimes following chains of logic far longer than any human could manage.

Modern AI uses a range of reasoning methods. For example, *probabilistic reasoning* allows systems to handle uncertainty by weighing the likelihood of different outcomes and *fuzzy reasoning* lets computers work with concepts that are vague or imprecise.

However, machines still struggle with *common sense reasoning.* Unlike humans, who bring broad, intuitive understanding to every task, computers are limited to the rules and data they are given. Bridging this gap—so AI can handle ambiguity, context, and the messiness of real life—remains a major challenge for the field.

Symbolic AI excels at representing knowledge using symbols and rules but struggles to adapt as human understanding expands. Early systems handled *instance growth* well—adding new examples or data within an existing structure, like new rows in a table. However, they found *knowledge growth*—adding new types or attributes, akin to new columns—much harder. Such structural changes challenge the coherence and flexibility of symbolic systems, making it difficult to keep pace with the evolving nature of real-world knowledge.

Triples are a simple but powerful way to represent knowledge: each fact is stored as a subject–predicate–object relationship (e.g., "Socrates is-a philosopher"). This structure keeps knowledge organised and easily expandable, supporting knowledge growth without major system changes. Triples underpin the Semantic Web, enabling machines to interpret relationships between data more intelligently.

Ontologies define the rules and relationships that structure triple-based knowledge, specifying how concepts connect and interact. They set boundaries, declare hierarchies, and ensure consistency, but computers can only reason within the limits of the information and rules provided. Together, triples and ontologies form the backbone of symbolic knowledge representation.

Decision trees are a core tool, structuring decisions as a series of branching questions that lead to outcomes. Their intuitive, tree-like format makes them easy to follow and ideal for incorporating domain knowledge. Binary decision trees, the most common type, efficiently narrow down possibilities and are widely used for tasks like classification and diagnosis.

Rules-based engines in AI use explicit sets of instructions to automate decisions and ensure consistency. Unlike decision trees, they can handle large, overlapping rule sets, making them ideal for domains where transparency, traceability, and explainability are essential, such as finance, compliance, and access control.

Expert systems are a core technology in symbolic AI, designed to emulate the decision-making of human specialists. Built around a knowledge base and an inference engine, they combine rules and domain expertise to solve complex problems, offering tailored recommendations in fields like medicine, engineering, and law.

Knowledge graphs organise information as networks of concepts and relationships, making connections explicit and enabling systems to infer new links. Their dynamic, scalable structure supports applications like search, recommendations, and scientific research, moving beyond static data to represent the rich web of real-world meaning.

Natural language processing (NLP) enables computers to understand and interpret human language. Symbolic NLP treats language as a structured system, using rules to analyse syntax and meaning, but struggles with ambiguity and context. While symbolic methods laid the foundation for NLP, the field now blends structured approaches with wider techniques for greater flexibility and accuracy.

In-depth

Building on the foundations of the overview, let's now dive deeper into the technologies and approaches of symbolic AI. Here we will explore, in straightforward language, how information can be represented symbolically within a computer, how rules and logic are applied to that information, and how the combination of symbols and rules allows computers to reason, build knowledge, and produce useful outcomes.

Computable Information

The first step in harnessing the power of computation is translating real-world information into a language that a computer can understand. This inevitably means converting information into a mathematical form. At their core, computers are mathematical machines, and numbers are not just their native language—they are the only form of internal understanding computers possess.

In practice, these numbers are represented using base two—a system known as binary. Humans are most familiar with base 10, almost certainly because we have ten fingers, and we learn the place value system at school using this decimal structure. However, base 10 is just one of many possible number bases. Computers, for reasons of simplicity and because of the mechanics of electronic circuitry and transistors, use only two symbols:

zero and one. This is why binary is the natural choice for computers—it matches the on and off states that are easy to implement in hardware.

It's a sobering thought that every task you have seen a computer perform—from spreadsheets to music streaming, family photos, social media, and even AI—ultimately boils down to the manipulation of just two binary digits, as seen from within the machine. Despite their outward familiarity, computers internally inhabit a world that we cannot easily grasp or comprehend.

Encoding

How can the astonishing variety of media we experience—text, images, audio, and video—all be encapsulated as numbers? The answer lies in a process called *encoding*: the act of transforming information from one format into another, in this case into numerical codes that computers can process.

The simplest case to understand is text. The characters you see on this page, when stored digitally, are each assigned a unique numerical value. For example, the letter A is assigned the value 65, B is 66, and so on. The same principle applies to punctuation marks and other special characters, as well as important but otherwise invisible characters like spaces and new lines. As long as everyone agrees on a common mapping scheme, we can reliably exchange text as a numerical representation.

The most widely adopted system for mapping letters and symbols to numbers is known as ASCII (pronounced "as-key"). Developed in the early 1960s, ASCII forms the bedrock of text processing in computing. It provides a standard set of codes for English letters, digits, punctuation, and control characters, ensuring that text can be interpreted consistently across different systems. Later systems like Unicode, built on ASCII to add support for a much wider range of characters, languages, and even emojis.

As can be seen in Figure 2.2, a multitude of encoding schemes exist to capture and store information in various formats, including text, images, audio, video, and more. The most common way you encounter these is through file extensions that indicate the encoding scheme in use—for example, `.jpg` for images, `.mp3` for audio, and `.mp4` for video.

Unlike text, complex media such as audio and video cannot be broken into discrete parts without some loss of information. To make this possible, computers use a process called *sampling*, in which continuous information is divided into small, discrete units for encoding—pixels in an image, or amplitude samples in audio. This process, while practical and effective, inevitably leads to some loss of information, depending on the sampling rate and resolution chosen. Higher sampling rates preserve more detail, but require more storage and processing power.

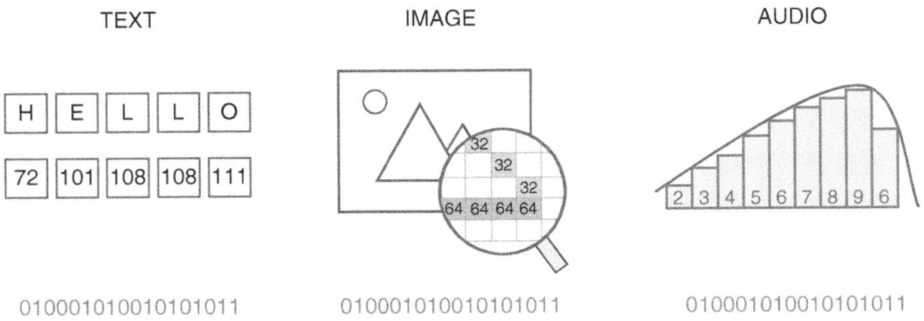

Figure 2.2: Media encoding schemes

Just as in text, where letters are mapped to numbers, a corresponding mapping is done for other types of media. Each image pixel is mapped to a set of three numbers, representing the red, green, and blue components of the colour. Each audio segment is mapped to numbers representing its amplitude and frequency. Other formats, like movies, are more complex, but the basic principle remains true.

Encoding schemes work best when they reflect a shared understanding among users, ensuring that different systems can operate with the same assumptions. This standardisation is why, for example, a video file can be played across many different media players. The file's headers and extension indicate to the player which encoding scheme has been used.

The practice of digital encoding—translating data into a numerical representation—is a cornerstone of computing, and hence AI. It forms the foundation on which all computational activities are built and executed.

Symbolic Representation

Numerical representation is one form of *symbolic representation*—a broad category of techniques where real-world information is captured using symbolic analogues. The use of symbols to convey everyday knowledge is neither new nor limited to computing.

On our roadways, we encounter a multitude of symbols that serve as important cues for drivers, imparting critical information like speed limits, potential hazards, movement restrictions, and more. In fact, the red–amber–green pattern of traffic lights is often cited as a canonical example of symbolic representation.

Such symbolic conventions are present in numerous areas of our everyday lives:

- **Media symbols:** Like play ▶, pause ⏸, and stop ■ icons, universally understood, facilitating common control over multimedia content.

- **Weather symbols:** Such as the sun ☼, rain ☔, and clouds ☁, succinctly communicating meteorological conditions and helping us plan our day.
- **Currency symbols:** Like the dollar $, pound £, and yen ¥, serving as shorthand for monetary units in global commerce.

It is important to note that symbolic representation is not limited to icons, images, or single characters. The field encompasses any scheme where symbols are used as substitutes for real-world entities. For example, there are many more intricate symbolic systems, often tailored to a specific domain:

- **Musical notation:** Employing symbols to represent musical elements like notes, rests, and dynamics, enabling the capture of complex compositions.
- **Chemical notation:** With its unique symbols for elements and compounds, allowing chemists to articulate chemical structures and reactions.
- **Mathematical notation:** Using symbols to convey key concepts, from basic arithmetic operations to calculus and algebraic expressions.

These more complex representation schemes often employ both symbols *and rules* as a coordinated set.

Consider chemical notation as an example: It not only provides a system for describing elements and compounds, but also incorporates rules governing how elements can react and combine. Similarly, in music, notation represents notes and rhythms, while rules of harmony and counterpoint determine which combinations are harmonious or discordant. Think of this like words and grammar—symbols and rules coexist to form a more complete system.

These examples highlight how deeply symbolic representation is woven into everyday life. The concept has roots in a well-studied field of human cognition and language known as *semiotics*—the systematic study of how we assign meaning to signs and symbols. It helps explain the central role symbols play in how we understand and communicate.

But why do humans and computers use symbols at all? Symbolic representation offers several advantages in various fields and applications:

- **Consistent:** They allow us to ascribe formal, precise, and consistent meaning to entities and concepts.
- **Enumerable:** They bind data to well-defined sets of possible values that are significant within a given domain.

- **Interpretable:** They represent complex concepts concisely, making it easier to interpret and work with information.
- **Modular:** They represent information in a manner that is discrete, reusable, and simpler to modify and maintain.
- **Scalable:** Once symbols are defined, they can be applied consistently across a wide range of situations and over vast data sets.
- **Interoperable:** They facilitate compatible operation between different systems and languages.

However, it's important to acknowledge that while symbolic representation offers numerous advantages, some its strengths can also be limitations—particularly when dealing with uncertain or incomplete information.

As we explored in the symbolic AI overview, deductive systems start from general principles and progress to specific conclusions. Attempting to reconcile the complicated realm of human information within systems rooted in the principles of precision and modularity can be a challenging endeavour, at times bordering on the impossible. Consequently, in contemporary AI, symbolic representation is often used in concert with later developments to address the spectrum of real-world challenges.

Knowledge Representation

Symbols, although essential, are not sufficient on their own to fully encompass the use cases required for effective information processing. *Symbolic systems* form an integral component of a broader field within computer science known as *knowledge representation*. This field encompasses a range of methodologies and structures used to organise and store information in a way that allows computational systems to process it efficiently and effectively.

Computers are excellent at handling data—but data on its own is raw and abstract. It only becomes useful when transformed into meaningful information. Knowledge representation schemes play a pivotal role in this transformation by defining how data is structured and organised to ascribe meaning to it.

Imagine I sent you a spreadsheet full of numbers but lacking any labels or context. In such a state, it would be of little use, and it's likely you would not be able to make sense of it. The moment I add column names like *date of birth*, *loan amount*, or *price*, however, the raw data in the document becomes meaningful. With the simple addition of such labels, it can now be interpreted, analysed, and acted upon.

Knowledge representation is a vast and diverse field, offering numerous ways to encode knowledge for computational purposes. Some common examples of knowledge representation schemes include:

- **Spreadsheets:** Use column and row names, workbook titles, formulas, and other structures to organise and interpret data.
- **Databases:** Rely on concepts like table names, column labels, and key identifiers to organise and make sense of data.
- **Software:** Function and variable names, call trees, and interfaces give structure and meaning to data within software programmes.
- **Data files:** Formats like comma-separated values, Microsoft Excel, and XML use specific structures to represent data effectively.
- **Charts and graphs:** Visual elements such as axis labels, chart titles, and colour keys provide context and interpretation to graphical data.

All of these approaches describe containers for information, not the information itself. We could take a single dataset—for example, a sports league table—and represent it using any or all of these methods. Each is a representational container for the information, with its own strengths, limitations, and intended purposes.

In each case, it is the surrounding scaffolding—labels, structures, and context—that gives data its meaning. This layering of interpretation onto raw data is a hallmark of knowledge representation, transforming otherwise abstract values into something useful and actionable.

Information Classification

The word *information* covers a wide spectrum of applications and use cases. There are many ways in which types of information can be classified for effective processing. Clear classification of information allows systems to operate with firmer expectations about what the data means and represents. Some common types of classification are:

- **Identifiers and keys:** Items used to (often uniquely) identify an entity within a wider data set. Examples include passport numbers, car licence plate numbers, staff payroll numbers, etc.
- **Attributes and properties:** Additional data associated with a given entity. Examples include name, date of birth, length, expiry date, etc.
- **Classes and types:** Entities can fit into an enumerated set of classes or types. Sometimes these are flat lists, such as car, truck, and bike.

Other times they are hierarchical, such as franchise » series » season » episode.

- **Relations and links:** Entities often share connections with one another. Examples include parent of, purchased, studies at, manufactured by, etc.
- **States and events:** Dynamic systems often have time-bound states and events associated with them. Examples include ready, flashing, out of service, overdrawn, etc.

Most often, information is rooted in the idea of *entities*, which are domain-specific items or concepts. For example, in the context of a medical system, the entities might be patients, doctors, treatments, medicines, symptoms, and so on. Entities often form the basis of data representation. For example, a table might represent a type of entity, each row an instance, and each column an attribute of that instance.

It's a common misconception that real-world information is always represented using standardised, neatly defined formats. While standards do exist, in practice people often adapt on the fly to meet the needs of the moment. Where data must be shared or widely understood across systems, standards can be formulated and agreed—for example, Health Level 7 (HL7) is a common standard for medical data exchange. However, strict compliance can sometimes be burdensome and may go beyond the immediate use cases.

Perhaps without realising it, you have been creating on-the-fly data classification schemes to meet your immediate data processing needs. For example, in a spreadsheet, you might use cells where **M** means *is a member* and **X** means *is not a member.* In doing so, you've informally created your own symbols within a knowledge representation framework tailored to your immediate task.

Classes, Instances, and Schemas

A key concept in information classification is the distinction between *classes* and *instances.* A class is an idealised representation of an entity—capturing the identifiers, attributes, relationships, and states expected to be relevant for a given context. Those familiar with philosophy may recognise a parallel with Platonic Forms, where the class represents the ideal essence of a thing.

Instances, by contrast, are real-world manifestations of a given class. For example, if the class is *mammals,* then instances might be dog, giraffe, whale, or human. If the class is *humans,* instances might be you and me.

A *schema* is a formal way to capture and structure data using classes and instances. For example, in a spreadsheet, we might use headings, formulas, and constraints that govern how the data will fit within it. The instances are then the data rows added later, each one conforming to the predefined structure.

Imagine sharing that empty spreadsheet with others and asking them to fill it in. There are no data rows yet, so no actual data is present. What you have shared is essentially a schema—a model that describes how information should be structured and organised. Without a single data item being present, you have nonetheless communicated a great deal of meta-information about the data space itself.

Schemas are central to deductive systems, particularly in databases. Defining a schema usually comes first in a project. It provides a blueprint for how data will be collected, stored, and understood—laying the groundwork for everything that follows.

But here lies both the power and fragility of deductive approaches. A schema lets systems be designed before any data is available, because it sets clear boundaries on what the data will look like. In formal terms, it supports *instance growth*—allowing new rows to be added while keeping the structure intact.

The difficulty comes when the schema itself has to change after data already exists—known as *knowledge growth*. It's like adding a new column to a spreadsheet that's already full of data—a structural change that affects every row.

Early deductive systems struggled with knowledge growth. Yet many foundational tools—such as relational databases—still rely on rigid, predefined schemas. They remain widely used because they encapsulate knowledge within tightly bounded domains, where new concepts do not routinely emerge. For example, a database designed for banking information today would be largely the same as one designed decades ago.

However, in more dynamic domains such as e-commerce or social media, schema evolution is more rapid and continuous. To help deal with this, later approaches—as we'll explore in the computational semantics section—were designed to offer greater flexibility.

Rules

Symbols, knowledge representation, schemas, and related constructs help us capture and store information in a machine-processable form—but how is that information actually to be processed?

In deductive systems, the core mechanism for acting on data is the use of *rules*. Such rules can take many forms and run in various engines, with software programmes being one of the most common. But whatever the format, each is essentially a conduit for executing defined logic.

Imperative vs. Declarative Rules

There is no universal standard for expressing rules in a computational context. The type, format, and structure of rules are typically tied to the technology used to define and execute them. While software programmes are the dominant format, they are not the only one.

Broadly speaking, rules fall into two main categories:

- **Imperative rules:** Describe *how* a goal should be achieved.
  - Specify step-by-step procedures.
  - Focus on defining the exact sequence of actions.
  - Use explicit control flow and manipulation of data.
  - Most often expressed as software programmes.
- **Declarative rules:** Describe *what* needs to be achieved.
  - Do not specify the step-by-step procedure.
  - Focus on defining relationships, conditions, and constraints.
  - Use states, predicates, and clauses.
  - Most often expressed as logical expressions.

For instance, a declarative rule might state, "If the light is red, then stop," whereas an imperative rule might dictate, "If the light is red, take foot off accelerator, apply brake, shift into neutral, apply parking brake."

Declarative rules, being nonprocedural, refrain from prescribing the exact sequence of actions or operations required to attain the goal, thereby allowing for greater flexibility in achieving that goal. In our example, the declarative rule applies equally to both automatic and manual cars, whereas the imperative rule may not.

Because declarative rules describe intent rather than procedure, they often express a higher-level truth—closer to requirements than processes. They are less rigid and more adaptable, but they depend on external systems to interpret and carry them out in practice.

Conditional Rules

Whether imperative or declarative, there are many formats of rules that machines can utilise to derive useful outcomes from information. In general, we can say that most rules are conditional and follow the pattern:

IF **CONDITION** THEN **IMPLICATION**

Where:

- **Condition** is a logical test, which normally resolves to *TRUE* or *FALSE*. These can be compound expressions using logical combinators like *AND* and *OR*.
- **Implication** might be an action in the real world, a change in the digital state of the system, or a conclusion to a question.

Here are some examples of typical rule types:

- **Domain rules:** Domain-specific knowledge.
  - *IF fever AND sore throat THEN possible throat infection.*
- **Temporal rules:** Time-dependent knowledge.
  - *IF the meeting time is after 18:00 THEN order pizza.*
- **Fuzzy rules:** Imprecise or uncertain information.
  - *IF cold (0 to 1) THEN increase heater power (0 to 10).*
- **Association rules:** Associations between data and entities.
  - *IF purchased bread AND milk THEN offer eggs.*
- **Meta rules:** Rules governing the execution of other rules.
  - *IF user not administrator THEN apply file restriction rules.*

While a few examples are listed here, it is important to note that this is not an exhaustive catalogue. The types and variations of rules are as diverse as the knowledge domains they attempt to model.

Rules typically don't exist in isolation; instead, they are often grouped into related collections known as *rule sets*. For example, a medical system might have one rule set for diagnosis and different rule set for appointment scheduling.

First-Order Logic

In everyday life, we use logic as a way of reasoning about what is true or false, often relying on words like *and*, *or*, and *not*. However, in mathematics and computer science, logic is a much more formal system, with precise rules and terminology.

The concept of `IF-THEN` statements is part of such a wider system known as *first-order logic (FOL)* (sometimes called *predicate logic*), which is a formal methodology for modelling domain knowledge. We will not go too deeply into FOL here, as it can be quite esoteric and unfamiliar. For example, what we referred to as *condition* and *implication* earlier are called *antecedent* and *consequent* in FOL.

However, we can outline the two key concepts in FOL that are used to model complicated domain knowledge in machine-processable forms:

- **Operators:** Combine parts of knowledge into logical expressions.
  - *AND*: Conjunction—conditions which all must be true.
  - *OR*: Disjunction—conditions where at least one must be true.
  - *NOT*: Negation—a condition which must be false.
- **Quantifiers:** Conditions and relationships between elements.
  - *FOR ALL*: Universal—true for every element.
  - *THERE EXISTS*: Existential—true for at least one element.

For example, the human language sentence:

There exists a student who is enrolled in both mathematics and physics courses.

Might be expressed more formally within a computer as:

$\exists$ x (x $\in$ students $\wedge$ ENROLLED(x, 'mathematics') $\wedge$ ENROLLED (x, 'physics'))

First-order logic is a powerful and expressive modelling language. It provides a formal structure for representing domain knowledge in a way that computers can interpret and process effectively. In practice, the concepts of FOL are most commonly expressed within software programmes—often without the authors being formally aware that they are working within the framework of first-order logic. This underlying structure enables complex reasoning and knowledge representation, even when the formal terminology is not explicitly used.

Reasoning

Capturing knowledge in symbolic form and specifying rules and relationships is inherently valuable. However, the true power of such concepts emerges when they form the basis of reasoning.

Computational reasoning refers to the processes where symbolic representations, rules, logic, and algorithms come together to enable machines to draw conclusions, make decisions, or infer information that hasn't been explicitly stated. Reasoning is a cornerstone of AI and underpins many of the remarkable outcomes we see machines performing today.

Inference

The process of *inference* is a fundamental element of computational reasoning. It refers to the act of drawing conclusions based on existing knowledge. In human terms, you might say that you made a deduction by "connecting the dots" from things you already knew.

A famous example illustrating inference is the *Man Is Mortal* syllogism, from the ancient Greek philosopher Aristotle. The syllogism goes like this:

- All men are mortal.
- Socrates is a man.
- Therefore, Socrates is mortal.

Drawing on terminology from earlier in the chapter, we can see that:

- Clause 1 is a rule (*a schematic universal quantifier for a class of entity*).
- Clause 2 is a declaration (*an instance of a specific class of entity*).
- Clause 3 is an inference.

This simple example, illustrated in Figure 2.3, shows how inference lets us derive new knowledge from existing facts. More generally, inference can be described as "If A leads to B, and B leads to C, then A leads to C."

Computers use inferential processes like this to make sense of data, answer questions, and solve problems. The real power comes from the fact that such inference chains can be enormous—sometimes involving thousands or millions of steps—revealing connections that even domain experts might not anticipate. Modern systems can perform inference at a scale and depth far beyond human ability.

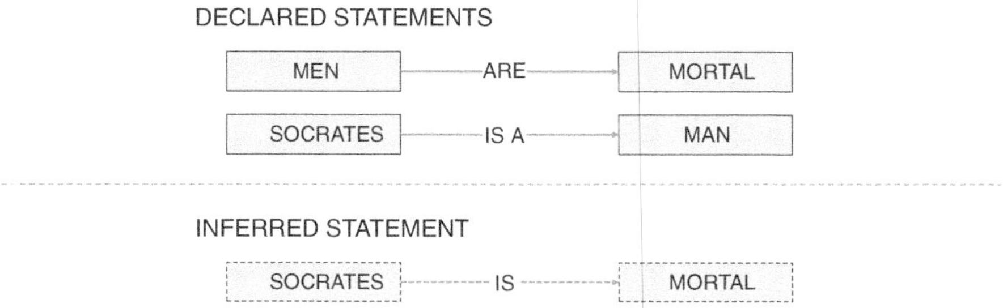

Figure 2.3: Simple inference example

Wider Reasoning

Beyond basic inference, modern AI systems engage in a wide array of sophisticated forms of reasoning, each tailored to specific challenges. A nonexhaustive list of examples is:

- **Probabilistic reasoning:** Assesses the likelihood of various outcomes.
- **Fuzzy logic:** Handles uncertainty and imprecise information.
- **Deductive reasoning:** Derives conclusions from general principles.
- **Inductive reasoning:** Derives structure from specific observations.

Reasoning is a vast and multifaceted field, encompassing many processes, algorithms, and techniques. Several concepts you'll encounter later in this book—such as machine learning and neural networks—can be viewed as reasoning engines in their own right. Together, they form the cognitive engines that allow machines to process information, make decisions, and uncover knowledge.

While such approaches echo aspects of human thinking, machines operate at immense scale—revealing insights and connections in data that might otherwise go unnoticed.

Common Sense Reasoning

A stark contrast between human cognition and machine intelligence lies in our ability to make common sense decisions. Unlike humans, who possess unbounded knowledge of the world, machines generally operate within a narrowly defined domain of expertise. This difference is at the heart of why machines sometimes make mistakes that may appear trivially simple to even children.

Drawing on millions of years of evolution, humans have a broad understanding of the world around them. This includes concepts like cause and effect, object permanence, spatial and temporal relations, and social dynamics. Our knowledge is applied to every aspect of our lives, enabling us to make intuitive and context-aware decisions across a multitude of scenarios.

In contrast, computational systems are constrained by the specific domains of interest for which they were designed. Since they were built to solve problems and provide outcomes within a specific domain, they often lack the inherent flexibility of human cognition and understanding.

We can see the limits of machine common sense when they encounter gaps that humans would easily fill using broader understanding. For example, if someone says, "I left my bike outside and it's wet now," a human immediately infers it probably rained—without needing explicit mention of the weather. This kind of implicit, background knowledge is second nature to us, but machines struggle with it.

When a machine encounters situations or questions outside its knowledge boundaries, it typically operates in one of two ways:

- **Closed-world assumption:** Unknown knowledge is assumed to be false.
- **Open-world assumption:** Unknown knowledge could be true or false.

Say, for example, I was searching for a street name in a comprehensive mapping catalogue. Not finding it would imply the street does not exist—a closed-world assumption. But searching for the same street name in an internet search might simply mean it is not found either way—an open-world assumption.

While such assumptions can be efficient for structured reasoning, both can lead to comical errors when applied to everyday situations that require common sense. This lack of common sense reasoning is why AIs often make mistakes that confuse us. On the one hand, they can process information like a PhD—on the other hand, they can make mistakes like a preschooler.

AI researchers continue to work on enhancing machine common sense reasoning abilities. This inevitably involves incorporating broader knowledge bases and hence moving from specific to more general capabilities.

Knowledge Growth

As we discussed earlier this chapter, symbolic AI had strengths but also carried inherent weaknesses. Its ability to represent knowledge as symbols and rules made it efficient at processing vast amounts of information. However, these rigid systems and rules became limiting when it came to accommodating the full breadth of human knowledge.

The ultimate result of such limitations was to help spur the development of inductive systems, which we will delve into in the next chapter. Yet, proponents of symbolic AI had one more innovative approach up their sleeve. They introduced symbolic representations that allowed knowledge to evolve and adapt with limited impact on structural elements.

Symbolic systems were primarily focused on what can be termed *instance growth*. This can be likened to adding more rows to an existing data table—expanding the number of examples or instances within a given knowledge framework. However, these systems faced challenges incorporating *knowledge growth*, which is more like adding new columns to a data table, as shown in Figure 2.4.

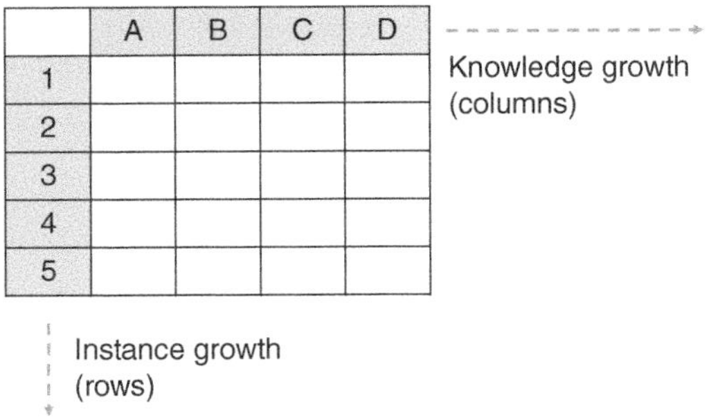

Figure 2.4: Knowledge vs. instance growth

Introducing new columns inevitably affects all existing rows, often in ways that are not easily reconciled. This phenomenon represents a significant shift in the underlying framework, commonly referred to as structural change.

This challenge underscored the need for symbolic systems that could gracefully adapt to evolving knowledge structures—as the complexity of the real world rarely fitted neatly into predefined rows and columns.

Triples

In the realm of knowledge representation, the idea of expressing information in the form of triples has proved to be a robust and flexible framework. This approach simplifies the process of knowledge growth by maintaining a consistent structure, which remains unchanged even as information evolves and grows.

At the heart of representing information as triples lies the concept of *subject–predicate–object* relationships: a statement consisting of three parts that expresses a single fact or assertion.

- **Subject:** The entity or concept that the statement is about.
- **Predicate:** The relationship which connects the *subject* to the *object*.
- **Object:** The entity or concept related to the *subject* via the *predicate*.

This simple and neat approach allows for the encoding of a vast range of information in a standardised format. Here are some example statements in triple form:

- Socrates ***is-a*** philosopher
- Socrates ***is-a*** teacher
- Socrates ***has-a*** mind
- Socrates ***teaches*** Plato

- Plato ***is-taught-by*** Socrates
- Aristotle ***is-taught-by*** Plato

The concept of representing information as triples has a long history, dating back to the work of logicians like Gottfried Wilhelm Leibniz in the 17th century. Leibniz proposed a symbolic language called *characteristica universalis,* which aimed to express all human knowledge through a universal set of symbols and relationships—akin to modern triple-based representations. In retrospect, Leibniz was way ahead of his time—but many of the concepts he outlined hundreds of years ago are in common use today.

In our rapidly evolving modern world, the proliferation of digital information has made triple-based approaches an invaluable method for organising, sharing, and expanding our collective knowledge. These approaches found formalisation within the framework of the *Semantic Web.*

Pioneered by Sir Tim Berners-Lee, the visionary behind the World Wide Web, this revolutionary concept proposed a system where information, encoded in triple form, could be interconnected and linked—akin to the way hyperlinks bind knowledge across web pages. The objective was to transform the web into a more intelligent and interconnected realm, one where data transcends human readability to facilitate machine understanding.

While the Semantic Web may not have achieved the same widespread success as its human-centred counterpart, it laid the foundation for formalising methods of representing information as triples. It addressed critical facets such as querying, security, encryption, and expressing concepts like trust and provenance, among others.

The elegance of representing information as triples lies in its simplicity and adaptability. As knowledge continues to expand and evolve, the triple structure itself remains constant, allowing for continuous refinement of understanding without the need for fundamental overhauls.

New instances can be accommodated simply by adding new statements. New knowledge, on the other hand, can be incorporated by introducing new predicates. However, managing an ever-growing list of predicates can be challenging, so careful control of this important enumeration is required. To address this challenge, people often use shared vocabularies of predicates to help manage the space and facilitate cross-system integration.

Ontologies

Looking more closely at the example triples we saw in the previous section, many meta-observations can be made:

- Socrates is the *subject* of multiple ***is-a*** statements.
- Plato appears as both a *subject* and an *object.*

- The predicate ***teaches*** is the opposite of ***is-taught-by***.
- Socrates ***has-a*** mind, but then all humans have minds.
- The *object* of an ***is-taught-by*** statement must always be a teacher.
- A person cannot be both *subject* and *object* of a ***teaches*** statement.

Many other insights can be drawn from this simple list of triples. These observations highlight that, while triples can capture information, they do not on their own describe an entire domain of knowledge. Other meta-rules exist outside of the triple structure—but operate upon it.

In modern computational semantics, this concept is formalised through something called an *ontology*. An ontology does not directly capture knowledge itself; rather, it defines the rules and boundaries that govern how information can interconnect, interact, and be understood.

Think of ontologies as precise sets of rules—akin to scaffolding—that provide structure and coherence to triple-based knowledge stores. They play a pivotal role in defining critical aspects such as relationships, attributes, restrictions, hierarchies, taxonomies, ranges, order, cardinality, and more.

Several shared ontologies exist and can be used to ease development and cross-system integration. Called *upper ontologies*, such models contain sets of shared relations and objects that are generally applicable across a wide range of domain ontologies.

As an example, using our earlier triples, an ontology might state:

- The *subject* of a ***teaches*** statement must be a human.
- The *object* of a ***teaches*** statement can be a human or a dog.
- Humans and dogs are disjoint classes.
- All humans have minds.
- If a *subject* ***teaches*** an *object*, then the *object* ***is-taught-by*** the *subject*.

From this trivial ontology and our existing triple set, we can now make some inferences. Let us ask ourselves: is Plato a dog? After all, since Plato is the object of a *teaches* statement, he could be either a human or a dog. But

- Since Aristotle ***is-taught-by*** Plato ...
  - We can infer that Plato ***teaches*** Aristotle.
- Since Plato is the *subject* of a ***teaches*** statement ...
  - We can infer that Plato is human.
- Since humans and dogs are disjoint sets ...
  - We can infer that Plato is not a dog!

Arriving at this seemingly obvious conclusion through the lens of triples and ontologies might appear unconventional—but it underscores a fundamental truth: Computers lack intrinsic common sense reasoning. They can only function based on the information and rules they are explicitly given.

The partnership between triples and ontologies equips machines with the capability to derive meaningful insights from raw information—bridging the gap between data and informed outcomes.

Common Tools and Techniques

As symbolic AI approaches have evolved, certain technologies have become widely adopted in practical solutions. The principal ones in use today are spreadsheets and relational databases. These two techniques are so pervasive and ubiquitous that they likely represent the largest segment of data management globally. Spreadsheets offer a user-friendly interface for organising, analysing, and visualising data, whereas relational databases provide a more robust and scalable solution for storing and retrieving large volumes of structured information.

However, it's important to recognise the significance of other, less well-known methodologies that also play a crucial role in symbolic AI. These methods are used across a wide range of applications, each contributing to the diverse landscape of structured data approaches.

Decision Trees

Decision trees play a critical role in the realm of symbolic AI, serving as a fundamental concept that offers a straightforward and intuitive way for computers to arrive at decisions and tackle complex problems. What makes decision trees particularly valuable is their ability to harness real-world domain knowledge, enabling the chain of reasoning they employ to be easily grasped, even by non-technical experts.

Think of decision trees as akin to the branches of a real tree, fanning out from a central point. At each branching juncture, there is a question or condition that guides the selection of the subsequent path. Ultimately, this journey culminates in a leaf node, representing a decision or outcome.

In its simplest form, each branch leads to two sub-branches, resulting from a binary true-or-false choice at each point. Consequently, with each step along the route, the number of potential outcomes is halved. These structures—known as binary decision trees or b-trees—form the most common type of decision tree used in symbolic systems. An example b-tree is shown in Figure 2.5.

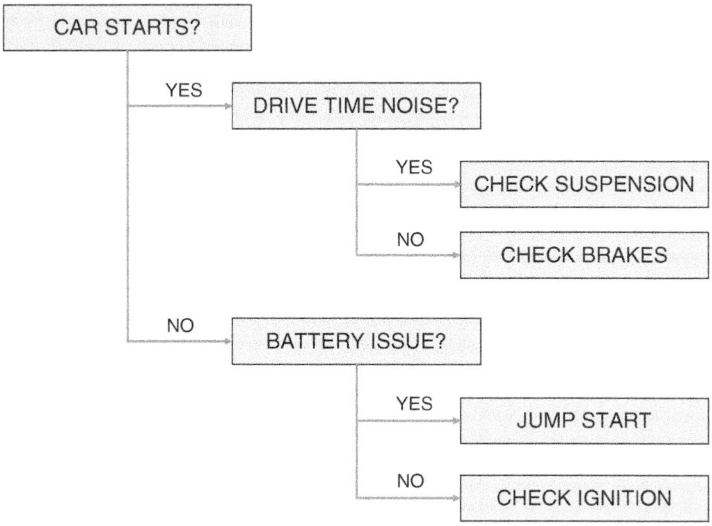

Figure 2.5: Example binary decision tree

Properly balanced b-trees have the remarkable capacity to segment vast solution spaces with millions of potential outcomes into just a few discerning conditions. For example, imagine trying to guess a number between one and a million. If each step of the decision tree asks "Is the number greater than X?," it can halve the possibilities with every answer. In just 20 steps, it can narrow it down to the exact number. This binary halving is the essence of how decision trees reduce complexity efficiently—even in enormous data spaces.

In AI, decision trees are a powerful tool for making decisions based on input data. They find applications in classification tasks, such as distinguishing between spam and legitimate emails, diagnosing faults, or predicting customer preferences.

Their attributes of simplicity, versatility, efficiency, and interpretability make decision trees a common element within computational systems. You may not even realise it, but you've likely encountered numerous systems employing decision trees in your day-to-day life.

Rules-Based Engines

Rules-based engines are a vital component of symbolic AI, playing a distinct yet complementary role alongside simpler decision trees. These engines are akin to having a set of well-defined rules that guide a system's behaviour—much like following a predefined protocol or guideline when handling specific situations.

Rules-based engines employ a variety of techniques to regulate their host systems:

- **Rule-based logic:** They operate on a set of rules, conditions, and actions that encapsulate domain knowledge and specify how the system should respond to different scenarios.
- **Structured decision-making:** Just as you might follow traffic rules while driving, rules-based engines ensure that systems adhere to predefined guidelines, maintaining smooth and predictable operation.
- **Transparency:** They offer clarity in their decision-making process, much like following a code of conduct or set of instructions.
- **Customisation:** They can be customised and extended to accommodate specific requirements. Much like tailoring your approach to different situations, rules can be added, modified, or removed to adapt the system's behaviour as needed.
- **Scalability:** They can be scaled to handle complex scenarios by adding more rules and conditions, just as laws and regulations evolve to address new societal challenges.

In our everyday lives, we encounter many situations where rules-based logic prevails. Consider the rules and regulations in sport, the etiquette that governs social interactions, or the procedural rules that ensure safety in aviation. Similarly, in the context of AI, rules-based engines provide a structured framework that guides decision-making, automates tasks, and ensures adherence to established principles.

For example, in the financial sector, a rules-based engine might be used to assess mortgage applications. It can evaluate dozens of conditions: credit score, income level, employment status, property type, loan amount, and more. Each rule contributes to a decision—approve, decline, or refer for manual review.

The engine ensures consistency across thousands of applications, applying the same criteria and logic to every case, which reduces human error and bias. Because rules-based engines operate automatically, they can work at a scale far beyond what human reviewers could manage, processing large volumes of applications quickly and efficiently. When regulations or business requirements change, the rules can be updated centrally, allowing the system to adapt rapidly without the need to redesign the entire process. This combination of scalability, consistency, and adaptability makes rules-based engines especially valuable in complex, high-volume domains.

Whether it's a chatbot providing customer support, an insurance system evaluating claims, or a manufacturing process following quality control rules, rules-based engines are the digital equivalents of structured rules and guidelines that help us navigate and operate in complex domains.

Expert Systems

Expert systems are another cornerstone of symbolic AI, offering a valuable and parallel concept to decision trees and rules-based engines. These systems are designed to encapsulate and emulate the expertise of human specialists, making them powerful tools for problem-solving and decision-making.

Like their simpler counterparts, expert systems leverage domain-specific knowledge. However, their approach is more akin to consulting a knowledgeable expert in a particular field. They go beyond simple tree-like branches to encompass a wider set of characteristics used to derive outcomes:

- **Knowledge-based:** They rely on an extensive knowledge base, comprising rules, facts, and heuristics derived from human experts in the field.
- **Inference engine:** They employ an inference engine to serve as the reasoning mechanism, mimicking the logical thinking and decision-making processes of human experts.
- **Interpretability:** They aim to provide transparent and interpretable responses, explaining the rationale behind their recommendations or decisions.
- **Problem-solving:** They use a wide range of methodologies to arrive at outcomes, making them ideal for complex and nondeterministic problems.
- **Automation:** They facilitate the automation of decision-making processes, offering the ability to work at scales and speeds beyond their human counterparts.

Expert systems are not a single, discrete tool; rather, they encompass an intricate and multifaceted set of reasoning processes, often involving a wide array of variables and considerations.

Just as a doctor considers a multitude of factors when diagnosing an illness, expert systems can evaluate complex scenarios and deliver tailored recommendations. In essence, when you consult a doctor for a medical condition, you are tapping into a human expert system—a knowledgeable professional who leverages their domain expertise and a structured thought process to arrive at a diagnosis and treatment plan.

Similarly, expert systems in the realm of AI leverage the accumulated wisdom of human experts to provide valuable insights and solutions across diverse domains, making them indispensable tools for solving complex problems.

Knowledge Graphs

Knowledge graphs are another critical component of symbolic AI, offering a versatile framework for representing information. Within these graphs, data is structured as nodes (representing concepts) connected by edges (representing relationships) that link them together.

A familiar example of a knowledge graph is a family tree, where people are connected by familial relationships. In such a setting, the types of relationships are relatively simple, including *parent of*, *married to*, and *sibling of*. Another common example is a social network graph, where nodes represent individuals and relationships might include *friend of*, *employed by*, or *follows*.

However, knowledge graphs extend these principles to encompass a vast array of potential relationships, such as *is a*, *has a*, *born on*, *studied at*, *current state*, *best before*, *length*, and many more. Their goal is to comprehensively represent knowledge within a specific domain—much like how our understanding of a subject deepens as we connect various pieces of information. An example knowledge graph is shown in Figure 2.6.

Information within knowledge graphs is interconnected, facilitating the exploration of related concepts, similar to how we make connections between seemingly unrelated ideas. Moreover, they adapt to evolving information by adding new nodes and edges, mirroring how our knowledge grows

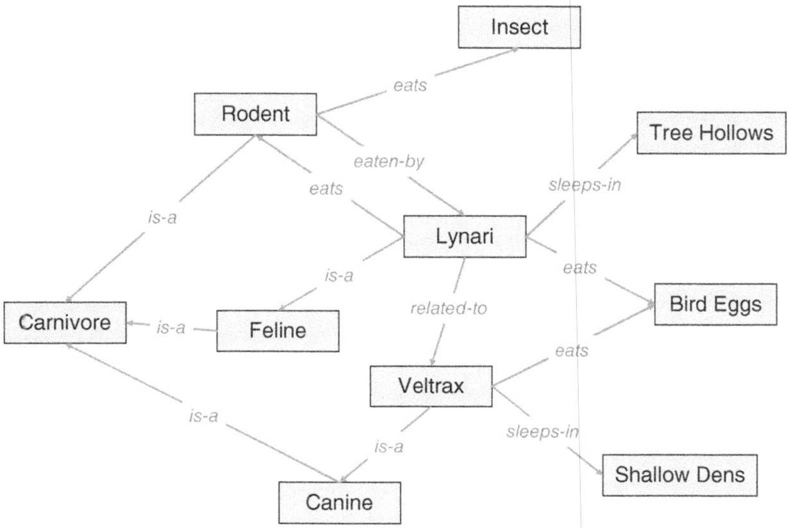

Figure 2.6: Example knowledge graph

with new insights. This scalability allows them to handle increasingly complex information.

Knowledge graphs enhance semantic understanding by giving concepts meaning via their relationships. This mirrors how we derive word meanings from their contextual usage. In essence, knowledge graphs serve as digital counterparts to how we mentally organise information and draw connections between ideas.

Recalling our earlier discussion on triple representation, you'll remember that information was captured as a subject–predicate–object set. It should now be clear that triple stores and knowledge graphs share an underlying structure: two entities connected by a relationship. However, they employ different spatial representations, and with this, different approaches to querying and using the data. Essentially, they are both approaching things via the same underlying model. A set of triples can be visualised as an interconnected graph, and graphs can be reduced to a set of triples.

One of the significant advantages of knowledge graphs is their ability to compute semantic distances between concepts—determining how closely related they are in meaning. In social network graphs, this notion is often referred to as *friend of a friend* distance.

This capability is useful in a wide range of scenarios. For example, in supply chain management, a knowledge graph can reveal how closely related different suppliers, manufacturers, and distributors are, helping to identify potential risks or alternative sources if a disruption occurs. In scientific research, semantic distances can highlight connections between related concepts, such as linking diseases to genes or treatments, thereby uncovering new avenues for investigation.

Knowledge graphs can also facilitate inference—the process of drawing new conclusions from existing information. For example, if a knowledge graph captures that *oranges* are a type of *fruit*, and *fruit* is typically *sweet*, it can infer that *oranges* are likely to be *sweet*—even if that specific connection was never explicitly stated. By following the links between related concepts, the system can draw useful conclusions that go beyond surface-level facts.

This ability to infer new knowledge is not limited to simple chains. It can encompass vast graphs to connect and reason across multiple layers of relationships, revealing insights that would otherwise remain hidden.

Knowledge graphs find applications in diverse fields, including search engines that understand the relationships between search queries and web content, recommendation systems that suggest movies and music based on user preferences, and scientific research where they model complex phenomena. Their adaptability, scalability, and ability to discern semantic relationships make them a valuable asset in the world of symbolic AI.

Natural Language Processing

In the context of AI, *natural language processing (NLP)* represents a fascinating field that focuses on enabling computers to understand, interpret, and even generate human language. While NLP has found its ultimate expression using later inductive methodologies, its roots trace back to symbolic AI.

Within symbolic AI-based NLP, language is treated as a structured entity with symbolic representation. This entails the creation of rules, grammatical frameworks, and ontologies that govern the relationships between words, phrases, and concepts. For instance, symbolic NLP systems employ parsing algorithms to dissect sentences into grammatical components like subjects, verbs, and objects, enabling computers to analyse the syntactic structure of language. Figure 2.7 illustrates how NLP might parse a simple sentence.

Concurrently, as AI was emerging, modern linguistics was also progressing. *Modern linguistics* is the scientific study of human language, delving into structure, usage, and the cognitive processes that underlie language production and comprehension.

In the 1950s, the influential linguist Noam Chomsky introduced the concept of *universal grammar*. This concept resonated with early AI researchers, as it aligned neatly with symbolic systems, particularly in terms of formal representations of grammar and grammatical rules. Chomsky's distinction between syntax (sentence structure) and semantics (sentence meaning) also dovetailed with symbolic AI, which similarly employed separate components for syntax and semantics.

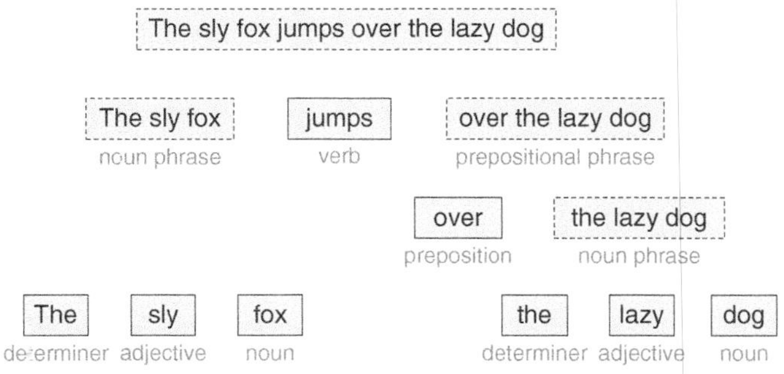

Figure 2.7: Breakdown by parts of speech

Once captured in such form, simple processing could be performed on the text, such as:

- **Sentence type classification:** Identifying whether a sentence is a question, command, or statement based on punctuation and word order.
- **Part-of-speech tagging:** Assigning labels like noun, verb, adjective based on word placement and syntactic rules.
- **Subject–verb agreement:** Ensuring that verbs match their subjects in number and person.
- **Pronoun resolution:** Determining what a pronoun like *he* or *it* refers to in short, rule-friendly contexts.
- **Simple sentence rephrasing:** Converting passive to active voice using grammar transformations.

More complex use cases—such as language translation, summarisation, or open-ended text generation—were ultimately beyond the reach of these early rule-based approaches. Tackling those challenges would require inductive techniques, which we explore later in the book.

Early symbolic AI approaches relied on predefined rules and heuristics to process and understand text. For instance, an NLP system might employ rules to comprehend and respond to user queries in a customer support context. Such systems could perform simple subject extraction—identifying the main subject of the customer's call—as well as basic sentiment analysis, where rules were used to determine whether a customer was expressing positive, negative, or neutral sentiment.

During this period, communities of researchers and practitioners began to build datasets of language words tagged with important concepts such as sentiment, meaning, and grammatical roles. These resources helped systems identify whether a word was positive or negative, or what part of speech it represented. However, even with these advances, such datasets still lacked the broader context that is often critical for full understanding—as meaning can depend heavily on surrounding words, intent, and situation.

Hence, it's important to acknowledge that symbolic NLP has its limitations. It struggles to cope with the inherent ambiguity and intricacy of natural language, especially as it can be highly context-dependent and nuanced. Subsequently, inductive and data-driven approaches—which gained prominence later—have tackled some of these challenges by harnessing extensive datasets and machine learning techniques to develop more context-aware NLP systems, a theme we will pick up in later chapters.

Symbolic AI played a pivotal role in the initial stages of NLP development, emphasising structured representations, rule-based systems, and symbolic reasoning. Nonetheless, as the field of NLP has advanced, the integration of wider techniques has expanded its capabilities, making systems more proficient at navigating the complexities of human discourse.

Use Cases

So far, we've delved into the fundamental components that constitute symbolic AI, gaining insights into the world of knowledge representation, logic, reasoning, and the other techniques used within this field. Now, let's bridge the gap between theory and practical application by examining how symbolic AI has been harnessed to create systems that tackle real-world challenges.

The scenarios that follow are described from a primarily symbolic AI perspective to help you clearly see how rules, logic, and structured representations drive problem-solving.

In modern systems, however, symbolic methods rarely operate alone. They are typically combined with statistical and machine-learning techniques. The descriptions here are intentionally narrower than the integrated reality of modern systems, allowing the symbolic elements to stand out before we explore hybrid approaches later in the book.

Real-world deployments involve much more than algorithms: Human oversight, organisational processes, quality assurance, regulatory constraints, bias mitigation, and safety considerations all play critical roles. For simplicity and clarity, those elements are omitted here so that the examples can concentrate on illustrating how symbolic AI contributes to solving practical problems.

Automated Medical Diagnosis

In the healthcare industry, the advent of automated medical diagnosis marks a significant advancement in augmenting patient care. These systems handle vast quantities of diagnostic data, quickly cross-referencing it with an expanding corpus of medical knowledge and research. They serve as invaluable assistants to human doctors by offering comprehensive analyses of patients' conditions, pinpointing probable causes, and suggesting appropriate treatment options.

Furthermore, these automated systems offer scalability far beyond human capabilities. They can operate around the clock, processing and analysing data from large numbers of patients simultaneously. This ability to work at such a vast scale is particularly beneficial in areas with limited medical personnel or in handling widespread health crises, where quick, accurate diagnoses are crucial.

These systems use expert systems and decision trees to help diagnose medical conditions in patients.

Expert Systems and Decision Trees

Medical expert systems rely on comprehensive knowledge bases and sophisticated inference engines. These knowledge bases are vast repositories of medical information, encompassing diseases, symptoms, patient histories, and the latest medical research. Inference engines interpret this data to make logical deductions. They process patient information through complex algorithms, inferring potential diagnoses by comparing individual cases against the accumulated medical knowledge.

Decision trees work by breaking down complex diagnostic processes into a set of often binary choices. Starting from the initial symptom or patient complaint, the decision tree branches out, considering various factors such as patient history, test results, and observed symptoms. At each node of the tree, a decision is made based on the information available, progressively leading to a more focused and accurate diagnosis.

Personalised Medical Assessments

The ability to offer highly personalised medical diagnoses marks a significant stride in patient-centred healthcare. By processing unique patient information—including symptoms, medication, history, and even genetics—these systems can identify the most likely causes of a patient's ailment. They go beyond generic diagnoses, offering personalised insights that resonate more closely with each patient's condition, and helping devise treatments that are specifically suited to the individual's health profile.

The integration of these expert systems into routine medical practice fosters a more nuanced understanding of patient health. They not only aid in diagnosing immediate issues but can also predict potential future health risks. This predictive aspect is particularly beneficial for proactive health management, allowing both patients and healthcare providers to address potential concerns before they manifest as serious conditions.

Outcome

The application of expert systems and decision trees in automated medical diagnosis represents a significant advancement in healthcare technology. These AI-driven tools are reshaping the landscape of medical diagnostics, offering high levels of accuracy, efficiency, and personalisation. By synthesising vast medical knowledge with patient-specific data, they enable more precise diagnoses and predictive health insights, significantly enhancing patient care.

As these technologies continue to evolve and integrate seamlessly into healthcare practices, they promise to further revolutionise patient diagnosis and treatment—making strides towards a future where healthcare is more responsive, informed, and tailored to individual needs.

Legal Case Analysis

The integration of rules-based engines for legal case analysis marks a substantial evolution in legal research. These systems efficiently process vast quantities of legal documents, extracting pertinent case law and precedents that are critical in shaping legal arguments and strategies. By providing rapid and comprehensive analyses of complex legal texts, they act as invaluable tools for lawyers, enhancing the thoroughness and efficacy of legal representation.

The scalability of these systems is a key advantage, particularly in handling large-scale legal research tasks that would be overwhelming for individual legal practitioners. They offer the ability to analyse extensive legal databases, delivering insights and relevant case references swiftly. This capability is especially beneficial in high-stakes legal scenarios or in jurisdictions with voluminous legal statutes and case histories, where exhaustive research is imperative.

These systems make use of rules-based engines to navigate through the intricate legal landscape.

Rules-Based Engines

Rules-based engines in legal analysis operate by applying a structured set of logical rules to identify relevant legal precedents and statutes. These engines parse legal documents, identifying key phrases and citations, and cross-referencing them with a vast repository of legal knowledge.

Each rule in these engines is crafted to detect specific legal phrases, terminologies, and citations that are crucial for understanding and applying legal principles. For instance, a rule might be designed to recognise references to precedent-setting cases or to detect the usage of particular legal terms that could indicate the relevance of a document to a specific case.

Enhanced Legal Strategy and Decision-Making

The implementation of these AI-driven systems in legal analysis significantly empowers legal professionals with deeper insights and strategic options. It facilitates a more nuanced understanding of legal precedents and their applicability to current cases, enabling practitioners to craft more robust legal arguments.

The predictive capability of these systems, based on historical legal outcomes, further aids strategic decision-making by providing lawyers with an informed perspective on potential case outcomes.

Outcome

The adoption of rules-based engines in legal case analysis marks a key shift in the legal field, introducing a higher level of precision, efficiency, and depth in legal research and strategy formulation.

As these technologies continue to advance, they are set to redefine the landscape of legal practice, offering increasingly sophisticated tools for legal analysis and decision-making. This evolution paves the way for a legal system that is more accessible, responsive, and equipped to handle the complexities of modern law.

Financial Fraud Detection

The use of decision trees for financial fraud detection has become an important tool for safeguarding assets and maintaining consumer trust. These systems efficiently analyse transaction patterns, identifying potential fraud by detecting anomalies and irregularities in banking and purchasing behaviours. This technological advancement plays a critical role in the early detection and prevention of fraudulent activities, thereby protecting both financial institutions and their customers.

The capability of these systems to process and analyse large volumes of transactions in real time is one of their most significant advantages. Unlike traditional methods, which may involve time-consuming manual reviews, decision trees can rapidly sift through data, providing immediate alerts on suspicious activities. This speed and efficiency are crucial in a domain where the timely detection of fraud can prevent substantial financial losses and reputational damage.

These systems employ decision trees to facilitate their financial data analysis.

Decision Tree

Decision trees work by categorising transaction data based on defined characteristics and patterns. Each branch of the tree represents a decision path, leading to a conclusion about the nature of a transaction—whether it's legitimate or potentially fraudulent.

The system considers various factors, such as transaction amount, frequency, geographical location, and user behaviour, to make informed decisions. This methodical approach allows for a nuanced analysis of transaction data, effectively pinpointing unusual patterns that may indicate fraudulent activities.

Enhancing Security and Trust

Decision trees in fraud detection not only enhance the security of financial transactions but also reinforce consumer trust. By proactively identifying and preventing fraud, these systems ensure a safer transaction environment for users.

Moreover, the precision of decision trees in distinguishing legitimate transactions from fraudulent ones minimises the inconvenience of false positives, where legitimate activities are mistakenly flagged as suspicious.

Outcome

The deployment of decision trees in financial fraud detection exemplifies the powerful application of symbolic AI in the financial industry. These systems have revolutionised the way financial fraud is identified and prevented, offering a more secure, efficient, and reliable approach to transaction analysis.

As financial technology continues to evolve, the role of AI in fraud detection is set to become increasingly crucial, offering more advanced and effective solutions for safeguarding financial assets and consumer trust.

Drug Discovery and Development

In the pharmaceutical industry, the use of knowledge graphs and ontologies for drug discovery and development has become a crucial element in advancing medical science. Such systems organise and interpret vast amounts of biomedical data, enabling researchers to uncover new drug interactions and therapies efficiently.

These systems utilise ontologies and knowledge graphs to help researchers make sense of biomedical data.

Ontologies and Knowledge Graphs

Ontologies in pharmaceutical research provide a standardised language and structure to represent biomedical concepts and their interrelations. They enable researchers to categorise and link diverse types of data in a meaningful way, enhancing the searchability and analysis of information relevant to drug development. For instance, an ontology might define a hierarchical structure of diseases, symptoms, and drug compounds, making it easier to explore potential therapeutic relationships.

Knowledge graphs act as a dynamic map of interconnected biomedical information. They link data points such as chemical properties of compounds, genetic information, clinical trial outcomes, and existing medical literature. This interconnectedness allows for a holistic view of the data, fostering breakthroughs in understanding complex drug interactions and disease mechanisms.

Accelerating Drug Development

The combination of knowledge graphs and ontologies accelerates the drug development process, from initial research to clinical trials. By offering a comprehensive and interconnected database of biomedical knowledge, these tools enable researchers to rapidly identify potential drug candidates and help anticipate their effects.

This not only speeds up the research phase, but also contributes to more targeted and effective clinical trials.

Outcome

The integration of structured approaches in drug discovery and development is a testament to the impact of AI in the pharmaceutical industry. These tools have revolutionised the way medical research is conducted, offering a more efficient, accurate, and comprehensive approach to developing new drugs.

As biomedical data continues to grow in volume and complexity, the role of AI in drug discovery promises to become even more pivotal, driving innovation and advancements in medical treatments and therapies.

Conclusion

Through the 1960s and '70s, there was a growing disillusionment with the idea of centrally planned infrastructure and economies. The hopes of the 1950s had crashed headlong into the messy realities of a complex and very human world. In retrospect, such strategies were seen as overly optimistic, failing to anticipate the complications and exceptions that inevitably arise in large-scale endeavours.

In computer science, too, the dreams of symbolic AI were beginning to unravel. A long list of issues had been building up throughout the '60s and '70s. Trivial knowledge could be encoded—but useful knowledge is rarely trivial.

It proved near-impossible to box off a subset of knowledge in clean, self-contained ways. An expert system couldn't easily be isolated to a narrow domain such as medicine, finance, or transport. Instead, knowledge branched out like the roots of a tree, sprawling across an ever-expanding surface area.

Worse, the systems depended on rigid, exhaustive sets of rules. But real-world knowledge is full of exceptions, outliers, and uncertainty—qualities that defy the neat categorisation required by strict logic.

In the rigid world of deductive systems, rule-breakers quickly became showstoppers. Deviations that are often essential to human understanding became stumbling blocks to progress.

Adding to the long list of practical difficulties, a significant challenge came from the philosophers, known as *the symbolic grounding problem*. In human cognition, symbols have meaning because they are tied to sensory perception and lived experience. When you think about an apple, you recall how it looks, feels, smells, and tastes. But symbolic AI lacked this connection. It could state facts about apples using predefined rules—but it had no idea what an apple *actually was*.

Although pioneering for its time, symbolic AI is now often described as something necessary, but not sufficient for machine intelligence. Modern computer scientists sometimes refer to it—affectionately but somewhat dismissively—as "good old-fashioned AI" (GOFAI).

Structured approaches alone proved inadequate for grappling with the messy complexity of the real world. The rigid rules they relied on struggled to handle the disorder, ambiguity, and rapid change typical of human-generated data.

Yet symbolic AI did not mark a dead end. The techniques it developed have been woven into the foundations of today's computing systems. Many of its ideas are so deeply embedded that modern developers rarely think about them consciously—they are simply part of the plumbing.

CHAPTER

3

Statistical AI

The early optimism about AI capabilities gave way to the realisation that the technology was not yet advanced enough to fulfil the grand expectations. Funding for AI research decreased, and there was a general decline in interest and research activity in the field. This period later became known as "The First AI Winter."

Something else was needed—something more flexible and adaptive than rule-based systems—something that could more comprehensively address the complicated and multifaceted world of human knowledge. Researchers increasingly understood that the datasets were not inert collections of numbers but narratives in their own right.

The data contained patterns, anomalies, and recurring structures—signals that often pointed to causal or correlational relationships worth investigating. Data could, to some extent, "describe itself," providing leads and hypotheses that expert intuition alone had missed.

Consequently, attention turned back to the classical toolkit of mathematics and statistics. Statisticians were already developing robust methods for sampling, testing, and quantifying uncertainty; these techniques proved ideal for extracting reliable inferences from messy, real-world data. By marrying exploratory discovery with formal statistical models, researchers could both uncover patterns and assess their significance, laying the foundations for the data-driven, inductive approaches that followed.

Overview

Before going into the depths of statistical AI, let's begin with a concise overview of the key ideas, techniques, and motivations behind statistical AI. We will start by introducing how statistical approaches treat data as the principal form of knowledge—using sampling, probabilistic models, inference, and methods for quantifying uncertainty to detect patterns, make predictions, and test hypotheses—giving you a clear sense of what statistical AI is and why it matters, without getting into the detailed mechanisms.

Data-Driven Approaches

Data, in its essence, is a tapestry of stories waiting to be told. Within its complex folds and intricate structures lie hidden patterns and concepts. These stories reveal themselves only to those who approach them with curiosity and an open mind.

It is akin to exploring a vast, uncharted landscape, where the features are not marked but are instead woven into the very fabric of the terrain. Those who arrive with preconceived notions, attempting to coerce the data to fit their expectations, often find themselves lost and disorientated.

Real-world data is dynamic and multifaceted; it does not conform to rigid expectations but instead unfolds in its own unique, sometimes surprising ways—offering insights to those willing to listen to its story.

As highlighted in Chapter 1, "The Evolution of AI," dating back to the Dartmouth workshop, computer scientists have recognised the distinction between deductive and inductive systems. While deductive systems initially garnered the attention of AI researchers, inductive systems were also quietly advancing in the background. Initially seen as separate approaches, today we recognise them as mutually complementary.

Inductive systems are characterised by their ability to derive generalised conclusions from specific observations or data. Unlike deductive reasoning, which starts with general premises and derives specific conclusions, inductive reasoning begins with specific instances and works towards general patterns or principles. Inductive systems aim to infer underlying rules, trends, or hypotheses from empirical evidence. Hence, they often yield probabilistic, rather than logically certain, conclusions.

Typical characteristics of inductive systems are:

- **Data-driven approaches:** A focus on learning from data, rather than relying upon predefined rules.
- **Handling uncertainty:** Use of statistical and probabilistic models to quantify and manage uncertainties and exceptions.

- **Pattern and feature recognition:** Use of statistical methodologies to automatically recognise patterns and relationships within data.
- **Learning from data:** Adapting to changing environments and data distributions as they are encountered.

The methodologies underpinning inductive systems were all about working from the bottom up—accepting the messy world of data and building patterns and rules from what was observed, rather than from what was expected to be seen.

Statistics

Inductive systems draw heavily on statistics—a field of study that involves collecting, analysing, interpreting, presenting, and organising data. Unlike mathematics in general, which focuses on abstract concepts and relationships, statistics deals with real-world data and variability. It provides tools and techniques for summarising and understanding data patterns, and it is particularly effective at addressing uncertainty and handling outliers. This is because it allows us to quantify and manage the inherent randomness and variability within data.

You may recall from your school days first encountering statistics and delving into concepts like mean, mode, median, range, and standard deviation. These fundamental techniques, known as descriptive statistics, are foundational to the field. They form the bedrock for the more sophisticated methods employed in AI, which we will outline later in this chapter.

Statistics has a long history that predates its adoption by AI researchers; the study of probability traces back to the 17th century with Pascal and Fermat, statistical methods were formalised over the following centuries—notably by Gauss and Laplace in the 18th–19th centuries, and later by Karl Pearson in the late 19th and early 20th centuries—and these developments laid the foundations for many techniques later used in inductive systems.

By using statistical methods, informed decisions can be made based on the available information, even when dealing with incomplete or noisy data. Outliers—data points that significantly differ from the rest of the dataset—can often be problematic during analysis. However, statistics provides methods to identify, understand, and handle outliers appropriately.

The combination of statistical methods with computing power enabled the AI community to create learning algorithms that could process and understand large datasets, leading to advancements in machine learning and data-driven AI.

While the term *learning* might evoke images of human education and growth, the concept takes on a distinct form within the realm of artificial intelligence. In AI, learning refers to the process by which algorithms and approaches adapt and improve based on earlier observations in data. This adaptation does not mirror human cognitive development—rather, it is more akin to a cycle of continuous refinement.

During the formative years of AI, many researchers worked to develop the area of inductive systems, although that name was not common at the time. More so than their deductive counterparts, these systems required copious amounts of data and substantial computational resources, often pushing the limits of available digital information and hardware at the time. Yet, incremental headway was achieved, particularly in domains distinct from symbolic AI.

Since inductive approaches were well suited to pattern discovery, new domains became amenable to computation. Edward Feigenbaum and Joshua Lederberg, for example, developed techniques to assist with problems in organic chemistry, while Donald Michie made early contributions to machine learning and to applying computational methods in scientific research. At the same time, researchers across the field—including John McCarthy, who helped define AI, and Richard Karp, noted for his work on algorithms and computational complexity—advanced the algorithms and theoretical frameworks that later supported basic reasoning, planning, and learning.

Board games were a prime target. Arthur Samuel and others developed the first self-learning checkers-playing programme. Richard Greenblatt, Alex Bernstein, and many others developed chess-playing systems that began to challenge human opponents.

A key area of research was natural language processing. Normal human discourse, like so much else about humanity, proved difficult to capture using rigid rule sets. Researchers such as Joseph Weizenbaum, Roger Schank, Terry Winograd, Karen Spärck Jones, and many others explored different ways for computers to handle language—some through symbolic reasoning, others through statistical or information-retrieval techniques. Although their systems did not yet learn grammatical rules from data in the modern sense, their pioneering work laid essential foundations for the more advanced, data-driven language processing methods used today.

Although AI researchers were making steady progress, problems were also mounting for the inductive approach. Among these were a lack of data, insufficient computational resources, noisy or biased datasets, and a dearth of theories and algorithms.

It can be hard for us today to understand the limitations under which these early researchers were working. Their world remained largely analogue—digital records were rare, narrowly focused, and often inaccessible to researchers. A typical computer used by a researcher might be outpaced by an inexpensive smartphone today.

Despite these formidable challenges, early inductive AI research paved the way for significant advancements. Over time, researchers developed techniques to address many of these issues. Through the relentless process of digitisation, an ever-increasing amount of data and computing power became available. The seeds laid by this early work led directly to the development of modern machine learning and data-driven AI approaches, which we will cover in later chapters.

Core Concepts and Mechanisms

Statistical AI is characterised by its data-driven approach, built upon several techniques and methodologies that leverage the vast quantities of digital data available today. By looking at a handful of these approaches in broad terms, you can gain a working sense of the toolkit and where each method fits.

note **Each of these concepts—along with several others—is covered in much more detail in the later "In-depth" section.**

Data is often described as either *structured* or *unstructured*. Structured data fits neatly into rows and columns (names, dates, IDs), making it easy for machines to search and analyse—like tidy bank statements—although it can be labour-intensive to clean and categorise. Unstructured data (documents, images, video) is more like a bag of mixed receipts: rich in information, but harder to interpret, and extracting meaning from it is one of the core challenges statistical AI is designed to tackle.

Two key attributes of data that often require special attention are *spatial* (geo-tagged) and *temporal* (time-series). Spatial data adds location and relationships like distance and proximity, while temporal data adds sequence and change over time—both of which demand specialised techniques to model properly. Together, these dimensions help AI uncover patterns, optimise systems, and make forecasts that reflect how the real world moves through space and time.

Sampling is the statistical art of learning about a whole population from a carefully chosen subset—like tasting a spoonful of well-stirred soup. Political polling estimates national opinion from a few thousand respondents, and AI systems similarly train and evaluate models on samples rather than entire populations. Good sampling is a balancing act: we want enough data to be reliable, while minimising bias and respecting data quality and ethical constraints.

In probability, events may be *independent* (one outcome doesn't affect another), *dependent* (earlier outcomes change later odds), or merely *correlated* (they tend to move together). These distinctions matter in AI because they shape how we model uncertainty and make forecasts. *Correlation*, however, is not *causation*: two things can rise together for a third reason, so treating correlation as proof of cause can lead to confidently wrong conclusions.

Statistical AI looks for *trends* (overall direction over time) and *patterns* (recurring regularities) so it can predict what may happen next. A useful rule of thumb is that a trend is a direction, while a pattern is a shape that repeats. Early systems relied heavily on human experts to spot these signals, but modern AI methods can search for them automatically at scale.

Distributions describe how probabilities are spread across possible outcomes. By adding the random numbers obtained from rolling two dice, not all totals are equally likely—seven is most common because it can be made in the greatest number of ways. Charting the frequency of each total traces out the distribution curve. A common and often naturally encountered example is the bell curve, a graphical representation of the normal distribution. AI uses such distributional patterns to forecast quantities and quantify uncertainty.

Clustering groups items into natural, unlabelled sets, while *classification* assigns items to predefined labels. A music service might cluster songs into emergent playlists based on similarity, or classify a new track as Rock or Jazz using patterns learned from tagged examples. The choice depends on whether you're discovering structure in the data or applying an existing taxonomy.

Features are the variables a model uses to recognise structure in data, and good feature choices make the difference between signal and noise. *Underfitting* happens when the model is too simple to capture important relationships, while *overfitting* happens when it matches the training data so closely that it performs poorly on new examples. Effective models balance both by selecting informative features and validating that they generalise.

Regression models learn relationships between variables to predict a numeric outcome, such as daily shop traffic from weather, weekday, and local events. Simple linear regression relates one input to an outcome with a best-fit line; multiple linear regression extends this to several inputs to capture combined effects. Modern computers can fit and evaluate these higher-dimensional relationships efficiently, revealing how different factors contribute. The aim is to quantify how independent variables relate to a dependent outcome.

Bayesian methods update an initial belief (a prior) as new evidence arrives, producing a revised belief (a posterior) that can support better predictions—for example, estimating the chance a customer buys after seeing promotion responses. They are well suited to uncertain, changing environments because the model can update continuously as more data arrives. An autonomous car, for instance, can combine prior knowledge (such as traffic rules) with live sensor data to maintain safe, probabilistic estimates of what is happening around it.

In-depth

Using that foundational information presented in the previous section, let's now take an in-depth look at statistical AI. Let's dig into how large datasets can be interpreted and analysed using statistical methods, allowing AI systems to make predictions, infer patterns, and deliver useful outcomes across a broad range of use cases.

Data, Data, Data . . .

A common definition of statistics is:

> The practice or science of collecting and analysing numerical data in large quantities, especially for inferring proportions in a whole from those in a representative sample.

A crucial aspect of this definition is "data in large quantities." For statistical methods to be effective, they require extensive datasets—generally, the bigger and more representative, the better.

In AI's early days, digital data was scarce, limited in both scope and depth. However, with the relentless rise of digitisation, the availability of data has skyrocketed, producing an unparalleled deluge of digital information. Every day, countless terabytes of data are generated—encompassing everything from documents, emails, social media posts, and photos, to sensor readings and more.

Astonishingly, more digital data has been produced in the last few years than in all previous human history, and this trend is accelerating. As a citizen of this digital age, you're likely inundated with data.

The explosion of data has been matched by advances in techniques to extract value from this growing trove of information. At the same time, computing capabilities have grown exponentially, enabling the processing of data at previously unthinkable scales. This synergy between data growth and computational power underpins the value unlocked by statistical approaches.

Data, Information, Knowledge, Wisdom

While *data* is a broad term, understanding it becomes easier when we look at a commonly used model among computer scientists: the Data–Information–Knowledge–Wisdom (DIKW) pyramid as shown in Figure 3.1.

The DIKW framework helps us differentiate between various stages of data processing and utilisation:

- **Data:** We start by collecting the raw, unprocessed figures and facts from different sources. Examples include temperature readings, pressure levels, wind speeds, and wind directions.
- **Information:** Here we add structure to raw data. This could involve compiling temperature ranges, calculating average wind speeds, or identifying the hottest places.
- **Knowledge:** Next, we apply algorithms to structured information to derive deeper insights. Examples are weather forecasts, seasonal predictions, or climate models.
- **Wisdom:** Finally, we come to the practical application of knowledge within a specific context—for instance, deciding to carry an umbrella because rain is predicted.

This hierarchy functions as a pyramid where the quantity decreases as we move up. The base, data, is abundant, but as we refine the data into higher states, the quantity decreases and the value increases. Each step builds on the previous one; a vast amount of data is needed to create information, which in turn is processed to develop knowledge, leading ultimately to wisdom.

Each transition up the pyramid relies on different approaches and methodologies—from collecting and cleaning raw measurements, to

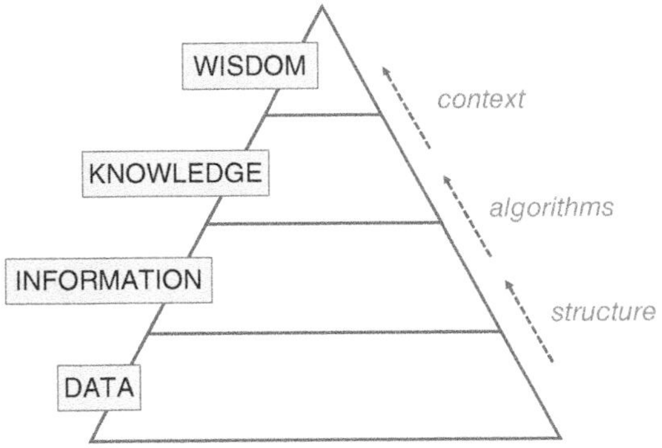

Figure 3.1: Data–Information–Knowledge–Wisdom (DIKW) pyramid

adding structure to create information, to applying algorithms and domain expertise to build knowledge, and finally to using that knowledge in context and exercising judgement about what to do with the result.

When an AI assistant offers a helpful suggestion to ease your day, it's the culmination of a vast pyramid of data, information, and knowledge, distilled into a single, insightful piece of wisdom.

Structured vs. Unstructured Data

In AI systems, data is typically categorised into two main types: *structured* and *unstructured*, as illustrated in Figure 3.2. Understanding this distinction is key to effectively processing, analysing, and applying data across AI applications.

Structured data is highly organised and follows a specific format, making it easily searchable and interpretable by machines—akin to a neatly arranged file system. It is typically stored in databases with well-defined schemas, with data arranged in tables, rows, and columns, similar to a spreadsheet.

Examples include names, dates, IDs, addresses, dimensions, classifications, locations, credit card numbers, passport numbers, and stock information. This clarity and organisation make structured data simpler to query, process, and analyse. It forms the foundation of the symbolic AI technologies outlined earlier in this book.

A good real-world analogy is personal finance. Structured data is like neatly ordered banking records—dates, amounts, and vendors all aligned in tidy columns. It's clean, searchable, and ready to use.

However, structuring data can be complex, labour-intensive, and costly. It involves categorising, tagging, and arranging raw data into coherent formats. This often requires specialised tools and algorithms, along with significant human effort to define schemas and classification schemes.

Consider the task of cataloguing a museum collection. Each item—from paintings to artefacts—must be recorded with structured attributes such as

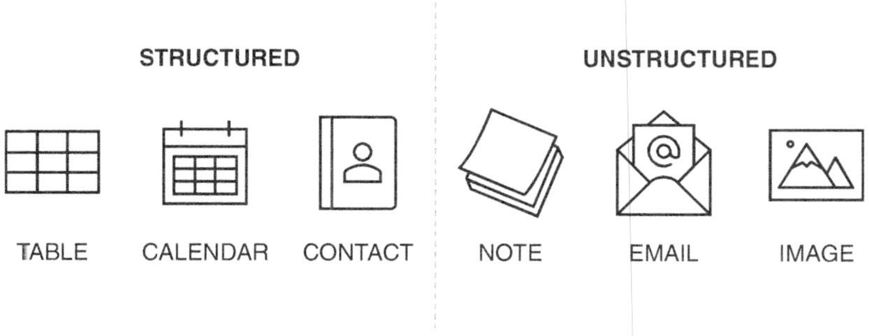

Figure 3.2: Structured vs. unstructured data sources

title, artist, date of creation, material, dimensions, and provenance. While this format enables easy search and analysis, the transformation process demands domain expertise, technical precision, and careful judgement.

Even then, not all data fits neatly into target structures. As discussed in the previous chapter, this rigidity has historically limited symbolic AI approaches.

Unstructured data presents a different challenge. It is less orderly, does not conform to standard formats, and is harder to categorise or organise. This includes free-form text, images, videos, and social media content—data typically created for a specific, narrow purpose. Returning to our personal finance analogy, unstructured data is more like a jumble of handwritten notes and crumpled receipts at the bottom of your bag—all the information is there, but making sense of it takes time, effort, and context.

Crucially, the vast majority of digital data today—including websites, tweets, emails, and audio or video recordings—is unstructured. While rich in information, it cannot be processed effectively using traditional methods without first applying more advanced techniques.

Extracting value from unstructured data requires sophisticated tools capable of interpreting complexity and nuance. This is the primary focus of statistical AI approaches, which are designed to work with the scale, variety, and ambiguity found in unstructured data.

Space and Time

Two special attributes that commonly arise and require specific attention are *spatial* (such as geo-tagged) data and *temporal* (such as time series) data as shown in the example use case in Figure 3.3. These are prevalent in a wide array of datasets and demand specialised algorithms and methodologies.

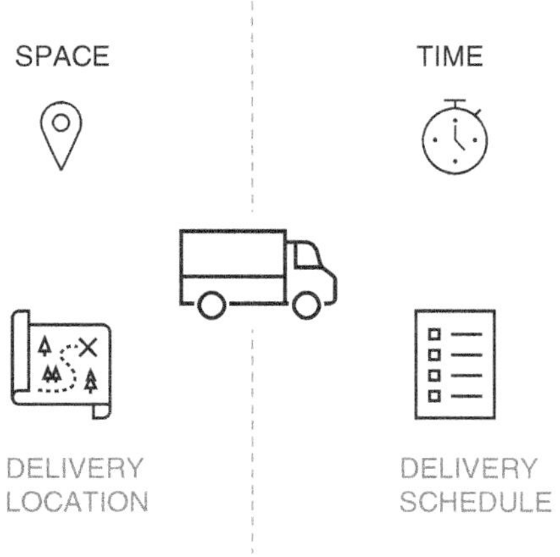

Figure 3.3: Space and time data

Geo-tagged data, or spatial data, is information directly linked to geographical locations. It has become increasingly common in the era of smartphones and GPS-enabled devices, where each data point is often accompanied by coordinates denoting its physical position. Examples include mapping services, social media check-ins, vehicle tracking, and geographic data from sensors.

Analysing spatial data can reveal patterns related to movement, demographic distributions, environmental change, and more. However, this data is often complex—it includes not just points, but also lines, polygons, and varying scales. Specialised algorithms are needed to account for geographical constraints and relationships such as distance, proximity, area, and even the curvature of the earth.

Typical questions we might ask of geo-tagged data include:

- Where are the "hotspots"—the clusters of incidents, demand, or activity?
- How do patterns differ by neighbourhood, region, or catchment area?
- What is the shortest path between two points—and how does it change with constraints and conditions?
- How far do people travel to reach a service, and which areas are underserved?

Time series data involves information linked to specific time points or intervals. It appears in many domains—from natural phenomena and economic activity to health monitoring—and captures how variables change over time.

Time series analysis is crucial for identifying trends, forecasting future events, and detecting anomalies. It uses statistical methods that account for sequential order, temporal dependencies, and causality, often incorporating factors like seasonality, trends, and periodicity.

Typical questions we might ask of time-stamped data include:

- What is changing over time—and is it a genuine trend or just noise?
- Are there cycles or seasonality (daily, weekly, yearly) that can be exploited?
- What happens before and after key events (a promotion, a policy change, a system outage)?
- Can what comes next be forecasted, and how confident should we be with the predictions?

These two classifications are often presented together, but they are not disjoint. Data can be both geo-tagged and time-stamped simultaneously.

For example, data describing the movements of a train along its route exhibits both attributes.

As both data types become increasingly prevalent, so too does the need for tailored approaches in AI and data science. Space and time are fundamental dimensions not only in data analysis but also in broader scientific inquiry.

Just as physics relies on space-time to understand the universe, data science leverages geo-tagged and time-stamped information to reveal patterns, optimise systems, and predict future outcomes—enabling breakthroughs in fields ranging from environmental monitoring and urban planning to logistics and public health.

Wider Data Classification Schemes

Our earlier distinctions—structured versus unstructured, and space and time—are useful, but they are not rigid boxes. Real-world datasets are messy and hybrid; a single source may combine tidy database fields with free-form text and images. A single dataset can be spatial, temporal, transactional, and streaming all at once, depending on how it is captured and used.

So the goal of classification is not to force data into one category, but to highlight the properties that matter for storage, processing, and interpretation. Hence, there are a great many classifications of data commonly used within AI systems. Some of the most frequent include:

- **Quantitative vs. qualitative data:** Quantitative data is numerical and measurable, like temperature readings. Qualitative data is descriptive and non-numerical, such as customer opinions or product reviews.
- **Primary vs. secondary data:** Primary data is collected first-hand for a specific purpose. Secondary data is preexisting information repurposed for a new use.
- **Big data:** Defined by its large volume, high velocity, and wide variety, big data refers to massive datasets that exceed the capacity of traditional data processing tools.
- **Transactional data:** Generated by financial or operational transactions, transactional data is key for analysing business activity and customer behaviour.
- **Streaming data:** Continuously produced and lacking natural boundaries, often by sensors or online interactions, streaming data requires real-time processing and analysis.

Many other such classification schemes are used, and none is definitive. The point is practical: Each lens highlights different constraints and opportunities—it can change what tools are used, what assumptions can safely be made, and which assumptions need to be carefully analysed.

Sampling

When you make a pot of soup, how do you ensure it has the correct seasoning? It would be strange indeed to consume the entire pot just to check if every part is seasoned as expected. Instead, as long as the soup is well stirred, a single spoonful is enough to assess the seasoning of the whole batch.

This technique, known as *sampling*, is a fundamental approach in statistical data processing. It relies on the idea illustrated in Figure 3.4 that a small, carefully chosen subset can preserve the important patterns of the whole—provided the sample is representative.

Consider, for example, political sentiment polling. Surveying an entire population would be impractical—so statisticians select a smaller, manageable sample. If chosen well, this sample can reflect broader public opinion. By chosen well, we mean designed to be representative: covering different regions and demographics, and accounting for non-response and other sources of bias.

Similarly, in AI, samples can be drawn from large datasets to train algorithms efficiently. If an AI system is learning to recognise images, it doesn't necessarily need to process every image available. In a modern setting, vast quantities of information are available, and the cost of processing each item—though small in isolation—can quickly scale up to huge amounts of time, energy, and money.

A carefully selected, representative sample is often enough to teach the underlying patterns and support useful predictions, because it captures much of the variation that exists in the full dataset.

Sampling offers major efficiencies in data processing. However, it comes with a trade-off: samples are never perfect, and some loss of fidelity—or increase in uncertainty—is inevitable. Robust sampling is also surprisingly

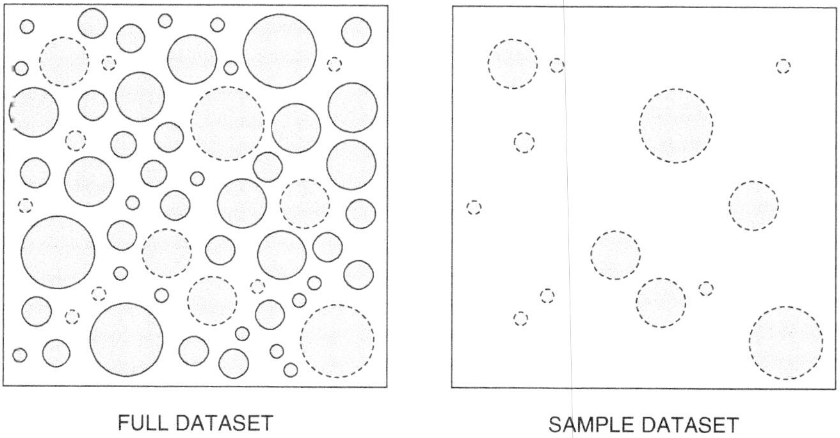

Figure 3.4: Data sampling

difficult, and it must be done carefully to ensure results remain valid and meaningful.

Types of Sampling

Real-world data is messy and hybrid. No single sampling method works well in every situation. Instead, different approaches are used depending on what needs to be are measured, how the data is collected, and practical constraints exist.

- **Random sampling:** Every member of a population has an equal chance of being selected. This method is ideal for achieving an unbiased sample, but it requires a complete list of the population—which isn't always feasible.
- **Stratified sampling:** A population is divided into subgroups (*strata*) based on shared characteristics, and samples are taken from each group. This ensures representation from each subgroup, making it useful when certain segments are of specific interest.
- **Cluster sampling:** A population is divided into clusters, and a few clusters are randomly selected. All members of the chosen clusters are then surveyed. This method is cost-effective, especially when the population is large and geographically dispersed.
- **Systematic sampling:** Members are selected at regular intervals from a list or sequence. This method is simple and quick, but it can introduce bias if there's an underlying pattern in the population.
- **Over and under sampling:** Imbalanced datasets are addressed by increasing minority representation (via duplication or generation) or reducing majority representation (via removal). Both help balance the dataset but carry trade-offs: oversampling risks overfitting, while undersampling may discard useful information.

Many other sampling methods exist and there's no single "best" method. Data scientists must make choices based on the specific needs of the study. The key is to understand the strengths and limitations of each approach, ensuring the sampling strategy fits both the research goals and the nature of the data.

Considerations and Challenges

Sampling can be remarkably powerful, but it is never free. The moment we work with a subset rather than the whole, we take on a set of practical and ethical decisions that shape what we can safely conclude.

In practice, good sampling depends on a few key considerations:

- **Sample size:** Determining the right sample size is crucial. Too small a sample might not capture the population's diversity, leading to inaccurate results. Too large, and it may be unnecessarily costly or time-consuming.
- **Sampling bias:** Bias can occur if the sample isn't representative of the population. This might result from poor selection methods or non-response bias—where certain individuals are less likely to participate.
- **Data quality:** The quality of data collected from the sample can significantly affect the study's conclusions. Inaccurate or misleading data can lead to incorrect inferences about the broader population.
- **Ethical considerations:** Especially in human research, ethics are essential. Informed consent, confidentiality, and respectful treatment of participants must be upheld.

Beyond these, one subtle challenge is that bias can come from what we never see—what isn't present in the corpus at all. For example, a political survey that relies on telephone polling will tend to exclude people without phones, people who don't pick up unknown callers, and people whose working patterns make them hard to reach.

Similar issues arise in AI. If the data under-represents certain communities or contexts, the system may perform poorly for them or fail to reflect their needs. Yet those same people may still be affected by the decisions the system helps to make. This is why knowing how data was generated and collected matters as much as analysing it.

Understanding these factors is vital for effective, ethical sampling—so that the patterns revealed are real, the uncertainty is understood, and the people affected by the analysis are not quietly excluded. As with soup tasting, the key is not just having a spoonful, but choosing it deliberately: large enough to be informative, balanced enough to be fair, and gathered with care.

Probability Theory

Probability theory, a fundamental branch of mathematics, focuses on quantifying the likelihood of different outcomes in various scenarios or experiments. It assesses, for example, the chances of rolling a double six with a pair of dice, drawing the ace of spades from a deck of cards, winning the lottery, or developing lung cancer after years of smoking.

This theory forms the cornerstone of statistical AI, offering a structured framework for measuring uncertainty. It equips AI algorithms with the ability to predict future events based on past data—even amidst randomness and variability. This is crucial for modelling and interpreting the randomness and variability present in real-world data.

The origins of probability theory stretch back centuries. Pioneers such as Gerolamo Cardano began analysing games of chance in quantitative terms, and in the mid-17th century Blaise Pascal and Pierre de Fermat developed foundational ideas while discussing gambling problems. Christiaan Huygens helped formalise these insights, transforming chance from a matter of luck into a discipline that could be measured.

In the 18th century, figures like Jacob Bernoulli and Abraham de Moivre expanded the field. Bernoulli introduced the Law of Large Numbers, while de Moivre's work on the normal distribution helped establish probability as a vital mathematical discipline—influencing domains as varied as insurance, finance, and the natural sciences, and showing that even games of chance follow discernible patterns.

Before diving deeper into probability theory, you might recall basic descriptive statistics from school—including mean, mode, median, range, and standard deviation. These foundational tools are essential for summarising and understanding datasets. They form the groundwork for more advanced topics in probability and inferential analysis—both pivotal in the context of statistical AI.

Independent, Dependent, and Correlated Events

When calculating the likelihood of an event, it's crucial to understand the type of event in question. These can be classified into the following three broad categories, which are also illustrated in Figure 3.5:

- **Independent events:** Events where the outcome is not influenced by previous or future outcomes. For instance, the probability of a coin toss resulting in heads or tails is always 50/50, regardless of earlier or later tosses.

Figure 3.5: Relationship between events

- **Dependent events:** Events where the outcome is affected by previous outcomes. For example, the probability of drawing the ace of spades from a deck increases each time a card is removed and not replaced.
- **Correlated events:** Events that are related to each other in some way. An example is the relationship between height and weight—generally, taller individuals tend to weigh more than shorter ones.

In probability theory, understanding the nature of the event is essential, as it determines the appropriate methods for analysing outcomes and making predictions.

While independent, dependent, and correlated events cover a wide range of scenarios, in the real world more nuanced relationships exist. For example, *conditionally independent* events may look related overall, but become independent once we take a third factor into account. As an example, carrying an umbrella and having wet shoes are correlated; but if we condition on whether it rained, the link largely disappears.

This brings us to another important consideration—especially when interpreting correlated events—namely the distinction between *correlation* and *causation*. Correlation implies a relationship or association between variables, but it does not necessarily mean that one causes the other.

This is often a source of confusion: correlation (when two things move together) is conflated with causation (when one thing drives the other). Just because two things happen at the same time doesn't mean that one causes the other. For example, both ice cream sales and drowning incidents rise in the summer, but buying ice cream doesn't cause drowning.

A more subtle example: Studies often find that children who eat breakfast regularly do better at school. But that does not mean breakfast alone causes better grades. Breakfast might be part of a broader pattern that includes sleep, routine, parental support, or household stability—factors that are correlated with both breakfast habits and academic performance.

Understanding such distinctions—and how events are related—is crucial for making accurate predictions using AI.

Trends, Patterns, and Predictions

A pivotal goal of AI and data science is the identification of trends and patterns to make useful predictions—projecting future outcomes from historical data. This process is closely linked to the core principles of probability theory and statistical analysis, particularly in the context of dependent and correlated events.

A *trend* in data signifies a general direction over time. AI uses trend analysis to understand long-term shifts or developments. In financial markets, this might involve analysing stock price movements to guide investment strategies. In healthcare, trends in patient data can indicate changes in disease prevalence. These often involve correlated events, which AI systems leverage to forecast future scenarios.

Patterns are recurring themes or regularities found within data. Pattern recognition is fundamental in AI, especially when working with dependent or correlated data. Retailers use it to analyse customer behaviour and tailor marketing strategies, while cybersecurity systems detect patterns associated with breaches. Recognising such patterns is essential for effective AI applications.

One practical way to understand the distinction is to think of a *trend* as a direction, and a *pattern* as a recurring shape. A trend might be a steady rise in energy use over several years; a pattern might be the predictable daily peaks that occur every morning and evening. In practice, the same dataset can contain both: long-term drift, and repeating cycles layered on top.

Distinguishing genuine trends and patterns from random fluctuations is difficult—particularly in datasets with strong dependency or correlation. Short runs of "good luck" can look like momentum; one-off events can look like a new regime; and searching across enough variables, we will almost always find something that appears meaningful. Robust analysis therefore depends on checking whether an apparent signal is stable over time, whether it holds in new data, and whether it survives plausible alternative explanations.

Traditionally, domain experts played a central role in this process: they framed the question, suggested which factors might matter, and sanity-checked results against real-world constraints. Many early statistical AI systems worked hand-in-hand with experts, narrowing the search space and reducing the risk of mistaking noise for insight.

However, many modern AI systems can analyse vast numbers of combinations, uncovering patterns and trends that may escape human attention. This can be valuable, but it introduces practical and ethical challenges. A model might latch onto proxy signals that reflect inequality rather than underlying causes, or it might discover a pattern that is real in one context but brittle in another—yet still drive consequential decisions.

Further, people may become uncomfortable with automated analysis—especially when the results influence jobs, credit, healthcare, or policing. Human oversight can help build trust and catch obvious mistakes, but it can also limit the scale and speed of what can be achieved. In practice, the goal usually requires a balance: Use automation to handle volume, and apply human judgement, governance, and auditing where the stakes are highest.

For these reasons, pattern and trend finding is not just a technical exercise. It requires transparency about how conclusions were reached, careful validation of what generalises beyond the training data, and accountability for the decisions made on the basis of those results.

Distributions

Distributions are a vital tool in statistical AI, offering insight into data behaviour and the probabilities that underlie it. Essentially, a *distribution* maps how the values of a variable are spread across a range of possible outcomes.

To illustrate, consider rolling two dice. Over many rolls, a total of 7 appears more often than a total 2 or 12 because there are more combinations of two dice that produce seven. The pattern of how often each total appears—from 2 to 12—forms a distribution. Literally how the possible values are distributed over the range.

The concept of distributions was first formalised by Carl Friedrich Gauss in the 19th century, building on work by Abraham de Moivre, and further developed by Francis Galton. Early applications included measurement and experimental error, astronomy, and the study of variation in human traits.

Of course, different distributions occur in different scenarios—dice throwing will look different from rainfall, call arrivals in a contact centre, or the number of faults on a production line. When we plot these distributions on a chart, each produces a distinctive curve.

A common and often recurring distribution is shown in Figure 3.6, which is the *normal distribution*—often called the *bell curve* due to the shape it plots out on a chart. The normal distribution is particularly important due to its frequent appearance in both natural and social data, and its central role in AI.

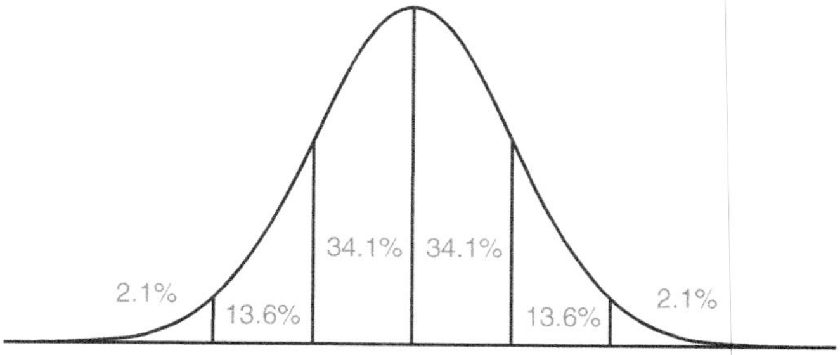

Figure 3.6: Normal distribution

Variations of the bell curve appear in many real-world scenarios—such as human height, exam scores, measurement errors, and manufacturing tolerances—making the normal distribution a central tool in statistical analysis.

But the spectrum of distributions goes well beyond the bell curve. A few other key distributions models include:

- **Binomial distribution:** Used for binary outcomes, such as success or failure, across repeated trials—for example, estimating the number of patients likely to recover after treatment in a medical study.
- **Poisson distribution:** Used for counting how often events occur within a given interval or space. Classic examples include the number of cars passing a sensor in one hour, or the number of calls received by a call centre per minute.
- **Uniform distribution:** Used when all outcomes in a range are equally likely. A simple example is a fair dice roll, where each face has the same chance of appearing.

Many other distribution models also exist. Understanding distributions is especially important for *independent events*, where outcomes have no influence on each other. This is because, when independent events are repeated many times, the overall behaviour becomes predictable in aggregate: The distribution tells the system what results to expect on average, and how much variation is normal.

These principles underpin many practical AI applications. For instance, an AI system might learn what "normal" network behaviour looks like over time. Later, it can flag large deviations from this distribution—a key approach in detecting cybersecurity breaches.

Mastering the subtleties of distributions enhances the performance and realism of AI systems, delivering better outcomes for users. It enables them to model the world more effectively, improving their ability to interpret complex and unpredictable real-world data.

Hypothesis Testing

Hypothesis testing is a fundamental statistical method used to make informed decisions and inferences based on data. It helps determine whether observed results reflect real effects or are simply due to random variation.

In AI, hypothesis testing is commonly used to evaluate whether a new model genuinely improves predictions—or if the observed improvement could have occurred by chance. It is not a technique that end-users of AI will apply themselves—rather it is a methodology used by AI researchers to test the value of the models they are building and operating. It helps ensure that deployed AI is delivering actual value and not phantom outcomes.

The process begins with a *null hypothesis,* which assumes no change or effect—for example, "The new drug has no impact on the disease." This is tested against an alternative hypothesis, such as "The new drug is effective." The goal is to assess whether the data provides strong enough evidence to reject the null hypothesis in favour of the alternative.

A key tool in this process is the *p-value,* which measures the probability of observing results as extreme as those in the sample, assuming the null hypothesis is true. By convention, a low p-value (typically below 0.05) suggests the observed effect is unlikely to be due to chance, and the null hypothesis may be rejected.

Take a simple example: Suppose a trial compares a new drug against a placebo, and researchers observe a difference in recovery rates. A p-value of 0.05 does not mean that there is a 95 percent chance the drug works. It means that if the drug truly had no effect, we would expect to see results at least this extreme about 5 times in 100 similar trials, purely by chance.

However, p-values alone don't tell the whole story. Factors such as *sample size* and *effect size* also matter—providing important context about the strength and significance of findings.

With a very large sample, even a tiny improvement can produce a low p-value. With a small sample, a genuinely useful improvement might look inconclusive because there isn't enough data to separate signal from noise. Effect size keeps the system honest about the practical impact; a "statistically significant" improvement can still be too small to matter in the real world.

Different hypothesis tests can be used depending on what is being measured. Each has its own assumptions and is used depending on the data and the question being asked:

- **t-tests:** Compare the means of two groups. For example, does Model B have a lower average error than Model A on the same test set?
- **chi-square tests:** Used for categorical data. For example, is click-through rate independent of device type (mobile vs. desktop), or are they associated?
- **ANOVA:** Compares means across three or more groups. For example, do three different marketing campaigns produce different average sales?

These tools provide structured ways to evaluate claims and improve decision-making in data-driven systems.

Understanding and quantifying potential errors is also vital. Producing results without corresponding error analysis would be like running a medical test without thinking about false alarms and missed cases. Errors are classified into two broad types:

- **Type I error:** Rejecting a true null hypothesis—indicating a significant result when there isn't one—a *false positive.*
- **Type II error:** Failing to reject a false null hypothesis—leading to a missed detection of a meaningful effect—a *false negative.*

For example, for AI model builders, a false positive might mean concluding a new model is better when it isn't, and rolling it out unnecessarily. A false negative might mean missing a real improvement—or failing to detect a genuine risk—because the test wasn't sensitive enough or there wasn't enough data. Minimising these errors helps ensure that conclusions drawn from data are accurate and robust, improving the reliability of AI systems that are being developed and deployed.

Hypothesis testing offers a rigorous, statistical foundation for evaluating models and guiding decisions in AI. It is a vital part of ensuring that progress in model performance reflects real improvements—not just noise.

Clusters and Classifications

Imagine you've been tasked with organising a brand-new bookshop. Dozens of large boxes filled with books await you—but there's a catch: The books are packed in no particular order. Your challenge is to arrange them on the shelves in a way that makes sense to future customers. One quick and simple method is to sort purely on physical appearance—size, hardback or paperback, page count, and so on. While efficient, it likely won't be very helpful for customers trying to find something specific.

A more useful approach is to consider metadata—details like author, publisher, or language. Using metadata adds some structure, but may still fall short when it comes to guiding customers to the books they want to read. The most effective—though also the most time-consuming—method would be to use a *semantic* approach: organising the books by subject and meaning. This might involve reading the blurb or even skimming the contents to understand what each book is really about.

This process mirrors a common challenge in statistical AI: how to group or label data in meaningful ways. These common use cases are known as *clustering* and *classification* problems, and they underpin many useful AI applications.

We'll return to clustering and classification concepts in the chapter on learning AI, where you'll see how they align with two key methodologies: *supervised* and *unsupervised learning.*

Clustering vs. Classifying

Clustering is the process of grouping a set of objects so that those within the same group are more similar to each other than to those in other groups. It does not rely on predefined categories or labels—the clusters are *discovered* through analysis of the data itself.

For example, consider a music streaming service that wants to categorise songs into playlists. Using clustering, it can group songs based on similarities in melody, beats, artist style, or even lyrics—all without any preset categories.

This method helps uncover natural groupings within data, such as organically identifying genres or sub-genres based on the characteristics of the songs.

Classification, by contrast, is a more human-directed process. The goal is to assign predefined labels to new data based on patterns learnt from a labelled training set. Returning to the music example: if we already have playlists like Rock, Jazz, or Classical, classification involves deciding which of these existing categories a new song belongs to. The system learns from examples that have already been categorised, and then uses those patterns to classify new songs.

While both clustering and classification group data, they do so in fundamentally different ways. Clustering is *exploratory*—it discovers patterns and forms new categories. Classification is *definitive*—it assigns data to existing categories using learnt rules. Each method has its own strengths. The choice between them depends on whether the data already has labels, and what the analysis is trying to achieve.

Discovering Object Clusters

Clustering involves the statistical discovery of similar objects within a large corpus—but how is that achieved?

Several methodologies support this process, each suited to different applications. We'll explore them in more detail in Chapter 5 on learning AI, specifically in the section on *unsupervised learning*. For now, here's a brief introduction to some common clustering techniques:

- **K-means clustering:** Partitions data into a predefined number of clusters by minimising the variance within each cluster. For example, a retailer might group customers into five segments based on buying behaviour, with each customer assigned to the "nearest" segment.
- **Hierarchical clustering:** Builds a hierarchy of clusters by either merging or splitting them step by step. For example, we might see

products first split into broad categories, then subcategories, and then finer groupings based on shared attributes.

- **Density-based spatial clustering:** Forms clusters based on the density of data points, separating dense regions from sparse ones. For example, it can find clusters of GPS points that represent popular venues, while treating occasional stray points as noise.
- **Mean shift clustering:** Locates clusters by shifting data points towards the densest regions in the data space. For example, in image processing it can group pixels into coherent regions by moving each pixel towards the nearest "peak" of similar colour.

Each method has its own strengths and use cases, depending on the nature of the data and the specific goals of the analysis.

Features, Underfitting, and Overfitting

The first critical step for both clustering and classification is effective feature selection. In this context, a *feature* is simply an attribute the model can use—a measurable aspect of an item or observation. For a book this might be genre, author, publication date, or the words in its blurb; for a customer it might be purchase history, browsing patterns, or how often they visit.

Choosing good features is less about finding a universal "right" list and more about matching features to goals. In our bookshop example, if the aim is to help someone choose a book to read, good features might include genre and reading age, whereas page count or cover colour may be less helpful. But if the goal is to decorate a cosy pub, cover design and physical size might be exactly what matters. What counts as a "good" feature depends on the desired outcome.

Once features are selected, two further challenges often arise: underfitting and overfitting.

Underfitting occurs when a model is too simplistic to capture the complexities and subtleties in the data. It's like having overly broad categories in a bookshop—such as classifying all books simply as "fiction" or "nonfiction"—which ignores the rich diversity within each section. Underfitting often results from a model that lacks complexity or is trained on insufficient data.

Overfitting, by contrast, happens when a model becomes too specific, fitting itself too closely to the training data. It's like treating every book as a separate category instead of recognising broader themes. An overfitted model performs well on training data but poorly on new, unseen data, as it has learnt the noise rather than the general patterns. This issue is common in models with many parameters and limited data.

In the real world, underfitting often looks like a model that can't capture obvious structure in the data—like always assuming a commute will take the average time, and missing the predictable peaks caused by school runs or rush hour. Overfitting, by contrast, looks like a model that learns the quirks of the training data too well—like planning tomorrow around last week's exact traffic pattern, and then being caught out when the weather changes or there's an unexpected road closure.

Both underfitting and overfitting highlight the need to balance model complexity with the quantity and quality of training data. In clustering, this balance helps form meaningful and distinct groups. In classification, it ensures the model can generalise accurately to new situations.

We will explore this topic in more detail in Chapter 5, when we look at machine learning.

Regression Analysis

Imagine you're now running that bookshop we spoke about earlier. You notice that some days are busier than others, and you wonder if there's a way to predict how many customers you might expect on a given day. This could help you manage inventory and staffing more effectively. This is where *regression* comes into play.

Regression, in its simplest form, is a method used to understand the relationship between variables. Regression analysis involves examining past data to forecast future outcomes.

In the context of your bookshop, it might help predict customer traffic based on factors like the day of the week, weather conditions, or nearby events. For example, you might find that sunny weekends attract more customers, or that a local street festival boosts footfall.

Historically, the concept of regression was formalised by Sir Francis Galton in the late 19th century while studying the relationship between the heights of fathers and sons, building on earlier mathematical work by Gauss and Legendre. He observed that sons of particularly tall fathers tended to be shorter than their fathers—and those of shorter fathers, taller—a pattern he called *regression towards mediocrity*.

The term regression might seem an odd fit, as it implies a step backward. Galton was referring to a tendency to revert to the average, not foreseeing the much broader role the method would later play in predicting future values.

In the AI world, regression plays a vital role. It underpins many models involved in prediction—from forecasting stock prices and estimating house values to personalising book recommendations in your online store.

Data Assumptions for Regression

Before we delve into the types of regression, it's important to understand some basic assumptions that this methodology relies on. Data used for regression analysis must demonstrate certain characteristics:

- **Linearity:** It must be a straight-line relationship between the variables being studied. In our bookshop example, this would mean that an increase in social media posts consistently leads to an increase in customer visits.
- **Independence:** Each observation should be independent of the others. In practical terms, the number of customers visiting the bookshop today should not be influenced by the number who visited yesterday.
- **Homoscedasticity:** A technical term referring to the idea that the variability in the data remains consistent across all levels of an independent variable. For instance, the variation in customer numbers shouldn't drastically change across different months of the year.

While these assumptions might sound technical, they serve as essential guidelines. If they aren't met, the predictions made by a regression model may be unreliable or misleading.

Simple vs. Multiple Linear Regression

The simplest and most common form of this technique is *simple linear regression*. Imagine you're charting the number of customers visiting your bookstore against the hours of sunshine per day. Plotting this data on a graph—with sunshine hours on the x-axis and customer count on the y-axis—simple linear regression can help draw a straight line that best represents this relationship.

This line, known as the *line of best fit*, minimises the distance between itself and all the points on the graph. It's like finding the average trend in the data, showing the general direction in which things are moving. This can be seen in the middle chart in Figure 3.7.

Now, suppose more factors are to be considered, like the day of the week or the number of promotional posts on social media. This is where *multiple linear regression* comes in. Instead of analysing the relationship between just two variables, it allows the system to include several independent variables to predict the outcome. For example, multiple linear regression could help clarify how sunshine hours, day of the week, and social media activity together influence footfall in the bookstore.

As more variables are added, the more complex the model becomes. This is where computers come into their own. Humans typically struggle to

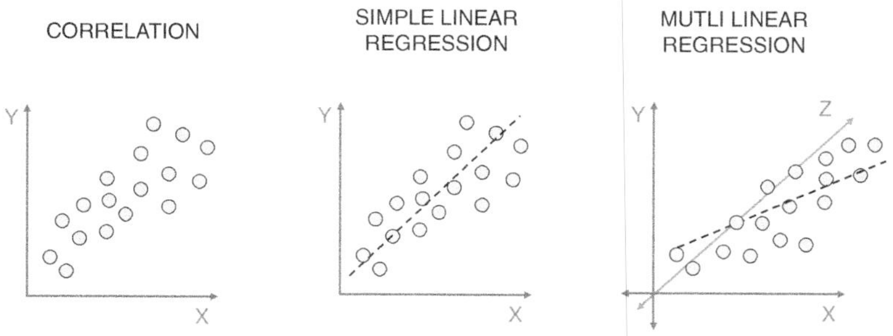

Figure 3.7: Types of regression analysis

visualise relationships in more than three dimensions. Because of the way our perception has evolved over millennia, it's difficult for us to imagine a graph with more than three axes. It simply does not fit within our cognitive capacity. This is illustrated in the rightmost chart in Figure 3.7. Even in this diagram we see the difficulties of representing a three-dimensional space on a two-dimensional page. Computers, however, excel in this space. They can process and analyse data in many dimensions, uncovering relationships and patterns that lie beyond our immediate comprehension. It is of no concern to them whether the graph has 2, 3, or 20 dimensions—the math still works.

In both simple and multiple linear regression, the key is understanding how the independent variables (like sunshine hours, day of the week, and social media posts) relate to the dependent variable (the number of customers). The power of regression lies in its ability to take these variables—however numerous—and reveal how they collectively influence real-world outcomes.

Challenges and Considerations

One of the most important considerations in regression analysis—and in any statistical modelling—is the distinction between *correlation* and *causation*. While regression can reveal a relationship between variables, it doesn't necessarily mean that one variable is causing the other to occur.

For instance, if your bookstore data shows more customers on sunny days, that doesn't definitively prove that good weather is causing more people to visit. It's a correlation—a link or association—but not necessarily a cause. This distinction is crucial, as mistaking correlation for causation can lead to flawed strategies and poor decision-making.

Another challenge in regression analysis is ensuring that the model accurately reflects the data without overfitting or underfitting—issues we explored in the previous section. For example, a system might use a regression model that fits last year's footfall perfectly because it has learnt the quirks of that particular period (a one-off festival or roadworks outside the shop). When those conditions disappear, the predictions fall apart. At the other extreme, a regression model that is too simple might miss obvious structure—such as weekday versus weekend patterns—and consistently under-predict the busiest days.

The quality of the data itself also matters: inaccuracies, inconsistencies, or biases can skew results and lead to misleading conclusions. Trying to apply regression techniques to poor or inaccurate data is like using a warped ruler: the math may be correct, but the measurements are wrong.

Bayesian Methods

Let's revisit our cosy bookstore to explore the intriguing world of Bayesian methods. Imagine you're trying to estimate the likelihood of a customer purchasing a novel from a particular genre. Based on experience, you have a general idea—a *prior* belief—about how popular that genre is. This is where Bayesian methods shine: they allow AI systems to update these initial beliefs with new evidence, leading to improved predictions.

Bayesian methods are named after the British mathematician and Presbyterian minister Thomas Bayes, who in the 18th century derived the foundational theorem now known as *Bayes' Theorem*. His ideas were later expanded by Pierre-Simon Laplace, who developed the modern Bayesian interpretation of updating beliefs with new evidence—a concept now central to statistics and AI.

In Bayesian terms, the *prior* is an initial belief about the probability of a customer buying, say, a science fiction novel. It's based on past experience or general trends in book sales.

Now, suppose you run a special promotion for science fiction books and observe how customers respond. The data from this promotion becomes new evidence. Bayesian methods let the system combine this evidence with the *prior* to form an updated belief—the *posterior* probability. This updated probability gives a more accurate prediction of future science fiction book sales.

The beauty of Bayesian methods lies in this continual updating. As more data is gathered—like customer preferences, seasonal trends, or the effects of marketing—the system's predictions become more refined.

As shown in Figure 3.8, the Bayesian analysis is a process of ongoing learning and adjustment, much like how a seasoned bookseller gets better at spotting trends and anticipating customer needs over time.

Bayesian methods represent a shift from a one-time calculation to an evolving process—one that reflects the dynamic nature of real-world

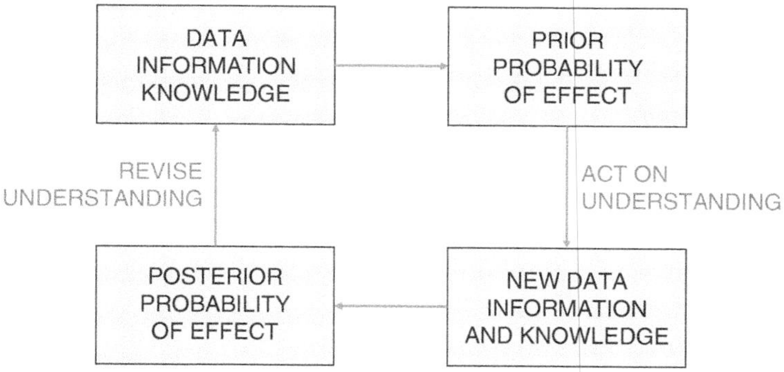

Figure 3.8: Bayesian analysis

scenarios. They offer a powerful framework for AI systems to adapt, learn, and make predictions based not just on static data, but on new information as that information becomes available.

This adaptability is crucial for building AI applications that remain responsive in changing environments.

Handling Uncertainties

Bayesian methods are particularly adept at handling uncertainty—a crucial aspect in the world of AI. They are especially valuable in situations where data is incomplete or ambiguous, making them a key component of AI systems operating in dynamic, real-world environments. The approach allows AI to deal with uncertainty in a structured and logical way.

Consider an autonomous car navigating city streets. It must make countless decisions based on uncertain and constantly changing information. Bayesian methods can enable the car's AI to combine prior knowledge—such as established traffic patterns and flows—with real-time data, including current traffic flow, pedestrian movements, or unexpected hazards.

By continuously updating its beliefs with incoming data, the AI can reassess risks and adapt its decisions to suit the evolving environment. This ongoing process of refinement based on new evidence is a core strength of Bayesian methods.

In our bookstore example, this translates to continually adjusting predictions about book sales as the system learns more about customer preferences and buying habits. Whether it's gauging the popularity of a new genre or measuring the impact of a promotion, Bayesian methods allow AI systems to incorporate new data, update uncertainty, and support better-informed decisions.

Bayesian Networks

Imagine expanding your bookstore's decision-making process to include Bayesian networks—a concept that adds a new dimension to understanding complex relationships. Bayesian networks are like intricate maps of probability, linking various factors that could influence the bookstore's success.

In simple terms, a Bayesian network is a graphical model that represents the conditional dependencies between different variables. Think of it as a conceptual tree, where each node represents a variable (such as book genres, customer demographics, or seasonal trends) and each edge depicts a probabilistic relationship between them.

For example, the likelihood of a customer buying a mystery novel might depend not only on the genre's popularity, but also on factors like the customer's age group, recent bestsellers, or the time of year. In a Bayesian network, these variables are interconnected, allowing AI systems to see how changes in one area can ripple through and affect others.

In AI, Bayesian networks are used to make complex decisions and predictions. They help systems process and analyse webs of interconnected information—making sense of scenarios where many factors interact in subtle, interdependent ways.

Challenges and Considerations

Bayesian methods encounter their own set of challenges, particularly when dealing with high-dimensional data. As AI systems increasingly work with more complex and multifaceted inputs, Bayesian analysis becomes correspondingly more intricate.

These high-dimensional models often stretch beyond what humans can intuitively grasp. The interplay between many variables creates a level of complexity that can be difficult to understand, even for experts.

One major hurdle is computational complexity. In high-dimensional spaces, calculating posterior probabilities—a cornerstone of Bayesian inference—demands substantial processing power and sophisticated algorithms. This not only strains resources but also makes optimisation more difficult.

Another challenge lies in selecting priors. In Bayesian analysis, priors reflect our initial assumptions before seeing new data. Choosing them introduces subjectivity, which can bias the results. A poorly chosen prior can distort learning and lead to suboptimal or misleading outcomes. In that sense, Bayesian methods are highly dependent on "starting off on the right foot": If the starting assumptions are badly wrong, the whole journey of updating can be pulled in the wrong direction.

Finally, as Bayesian models grow in complexity, they often become less interpretable. This is a serious concern in fields where it's important to understand how and why a system reached its conclusions. Balancing accuracy with transparency and interpretability remains a core challenge for Bayesian approaches in AI.

Use Cases

Now that we've explored the foundational elements of statistical AI—from data dynamics and sampling methods to probability theory, clustering, classification, regression, and Bayesian approaches—let's now turn to the practical side: how these statistical techniques are used to solve real-world problems. This section will highlight the versatility and impact of statistical AI, helping to connect abstract ideas with tangible applications.

While we've treated statistical AI as a distinct domain, in practice, its principles are deeply embedded in more advanced AI systems. The sophisticated realms of neural networks, machine learning, and generative AI—covered in later chapters—are all built on the statistical foundations we've just examined.

The descriptions here are intentionally narrower than the integrated reality of modern systems, allowing the statistical elements to stand out before we explore hybrid approaches later in the book.

Real-world deployments involve much more than algorithms: Human oversight, organisational processes, quality assurance, regulatory constraints, bias mitigation, and safety considerations all play critical roles. For simplicity and clarity, those elements are omitted here so that the examples can concentrate on illustrating how statistical AI contributes to solving practical problems.

Movie Recommendations

Movie streaming service users will be familiar with receiving personalised recommendations while navigating through the app. The service surfaces items from its catalogue that it believes will appeal to the current user. These recommendations not only enhance the user's experience by simplifying content discovery, but also provide opportunities for the service to promote items the user hasn't yet explored or purchased.

These systems employ clustering and classification algorithms to tailor such movie suggestions.

Clustering and Classifying

Clustering plays a vital role in these systems. Users are grouped based on their viewing habits—such as preferred genres, specific shows watched, or ratings given. For example, one cluster might consist of users who frequently watch romantic comedies, while another might be made up of sci-fi enthusiasts. These groupings are not static; they evolve as user habits change, ensuring recommendations remain relevant and engaging.

Classification complements clustering by categorising movies and shows into predefined genres. When a new title is added, the algorithm analyses its characteristics—such as plot, cast, and user reviews—to assign it to the relevant categories.

Personalised Recommendations

The core of these systems lies in their ability to not only understand individual preferences, but also compare your profile with others like you. If the system identifies that users in your cluster highly rated a particular film, it's likely to recommend that film to you. This approach draws on the collective preferences of similar users, making recommendations more accurate and diverse.

An essential feature of these AI systems is their dynamic nature. As your interactions evolve—by rating new films or exploring different genres—the system updates your user profile and adapts your recommendations accordingly. This ensures that the suggestions you receive reflect both your long-term preferences and your current interests.

Outcome

Media recommendation systems in streaming services are a prime example of the practical application of statistical AI—specifically through clustering and classification. They show how AI can analyse and compare complex user data to deliver a personalised and continually evolving viewing experience.

Health Risk Assessment

Forecasting an individual's risk for specific health conditions is both worthwhile and potentially profitable. Such predictive insight empowers people to make informed decisions about their well-being.

For healthcare professionals, it enables more effective preventive strategies and earlier interventions that can significantly improve patient outcomes. For insurers, it supports the setting of premiums that more accurately reflect the risks being assessed.

These systems employ sampling and regression analysis to help assess individual health risks.

Sampling and Regression Analysis

Sampling plays a critical role by enabling the analysis of representative subsets of data. Since analysing entire populations is impractical, sampling allows researchers to collect data from a smaller group that reflects broader health trends—leading to reliable, generalisable insights.

Regression analysis is vital for modelling relationships between health indicators and outcomes. For example, it can help predict a patient's risk of developing heart disease or diabetes based on factors like age, weight, blood pressure, and lifestyle.

Personalised Risk Profiles

A major benefit of these techniques is the ability to create personalised risk profiles. By comparing individual health data against broader population trends, healthcare providers can offer tailored advice and treatment plans. This personalised approach is far more effective than generic, one-size-fits-all solutions.

Healthcare is a rapidly evolving field, with new data and research emerging constantly. Sampling and regression methods are highly adaptable, allowing updated findings to be integrated into risk models. This keeps assessments current and relevant, ensuring patients receive the most accurate insights available.

Outcome

The use of sampling and regression analysis in health risk assessment is a powerful example of statistical AI in action. These tools support the development of predictive models and personalised strategies that enhance patient care. As health data continues to expand, the role of AI in risk assessment and preventive medicine will only grow—enabling smarter, more proactive, and data-driven healthcare.

Financial Market Forecasting

Forecasting movements in stock markets and other financial instruments ranks among the most lucrative applications in any sector. Many of the world's most capable organisations dedicate substantial computing resources to predicting market trends and identifying emerging risks.

The insights gleaned from these efforts are invaluable to investors and financial analysts, guiding key decision-making processes.

These systems employ probability theory and Bayesian methods to help forecast movements in financial markets.

Probability Theory and Bayesian Methods

Probability theory is fundamental to assessing the likelihood of different market outcomes. By quantifying uncertainty, it helps evaluate risks and potential rewards. For instance, probability models might analyse historical price data to estimate the chances of a stock rising or falling—supporting decisions that balance potential gains against known risks.

Bayesian methods add a dynamic layer to market analysis. They update initial assumptions with incoming data to refine predictions. For example, an investor might begin with a prior belief about a stock's growth potential. As new information arrives—such as quarterly earnings or market shifts—Bayesian methods adjust that belief, leading to more accurate, data-informed forecasts.

Comparative Analysis, Uncertainty, and Volatility

A key advantage of these methods is their ability to support comparative analysis. Bayesian models can weigh multiple stocks or sectors, constantly refining predictions as new data flows in. This adaptability is critical in fast-moving financial markets, where yesterday's patterns may not hold tomorrow.

Markets are inherently volatile, and forecasting is never free from uncertainty. Probability theory and Bayesian methods excel in this environment by offering nuanced, probabilistic forecasts—not fixed answers. This flexible approach is essential for navigating the unpredictable nature of financial markets.

Outcome

Stock market forecasting illustrates the practical power of probability theory and Bayesian methods in a high-stakes environment. By quantifying uncertainty and incorporating new information, these techniques offer a structured, adaptive approach to market prediction—essential for strategic investment decisions. As financial markets continue to evolve, the role of AI in forecasting will become even more critical, providing increasingly sophisticated tools for market analysis and decision-making.

Credit Scoring

Credit scoring allows financial institutions to assess an individual's creditworthiness—quantifying the risk involved in lending. This is achieved using sophisticated algorithms that evaluate a range of factors, from payment history to credit utilisation. The process requires a careful balance between risk management and customer service. Effective credit scoring helps lenders make informed decisions, reducing defaults while ensuring fair access to credit for consumers.

These systems employ regression analysis and Bayesian methods to help quantify risk for lenders.

Regression Analysis and Bayesian Methods

Regression analysis is used to uncover relationships between financial indicators and credit risk. By analysing variables such as income, credit history, employment status, and outstanding debts, institutions can estimate the likelihood of a borrower defaulting on a loan.

Bayesian methods enhance this by allowing predictions to update dynamically as new financial data becomes available. A borrower's credit score can adjust with life changes—a new job, increased debt, or changes in repayment behaviour. This approach ensures that credit scores reflect current realities, offering a more accurate and responsive risk assessment.

Comparative Analysis and Market Adaptation

A key strength of statistical AI in credit scoring is its ability to compare individual financial profiles with broader trends. Borrowers can be grouped into risk categories by analysing their behaviour against historical data. This helps lenders manage risk more effectively and personalise lending strategies.

The financial landscape is also shaped by regulatory changes and market fluctuations. Regression and Bayesian models can adapt to new conditions, incorporating updated criteria to keep credit scoring relevant and compliant.

Outcome

The use of regression and Bayesian methods in credit scoring is a clear example of statistical AI in action. These techniques provide a structured yet flexible approach to risk assessment, enabling decisions that are both accurate and adaptable. As the financial sector continues to evolve, AI's role in credit scoring and risk management will only grow—offering more nuanced, real-time insights for lenders and fairer outcomes for borrowers.

Conclusion

Statistical AI has driven rapid and practical advances, enabling systems to extract value from messy, large-scale datasets and to deliver entirely new applications across science, medicine, commerce and public services. By combining various statistical methods researchers and engineers have turned previously intractable problems into deployable systems—opening up new use cases and services that were previously out of reach.

But as we explore the use of statistical methods in AI, it's essential to also consider their limitations and ethical implications. While these methods have transformed the landscape of AI, they introduce challenges and responsibilities that require careful attention.

AI systems process vast amounts of personal and sensitive information, raising important questions about the ethical use of this data. Issues such as consent, data ownership, and the protection of personal information are critical. Ensuring that AI systems respect privacy rights and follow strict data governance protocols is not just a legal requirement—it's a moral obligation.

The data used in AI systems can often be biased, reflecting existing historical or societal prejudices. This can lead to AI outcomes that are unfair or discriminatory, with significant consequences for individuals, particularly in areas like recruitment, law enforcement, and credit scoring.

Ensuring AI systems are fair and unbiased is essential. This requires careful data selection, preprocessing, and continuous monitoring to detect and address any bias in AI decisions.

As statistical AI models grow more complex, understanding how they make decisions becomes more difficult. This lack of interpretability and explainability can be problematic, especially in high-stakes fields like healthcare or criminal justice, where knowing the *why* behind a decision is as important as the decision itself.

Developing AI systems that are not only accurate but also transparent is crucial for building trust and ensuring ethical accountability.

Even when patterns are identified and interpretable, determining what *causes* those patterns remains challenging. An emerging area called *causal inference* seeks genuine cause-and-effect relationships by isolating variable effects while controlling for confounding factors. However, real-world events involve many interacting factors, and our data is often partial—true causes may lie in the wider "open world" beyond our dataset. This means AI systems excel at predicting *what* may happen, but are less reliable at explaining *why* it happens or what interventions might change outcomes.

The power of these methods must be tempered with a commitment to ethical principles—fairness, transparency, and respect for privacy—and a realistic understanding of their limits.

CHAPTER

4

Connected AI

As pioneers in artificial intelligence worked to build increasingly intelligent machines, a recurring theme emerged: *connectivity*. Many elements of the real world are inherently connected—and researchers soon realised their digital models needed to reflect this.

A key motivation behind connected AI lies in its ability to capture the richness of real-world relationships. By modelling data as networks of interacting elements, connected AI systems can reveal hidden patterns, propagate information, and solve problems that are difficult or impossible for isolated or linear approaches.

At first, this took the form of simple linear lists, which later evolved into more complex structures like graphs and trees. Each step forward in connectivity brought new capabilities and better outcomes.

A major turning point came when researchers began to study and replicate the most intricately connected system known to us—the human brain. This line of inquiry led to the development of models that were inspired by the structure of neural pathways and also mimicked their function. These breakthroughs laid the foundation for many of the most powerful advances in AI today.

Overview

Let's begin with a concise overview of the key ideas, techniques, and motivations behind connected AI. We'll start by introducing how connected approaches model information as networks of relationships—using nodes, links, and layered structures to represent and process complex connections.

This gives you a clear sense of what connected AI is and why it matters, without delving into the detailed mechanisms.

Connections

A core tenet of Buddhism is the belief that all things are interconnected—that nothing exists as a solitary, independent entity. This foundational principle found practical expression in artificial intelligence, as researchers began digitally modelling the connected nature of the world around them.

The first and most obvious connections we encounter are physical ones—railway lines linking train stations or bridges connecting landmasses. The latter inspired the development of a key mathematical concept known as *graph theory*, which we will explore later in this chapter.

Other types of connections soon emerged. A family tree, for example, is a connected graph where nodes link to further nodes, each representing a person and their relationships. These connections are not physical but *relational*—in this case, familial.

As discussed in Chapter 2, "Symbolic AI," these types of connected structures—known as *knowledge graphs*—form the foundation of many AI applications. In a knowledge graph, the connections are relationships (called *predicates*) linking two entities or connecting an entity to a piece of information.

Relationships are not the only kind of connection found in AI. A *decision tree*, as we also discussed earlier in Chapter 2, is another example. Here, connections take the form of rules—guiding the system from one condition to the next, such as moving from symptoms to a medical diagnosis.

Connections themselves also have attributes. Some are *bidirectional* (traversable in both directions), while others are *unidirectional* (can only be traversed in the forward direction). Some structures allow connections to loop back and rejoin earlier nodes, whereas others strictly forbid such cycles. Indeed, connected systems in AI take many shapes and serve many functions.

A significant breakthrough came when researchers turned to the connections within biological brains for inspiration. In hindsight, the brain was an obvious model—a living system capable of processing information, recognising patterns, reasoning, learning, and adapting. These are exactly the kinds of capabilities AI researchers aim to replicate in silicon.

The Human Brain

In the second half of the 20th century, our understanding of the human brain was still evolving. Yet, despite many unknowns, scientists had uncovered the basic workings of two of its fundamental components: *neurons* and *synapses*.

For centuries, researchers had made slow and painstaking progress in understanding how the brain functions. Many people across diverse disciplines contributed to this work—too many to name here. The limited insights they gained into the brain's mechanics laid the foundation for early AI researchers, who sought to replicate these neural structures in silicon.

Neurons are specialised cells that transmit electrical signals, allowing information to travel throughout the body. These impulses flow through complex networks of interconnected neurons, forming pathways that underpin a wide range of cognitive and physiological functions.

Synapses, meanwhile, are the junctions where two neurons meet. These tiny gaps facilitate the transmission of signals between neurons through both chemical and electrical processes.

Understanding how neurons and synapses worked was pivotal for early AI researchers, who aimed to emulate the brain's information-processing capabilities.

Simulating Biological Neurons

Astonishingly, this area of AI began as early as World War II, with a pioneering study into artificial neurons by Warren McCulloch and Walter Pitts. McCulloch was a neuroscientist and psychiatrist; Pitts, a logician and mathematician. Their collaboration combined expertise from both neuroscience and mathematics.

In 1943, they published a groundbreaking paper that laid the foundation for understanding how simple mathematical models could simulate the behaviour of biological neurons. Their work introduced the concept of a computational model that mimicked the basic functioning of a neuron.

McCulloch and Pitts proposed a simple binary-threshold model, where individual neurons would either *fire* (output a signal) or not, depending on the input signals they received and a defined threshold. This model could perform logical operations and could be interconnected to carry out more complex computations.

They demonstrated that networks of interconnected artificial neurons could emulate logical and algorithmic functions—showcasing the potential of these models to perform meaningful computation.

The Perceptron

Having bridged the gap between neuroscience and computation, other researchers became inspired to work in this promising overlap. In the late 1950s, Frank Rosenblatt developed a pioneering concept in this space called *the perceptron*. This was an early artificial neural network inspired by the processing of information in the brain. It comprised interconnected nodes in a single layer, each with inputs, weights, and an output. Just as neurons in the brain transmit signals through synapses, perceptrons manipulate input data through weighted connections to produce an output.

The perceptron's key innovation lay in its ability to *learn and adapt*. By adjusting the weights associated with inputs, it could fine-tune its responses based on the data it encountered. Rosenblatt's work demonstrated that a perceptron could be trained to distinguish between different patterns—marking a significant step towards pattern recognition and machine learning.

Early work on neural networks focused primarily on solving *classification problems*. These involve dividing a data space into disjoint, well-defined sets or classes. The goal is to create a *decision boundary*, where different classes lie on opposite sides of that boundary. These boundaries—represented by lines, curves, or surfaces—effectively separate distinct categories within the data.

Problems and Limitations

While perceptrons showed promise, their limitations became apparent when faced with complex problems involving non-straight-line decision boundaries. As we saw in Chapter 2, the messy human world refused to be tamed by rigid rules and well-defined edges. Only patterns that conformed to simple linear separations could be handled by this approach.

Marvin Minsky and Seymour Papert wrote a detailed analysis demonstrating that Rosenblatt's single-layer perceptrons were limited to simple, linear decision boundaries only. This critique, later known as the *perceptron controversy*, dampened enthusiasm for neural network research for over a decade.

Resurgence and Later Developments

However, by the 1980s there was a resurgence in the field of neural networks, led by Geoffrey Hinton, Yann LeCun, Yoshua Bengio, and others. Researchers began to realise that neural nets could be applied to a much broader range of problems beyond simple classification. Alongside this realisation, there had been substantial improvements in computational power and technology. This allowed researchers to explore more complex neural network architectures and to conduct larger and more sophisticated training processes.

A key advance in neural network research was the development of multi-layer neural networks. Rosenblatt's single-layer perceptrons were not capable of tasks beyond basic binary classification, where data points are separated using a straight-line decision boundary. Multilayer neural networks allow for the modelling of nonlinear relationships, making them well suited to tasks such as image recognition and natural language processing. These architectures increased both the range of use cases and the depth to which they could be explored.

Another major development was the popularisation of back-propagation—a key algorithm for training neural networks. While first proposed by Paul Werbos in the 1970s, it was Hinton, David Rumelhart, and Ronald Williams who helped bring it to prominence in a landmark 1986 paper. Back-propagation works by adjusting the connection weights between neurons to minimise the difference between the network's predicted outputs and the actual target values.

Alongside back-propagation, entirely new network architectures were also being developed. These included convolutional neural networks (CNNs) for image processing and recurrent neural networks (RNNs) for sequence data—early precursors and contributors included Kunihiko Fukushima's neocognitron and John Hopfield's associative networks. These architectures proved highly effective at capturing spatial and temporal relationships within data. We'll explore their workings in detail later in this chapter.

Core Concepts and Mechanisms

Connected AI consists of several key components that collectively define its interconnected approach, beginning with simple structures such as lists, graphs, and trees, and extending to more complex architectures that mirror aspects of biological brains. In the following, we outline a handful of these approaches in broad terms, to give you a working sense of the toolkit, and where each method fits.

note **Each of these concepts—along with several others—is covered in much more detail in the later "In-depth" section.**

To model relationships between objects, computers use *graph theory*—a mathematical framework that represents items as *nodes* and their connections as *links*. By focusing on how elements are linked, rather than their physical arrangement, graph theory enables complex problems to be simplified and solved through logical diagrams. This abstraction highlights essential properties like connectivity, traversal, and adjacency, making it easier to analyse networks in a wide range of fields.

A powerful real-world example is the London Underground map, redesigned by Harry Beck using graph theory principles. By abstracting tangled geography into a clean, readable network, Beck's map revolutionised transit mapping and made navigation more intuitive. This approach shows how graph theory helps us understand and manage complex systems in everyday life.

To organise and process information, computers use structures such as *linked lists*, *trees*, and more complex *graphs* and *networks*. Linked lists capture simple, linear connections, while trees arrange data hierarchically, with each node branching to others. Graphs and networks extend these ideas, modelling intricate webs of relationships across vast systems like the World Wide Web or social media, where the pattern and flow of connections shape how the system behaves.

In these networks, links between nodes can be one-way, two-way, or even form loops, depending on the needs of the system. Some structures, like *directed acyclic graphs* (DAGs), prevent cycles to maintain clear direction, which is vital in areas like scheduling and version control. As graph theory evolved, links became more than just connectors—they now act as agents of logic and process, enabling AI to solve problems, optimise routes, and manage complex tasks in fields such as project planning and supply chain management.

Neural networks are the backbone of many modern AI systems, from music recommendations to medical diagnostics. They are made up of *nodes* (which make decisions) and *links* (which carry signals), arranged in *layers* that pass information forward. By processing data through these layers, neural networks build up complex representations, allowing them to recognise patterns, make predictions, and solve problems that are difficult for traditional algorithms.

What makes neural networks powerful is their ability to learn. Each input is given a *weight* that determines its importance, and these weights are adjusted as the network is trained on data. Additional features like *biases*, *attention*, and *gating* help the network focus on what matters and filter out noise. This interconnected structure enables neural networks to handle vast amounts of information quickly. Despite their complexity, neural networks are built on simple principles inspired by both mathematics and the structure of the human brain.

Modern neural networks have grown from simple models into vast systems with millions or even billions of parameters, enabling them to extract features and make decisions with remarkable accuracy. These powerful networks now underpin a wide range of industries. Their ability to handle complex data at scale makes them indispensable tools for solving some of the most challenging problems we face today.

As neural networks have advanced, specialist architectures have emerged to tackle particular types of data and problems, much like the brain has regions for vision or hearing. Two of the most important are convolutional neural networks and recurrent neural networks.

Convolutional neural networks (CNNs) are designed to process spatial data, especially images. They use layers of filters to scan and extract features, starting with simple elements like edges and colours, and building up to complex patterns. This makes CNNs highly effective for tasks such as facial recognition, object detection, and medical image analysis, as well as for real-time applications like autonomous driving, where recognising visual details quickly is essential.

Recurrent neural networks (RNNs) are built to handle sequential data by maintaining a memory of previous inputs, allowing them to understand context and order. This makes RNNs invaluable for language translation, speech recognition, and text generation, as well as for analysing time-based data in fields like finance. By updating their internal state with each new input, RNNs can make informed predictions about what comes next in a sequence, capturing patterns that unfold over time.

The field of neural networks remains vibrant and fast-moving, with researchers around the world continually pushing boundaries, refining techniques, and uncovering new possibilities that promise to shape the future of AI for years to come.

In-depth

Building on the foundations of the overview, let's now dive deeper into the technologies and approaches of connected AI. In this section, we will explore how computers model and process information by representing it as networks of interconnected elements—such as nodes, links, and layers. We'll see how these connections enable systems to capture relationships, propagate signals, and learn from data, ultimately allowing AI to recognise patterns, make decisions, and solve complex problems by harnessing the power of connectivity.

Graph Theory

In the mid-18th century, Königsberg was a vibrant and bustling Prussian city. Its prestigious university attracted some of Europe's greatest minds, especially mathematicians.

The city had an unusual layout, with four land masses separated by water and connected by seven bridges. On Sunday afternoons, residents often went for long walks, attempting to solve a navigational challenge known as the Bridges of Königsberg. The aim was to find a route that would visit all the land masses and cross each bridge once—and only once.

One day, a skilled mathematician named Leonhard Euler decided to take on the challenge. Perhaps feeling lazy that day, instead of strolling around the city, he reached for the tools of his trade—a piece of paper and a pencil. He sketched four circles, representing the land masses, and drew lines between them to represent the bridges. Euler made a simple yet profound realisation: The actual geography of the city was irrelevant to the problem.

The layout of the land, its size and shape, the length of the bridges, even the materials they were made from—none of it mattered. What counted was the number of land masses (nodes) and how they were interconnected by bridges (links). The diagram Euler drew that day is now regarded as a precursor to what we would call a *topological map*. Figure 4.1 shows the space represented as a geographic and topological map.

This type of map, where geographic accuracy is sacrificed for clarity of structure, would find wide application in the years ahead. A canonical example is Harry Beck's iconic map of the London Underground.

Using his simplified but powerful diagram, Euler mathematically proved that no route existed that satisfied the conditions of the Bridges of Königsberg puzzle—though this didn't stop locals from continuing to try. With this work, Euler laid vital groundwork for two important new areas of mathematics: *topology*, the study of geometrical properties and spatial relations, and—more relevant for us—*graph theory*.

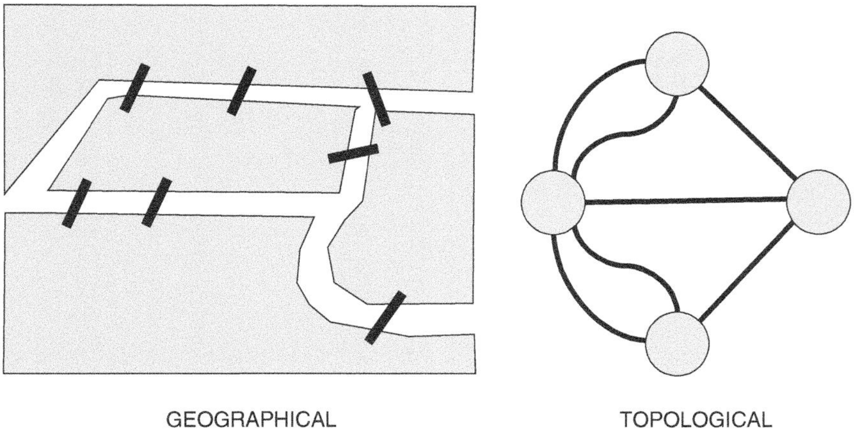

Figure 4.1: Geographical vs. topological graph

Nodes, Links, Graphs, and Networks

From the earliest days of computer science, engineers recognised the value of using Euler's representational model in their solutions. While Euler had begun by using graphs to depict simplified views of physical geography, computer engineers realised they could apply the same technique to represent the structure, arrangement, and navigability of information.

Over the years, many systems have emerged that use graphs as their core model. Some examples will be familiar to you from the earlier Chapter 2 on symbolic AI.

- **Linked lists:** A linear sequence of nodes where each node is linked to the next, representing a straightforward, sequential connection of elements.
- **Trees:** A structure where nodes are connected by parent–child relationships, ideal for representing nested or hierarchical data. A common variant, the binary tree, features each parent node linked to two child nodes.
- **Graphs:** Complex networks of nodes interconnected by links, well suited to modelling diverse relationships and interconnections—a canonical example being the World Wide Web, with its vast body of interconnected hyperlinks.
- **Networks:** More elaborate graphs often used to represent real-world systems like social networks or transportation systems, where the interplay between nodes and links is critical for functionality and analysis.

Some of these types of connections are illustrated in Figure 4.2.

The general principles of graph theory are widely applied, transcending any one specific method or domain. A few key characteristics persist across many graph-based systems—particularly in the nature of links, including directionality and cyclic behaviour:

- **Directionality:** In some graphs, links can be navigated in both directions, where one direction typically has an inverse meaning—for example, *parent of* versus *child of.* In other cases, direction makes most sense in one primary way, such as *subscribes to* or *depends on.*
- **Cyclic behaviour:** Some graph structures allow links to loop back to earlier nodes, forming cycles. In social networks, for instance, a person might follow someone who follows another, eventually creating a loop. Other graph types disallow such cycles to preserve a strictly hierarchical or linear structure.

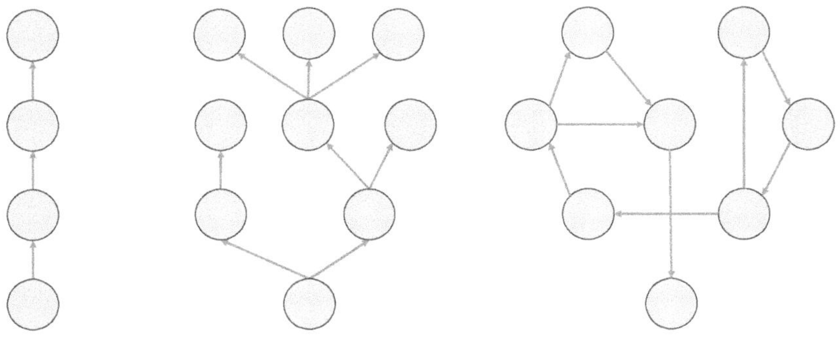

Figure 4.2: Types of connections

One particularly important formulation is the *directed acyclic graph*. In a DAG, links move only forward, and cycles are never allowed. These structures are especially prevalent due to their natural alignment with real-world scenarios. In domains such as project scheduling, supply chain management, and event planning, DAGs occur naturally, representing sequences where certain tasks or processes must precede others. Their unidirectional, non-cyclic nature simplifies computation, making tasks like sorting, searching, and path-finding far more efficient.

Graph theory equips AI engineers with a rich toolkit for analysing and processing data, enabling solutions to a wide range of real-world problems. For example, finding the shortest path in a network is essential for route planning in transport systems, such as GPS navigation apps that calculate the quickest way to reach your destination. In social networks, algorithms use graph theory to evaluate node centrality—identifying influential people or key connectors, which is vital for marketing, information spread, or detecting communities.

Graph traversals, such as depth-first and breadth-first searches, are used in everything from web crawling (systematically exploring websites), to solving puzzles and games, and even in project management tools that map dependencies between tasks. For example, depth-first search is like exploring a maze by following one path as far as possible before back-tracking, while breadth-first search is like checking all rooms on one floor before moving to the next.

These techniques are not just theoretical—they power practical applications across industries. For instance, supply chain optimisation relies on shortest path algorithms to minimise delivery times and costs, while fraud detection systems use centrality measures to spot unusual activity in financial transaction networks.

Importantly, graph theory also underpins a key area of AI: neural networks—a theme we will come to shortly.

Relationships, Rules, and Signals

When Euler first drew out his diagram, the links represented tangible geographical connections. This physical connectivity is the most obvious use of graphs—for example, stations (nodes) along a railway track (links), or cities (nodes) connected by roads (links). However, as AI researchers adapted his model, they employed more abstract interpretations for links.

One approach was to use links to represent relationships between connected nodes. For instance, in the realm of movies, nodes might be connected by links such as *starred-in* or *directed-by*. A prime example of this approach is the *knowledge graph*, which was detailed in Chapter 2. This subtle respinning of graphs is very powerful—they have moved from modelling the physical world into an abstract information space.

Another prevalent usage of links in graphs, particularly in tree structures, is to embody domain-specific rules. In this model, the nodes encapsulate rules or conditions that must be met. The links signify the result of the rule—typically with binary true or false outcomes. The traversal of the graph then halts or proceeds based on these rule outcomes. Take, for example, a decision tree in medical diagnostics: The rules represent symptoms that must be present for the traversal to continue towards a diagnosis. Absence of a symptom halts progression along that diagnostic path.

This reimagining of links—from mere informational descriptors to active causal agents—marked a significant shift. *Linked rules* became not just repositories of information but drivers of processes. This evolution has been crucial in the proliferation of symbolic AI applications, where linked rules play a foundational role.

But it was in the field of neural networks that a novel interpretation of links found greatest utility. In this context, links represent signals collectively fed into a node, enabling more comprehensive interpretations and decision-making. This mechanism was inspired by the human brain, where neurons transmit signals through synapses. Similarly, in a neural network, each link carries information in the form of a weighted signal to a node, which then uses the signals to make a determination.

Neural Nets

Imagine you are planning a movie night out with friends. There are many things to consider to ensure the night is a success. First, you must determine a day that works best for most of your friends, then identify a movie that matches their tastes, and finally choose a restaurant to visit after the movie. Organising such an event can be a major undertaking in its own right. Let's break it down and see how a formal structure might help us reach the best outcome.

Starting with the date, suppose you ask your friends to nominate the days from Monday to Saturday when they are available. You gather all their responses and calculate the day with the greatest overlap. Perhaps Thursday emerges as the top contender.

But there's a problem: Your best friend can't make it that day. You do not want to go to all the trouble of arranging the event if they cannot be there. So, you recalculate the best overlapping day, giving greater weight to your best friend's availability. Similarly, you might apply positive or negative weights to other friends' submissions—perhaps there is someone you would not mind missing the event. This weight-based calculation might lead to a new day choice that better reflects what matters most to you.

Next comes the movie. Along with their availability, your friends also provided their movie preferences. As before, you identify the option with the greatest overlap. But once again, there's a hitch: The most popular film isn't showing on your chosen night. So, you apply weighting again—assigning a weight of zero to films not playing that evening and lower ratings to films showing at awkward times. Eventually, you land on a combination of date and film that works.

Finally, the post-film restaurant. This time, you might weigh choices based on distance from the cinema and perhaps the price of menu items.

In this example, we've taken a multifaceted problem and broken it into discrete stages. Each stage involves a decision—a *node*—informed by inputs from your friends, which act as *signals* coming into those nodes.

The flow from node to node depends on whether earlier choices activate later ones. If no date is found, there's no point picking a film. If no film is chosen, choosing a restaurant becomes irrelevant.

While this is a simplified analogy, it captures the essential elements of a *neural network*. Such networks are the bedrock of modern AI, used in everything from recommending music to helping diagnose cancer. A high-level diagram of a neural network is shown in Figure 4.3.

At the heart of neural networks lies the familiar concept of *nodes* and *links*. Just as the nodes in our example represented decisions—like choosing a date, film, or restaurant—so too do nodes in a neural network represent computational units making decisions based on incoming data. And just as our example used weighted preferences to influence the outcome, neural networks use *weighted connections* to determine how strongly each input affects a decision.

Just as you chose a date, then a movie, then a restaurant—in a set sequence—so too do neural networks pass outputs from one node to the next, forming an interconnected flow of decisions. Earlier choices influence later ones, helping the system converge on the best outcome.

While individual nodes make local decisions, it's often more helpful to think of connected groups of nodes working together. In our analogy, we might call all the decision nodes a single *layer* called "movie night." Many such layers can

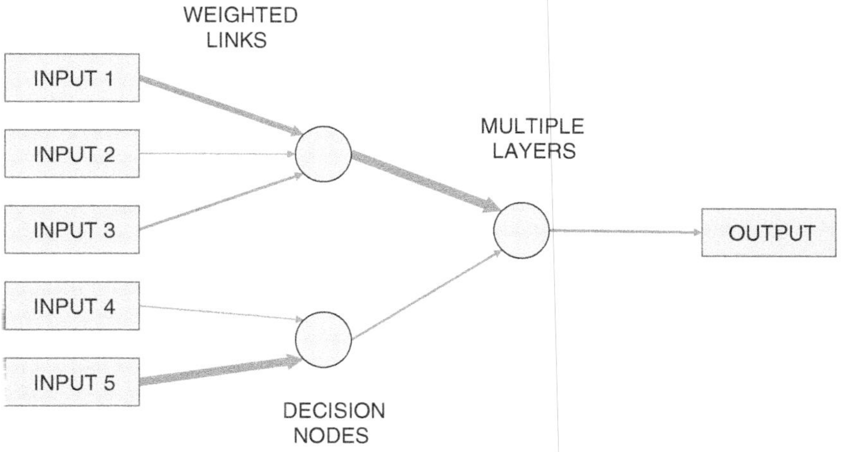

Figure 4.3: A simple neural network

be connected to form a large—sometimes immense—network. For example, the movie night layer may itself form part of a larger event-planning system that coordinates bookings, calendars, transport, and budgets.

In our example, weights were manually set based on personal priorities. But in a neural network, weights can be *learned* from data. By feeding on many past scenarios, the system can "learn" a set of weights that accurately model the space. Then those weightings will work when new, as yet unencountered scenarios arise. We will explore learning AI in depth in the next chapter. This key ability to adjust weights is what allows neural networks to improve accuracy over time through training and iteration.

In a modern neural network, weights are not the only types of parameters at play. Several other different elements can be deployed and adjusted through learning to gain better outcomes.

These elements are:

- **Bias:** Used for boosting weak signals that might otherwise be ignored, so a unit can respond even when its inputs are small. For example, in image recognition, a bias can help a neural network detect faint features in a low-contrast photo that would otherwise be missed.
- **Attention:** Useful for pointing the model at the most relevant pieces of information so it can ignore distractions and make better decisions. For instance, in language translation, attention mechanisms allow the model to focus on the most important words in a sentence, improving translation accuracy.
- **Gating:** Useful for opening or closing information pathways, letting the model keep what matters and discard what does not.

For example, in speech recognition, gating helps the network filter out background noise and focus on the speaker's voice.

- **Normalisation:** Useful for keeping signal sizes steady so training is faster, more stable and less prone to odd failures. For instance, in training deep networks for medical image analysis, normalisation ensures that signals do not become too large or too small, preventing instability and improving learning speed.

Neural networks are well suited to handling *sequential decisions*, where one layer's output becomes the next layer's input—allowing them to build up understanding over several stages. This approach reflects a broader principle in tackling today's complex problems: It is often more effective to divide a large challenge into smaller, manageable units and solve them as a set of interconnected problems, rather than attempting to address everything as a single monolithic task.

The interdependence of decisions in our planning example mirrors another vital trait of neural networks: the way nodes influence one another across layers. Once we have decided to divide a large problem into smaller units, the way those units influence and interact with one another becomes pivotal. The final outcome is shaped by a complex interplay of factors, each one weighted by its relevance and importance.

This analogy, while simplified, offers a helpful window into how neural networks work. In reality, today's networks are vast and highly sophisticated. A modern neural network might contain millions or even billions of nodes and parameters, interconnected across hundreds of layers. These immense structures enable the network to process vast amounts of data and solve highly complex problems. Their internal workings are often far beyond direct human comprehension. Yet, despite their complexity, they still trace their lineage back to Euler's pencil and paper sketch.

Contrasts with Biological Brains

While the term *neural network* suggests a close resemblance to human brain function, it is important to recognise that this terminology, though useful, is not entirely accurate. The linguistic borrowing perhaps implies more overlap than the technology itself can justify.

Neural networks in AI are inspired by the brain's structure, but they are fundamentally simpler and more deterministic. Unlike neural networks, which perform specific computations through clearly defined algorithms, the human brain operates through a vast network of neurons and complex biochemical processes that contribute to learning, memory, and cognition—in ways not yet fully understood by science.

AI neural networks typically follow deterministic processes, where the same input consistently produces the same output. In contrast, the human brain exhibits a degree of unpredictability and variability in its responses, influenced by factors such as emotional state, physical health, and prior experiences.

The brain's capabilities are not just defined by synaptic connections, but also by an intricate interplay of biological, chemical, and physical mechanisms—all of which contribute to the emergent properties of consciousness and thought. These are not paralleled in artificial systems.

The goals of a neural network are simple, directed, and enumerable. In contrast, the human mind operates with a complex set of goals—some external, some internal, some contextual, and some long term. For example, even if you are asked to perform a simple task like answering a question about your day, you cannot separate that from an emotional response, meta-thoughts about why you are being asked and what you should reveal, and concerns about what the asker might think of you based on your response, and so on.

While neural networks are powerful tools for pattern recognition, decision-making, and learning, they do not replicate the depth or nuanced flexibility of the human brain. Making a direct comparison is like comparing a map of a city to the city itself—a useful abstraction, but not a direct parallel. As technology continues to advance, neural networks grow in complexity and application—yet they continue to remain distinct from the biological intricacies of human neural processes.

Modern Neural Networks in Practice

Neural networks today have evolved far beyond the simple movie night model we discussed earlier. Modern networks can consist of millions—or even billions—of nodes, interconnected by a vast web of links spanning multiple layers. These layers enable neural networks to perform complex feature extraction and decision-making processes. Indeed, neural networks (teamed with machine learning, which we cover in the next chapter) are the bedrock of most modern AI systems.

For instance, OpenAI's GPT-3, an early large language model, comprises 175 billion parameters—effectively the *weights* and *biases* in the links of the network—which allow it to understand and generate human-like text based on the input it receives. Later models, such as GPT-4 and GPT-4.1, have parameter counts that remain undisclosed, but are widely believed to be significantly larger. We will cover these technologies in depth in Chapter 6 on generative AI.

These large-scale networks are at the heart of many cutting-edge technologies, impacting industries from healthcare to entertainment. Here's a look at how neural networks operate in practice:

- **Healthcare:** Neural networks are employed to analyse medical images, such as X-rays and MRIs, to detect abnormal signs. For example, modern AI systems can detect many types of eye disease from 3D scans by recognising subtle patterns that might be missed by human experts.
- **Autonomous vehicles:** Neural networks are crucial in autonomous driving technologies, processing vast amounts of sensor data in real time. These networks need to make timely decisions about steering, speed, and route planning—recognising static objects and predicting the movements of pedestrians and other vehicles.
- **Finance:** Neural networks in the financial sector manage tasks like high-frequency trading, fraud detection, and risk management. They analyse financial market patterns to predict stock movements and identify transactions that may indicate fraud.

Such applications—and many others—demonstrate neural networks' capacity to handle and interpret data at scales and speeds far beyond human capabilities. These examples highlight their ability to integrate vast datasets, making them indispensable in fields where large-scale analysis and real-time decision-making are crucial.

As technology continues to advance, these networks grow in both size and sophistication—expanding their capabilities and applications across an ever-wider range of industries. While future breakthroughs will no doubt involve ever more creative and specialised uses of neural networks, the core concept of the neural network itself is likely to remain a fundamental pillar of AI for many years to come.

Convolutional Neural Networks

Imagine you're looking at a vast, high-resolution photograph of a crowd at a concert. Your task is to find your friend's face among thousands of others. This is a bit like a real-life version of *Where's Waldo*—it requires scanning the crowd and identifying distinguishing features to pinpoint your friend among a sea of faces.

Initially, you take a general view of the entire photograph. This broad scan isn't about finding your friend immediately, but about understanding the layout of the crowd—identifying dense areas and noting spots more likely to include your friend based on past experience. You might mentally mark places near landmarks, perhaps the bar where your friend usually stands.

Next, to help focus on parts of the image, you cut a small hole in a card and overlay it onto the main image—so you see only the section revealed by the cutout. This lets you concentrate on small parts at a time, inspecting faces and clothing in more detail. As you move the card to reveal other parts of the base image, you look for specific features—your friend's hair colour, clothing style, or distinctive accessories. Each fragment you examine helps you confirm or rule out your friend's presence.

Each time you shift the card, you make slight adjustments based on what you observe. This step-by-step adjustment is crucial for thoroughly combing through potential spots without missing any details. If you spot something promising—like a piece of clothing your friend was wearing—you concentrate more on that area to gather additional clues.

The process outlined here draws parallels with *convolutional neural networks*. Like the human brain, which has specialised neural structures for processing visual information, a CNN is a specialised neural network crafted to interpret visual data. A high-level illustration of a CNN is presented in Figure 4.4.

Just as areas like the human visual cortex are tuned to detect colours, shapes, and motion, CNNs are built with layers that identify and interpret visual patterns from raw images. This specialisation allows CNNs to excel at tasks ranging from facial recognition to autonomous driving. In both nature and technology, this kind of specialisation enables more efficient processing of complex inputs. Each layer in a CNN, like regions of the brain, is interconnected yet purpose-built—collectively enhancing understanding of a visual scene.

The first layers of a CNN capture general, local features from the image—edges, colours, and textures—while deeper layers aggregate broader context as the network's effective *receptive field* grows. Together, these layers enable the network to build up a detailed understanding of the image,

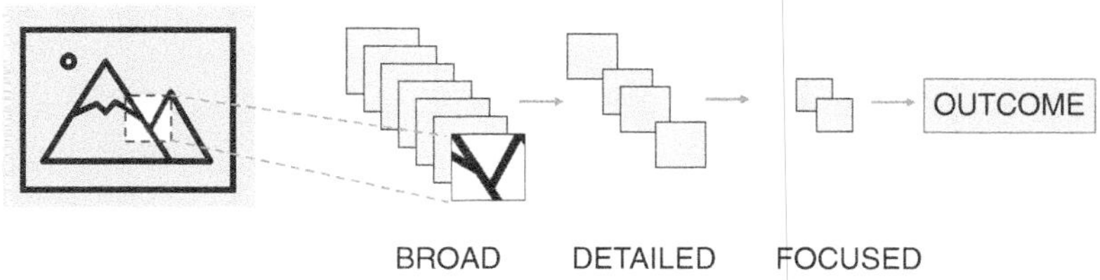

Figure 4.4: Simplified convolutional neural network

progressing from simple patterns to complex objects and scenes. This hierarchical approach is what allows CNNs to recognise and identify objects, and interpret visual information with remarkable accuracy.

The term *convolution* refers to the mathematical operation used to process parts of the input image. Like the card with a hole we spoke about earlier, CNNs apply such filters to zero-in on specific features. This process "slides" the filter across the image, revealing and then examining sections and detecting patterns like facial structures.

As each new section is processed, the network adjusts its focus based on features already detected. This is akin to how you adjust your search based on earlier observations. In CNNs, this is managed through *stride* (how far the filter moves on each step) and *padding* (how the image borders are handled so edge pixels are processed), ensuring the image is thoroughly scanned.

CNNs are a canonical example of *deep learning*. These systems break problems into layers: Lower layers extract simple features, while deeper layers form broader judgements that are passed onward or read out by the output layer. We'll explore deep learning more in the next chapter.

The CNN's ability to break down an image and analyse it methodically makes it exceptionally powerful for visual recognition. Unlike the relatively simple task of finding your friend, CNNs perform complex tasks—such as detecting disease in 3D scans or identifying pedestrians in real time for autonomous vehicles.

Recurrent Neural Networks

Imagine you are deep into a riveting novel with a complex plot and a rich tapestry of characters. As you read, your understanding of the narrative depends heavily on remembering what has happened before. This ongoing accumulation of context helps you make sense of each new development as the story unfolds.

You retain key details about the characters and plot—such as a character's motives, past actions, or relationships that influence their decisions. Each chapter builds on the last. You integrate new information with what you already know, helping you anticipate future twists or understand deeper character developments. Based on this accumulated knowledge and narrative patterns, you might try to predict future outcomes—the resolution of a conflict, or how a character might react to an event.

Imagine now you stop reading the book for an extended period of time, say many months. You still retain memory of the overall plot, but nuanced details of the characters, specific episodes or motivations are forgotten. Now, if you were to begin reading where you left off, your experience of

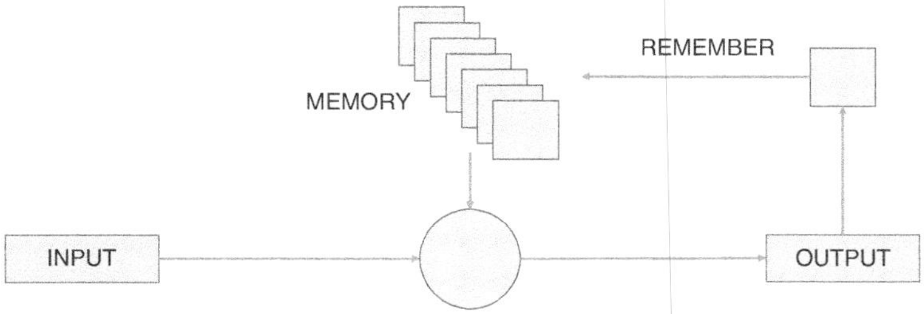

Figure 4.5: Simplified recurrent neural network

the novel would be very much degraded. You would not fully understand all the elements that the author has created after you lose much of the backstory they used to build their work.

This process draws a close parallel with *recurrent neural networks*. These neural networks process sequences of data by maintaining a "memory" of previous inputs in their internal state, which in turn influences their understanding of new data. A high-level illustration of an RNN is shown in Figure 4.5.

The term *recurrent* refers to the architecture of these networks, where outputs from certain processing steps are fed back into the system. This recurrence—or looping back—allows the network to retain memory of earlier inputs.

This architecture echoes aspects of the human brain, where neurons fire in patterns that both respond to new stimuli and recall past experiences. This process enables not just memory, but contextual understanding—and the ability to learn from sequences. By mimicking this behaviour, RNNs achieve a form of "digital memory," crucial for tasks requiring a nuanced understanding of time and order.

Just as you track the plot and characters over the course of a novel, an RNN retains past data using elements called "hidden layers"—which in turn influence how it processes new inputs. And like reading a story from beginning to end, RNNs handle data sequences in order and one unit at a time, updating their internal state as they go.

Just as you might anticipate a twist in the story, RNNs can predict the next data point in a given sequence. This is vital for tasks like language translation, where each word depends heavily on the ones that came before. Prediction like this helps to focus the RNN on the most relevant context, allowing it to generate accurate and coherent outputs. By maintaining and updating its internal memory, the network can adapt to new information and refine its predictions as the sequence unfolds.

RNNs are well suited to problems that require memory and context. They are widely used in applications such as speech recognition—where each phoneme depends on those before it—and text generation, where every new word is shaped by earlier ones.

In a more consequential domain, RNNs are sometimes deployed in financial markets, where they are used to predict stock prices, cryptocurrency values, and other economic indicators. The performance of a financial instrument is shaped by a sequence of past prices and market signals. RNNs analyse these historical sequences to forecast future trends—allowing analysts and traders to make informed decisions grounded in learned patterns and fluctuations over time.

Advanced Connected Techniques

While we have covered the basics of neural network architectures, the field of connected AI is continually evolving, with new methodologies and enhancements being developed to address increasingly complex challenges. Here are a few advanced topics that represent active research and application in connected AI:

- **Gradient descent:** This fundamental optimisation algorithm is crucial for training all types of neural networks. It helps find the minimum of a loss function (which measures how far the model's predictions are from the actual results). It's directly related to how networks learn from data during training, adjusting weights to minimise error.
- **Regularisation:** This technique enhances the generalisation of neural networks to new, unseen data by preventing overfitting. It ensures that the model's connectivity and learnt weights do not simply memorise the training data, but can perform well across varied inputs.
- **Attention mechanisms:** Originally used in the context of RNNs for sequential data processing, attention mechanisms help models focus on the most important elements of input data. This is crucial for tasks like machine translation.
- **Capsule networks:** Capsule networks introduce a novel approach to data processing in neural networks, addressing some limitations of CNNs in recognising spatial relationships and handling different viewpoints. They look to enhance the ability to capture hierarchical structures and positional information, improving upon the traditional CNN framework.

Another key topic, called *transformer architectures,* is a pivotal aspect of generative AI, and we will cover these in Chapter 6, "Generative AI." These topics illustrate just a few of the avenues through which connected AI is advancing. As researchers and engineers continue to push the boundaries of what's possible, we can expect even more innovative solutions that further enhance the capabilities of neural networks in processing and understanding complex data.

Use Cases

In the preceding sections, we delved into the foundational elements of connected AI, exploring the concepts of nodes and links, graph theory, and the intricacies of neural networks, including specialised architectures for specific use cases. As we move from theory to practical application, it's time to illustrate how these elements of connected AI are employed to solve real-world problems. In this section, we highlight the versatility and power of connected AI, demonstrating how these models structure and interpret complex data relationships to drive impactful outcomes.

It is important to note, however, that many of these systems depend heavily on learned weights and biases. These elements are crucial for the functionality and accuracy of AI models but also introduce potential challenges, such as data bias and the need for extensive training data. While we will touch on these issues here, a more detailed discussion on the implications and management of these factors will be covered in the next chapter on learning AI.

The following use cases will showcase how connected AI models are applied across various domains, emphasising their role in advancing technology and enhancing decision-making processes. As we explore these applications, we will see how connected AI not only stands on its own but also serves as a crucial component in the broader AI landscape.

Real-world deployments involve much more than algorithms: human oversight, organisational processes, quality assurance, regulatory constraints, bias mitigation, and safety considerations all play critical roles. For simplicity and clarity, those elements are omitted here so that the examples can concentrate on illustrating how connected AI contributes to solving practical problems.

Inventory Management Systems

Enterprises often possess large volumes of stock to support processes such as retail stores or manufacturing facilities. Managing this inventory can be a complex and multifaceted endeavour.

Increasingly, AI is being used to enhance these systems by predicting stock levels, optimising reordering, proactively moving stock to the best locations, and more. These enhancements are crucial for businesses to maintain adequate inventory, minimise holding costs, and prevent stockouts.

These systems can employ neural nets and knowledge graphs to facilitate stock management.

Basic Neural Nets and Knowledge Graphs

These applications often use neural networks to analyse sales data, seasonal trends, and supply chain variables to forecast future inventory requirements and movements. Since these systems process large datasets to identify patterns and make predictions, neural networks are well suited for the task.

Knowledge graphs are also used to represent relationships between products, suppliers, and other relevant entities, providing additional context that aids decision-making. By representing complex relationships and hierarchies, knowledge graphs help structure this information effectively. This example demonstrates how multiple AI architectures are often used together to achieve a comprehensive outcome.

Optimised Stock Levels and Movements

Together, neural networks and knowledge graphs ensure that stock levels are maintained at optimal levels. Neural networks predict future inventory needs based on historical data, considering factors such as seasonal demand and sales trends. These predictions inform reordering processes, ensuring that stock is replenished just-in-time to meet demand.

Knowledge graphs enhance this system by mapping the relationships between products, suppliers, and storage locations. This mapping helps businesses identify the most efficient routes for stock movement, optimise storage space, and quickly adapt to changes in supplier availability or transportation disruptions.

For example, if a surge in demand for a particular product is detected, the system can automatically adjust stock levels by sourcing additional units from alternative suppliers within the knowledge graph. Similarly, if a primary supplier faces delays, the system can quickly identify and switch to a backup supplier.

Outcome

The combined use of neural networks and knowledge graphs in inventory management provides a powerful tool for businesses. It helps maintain optimal stock levels, improves efficiency, and enhances the ability to respond to supply chain disruptions. Like many real-world systems, inventory management is inherently interconnected, making the use of connected AI technologies essential.

Financial Fraud Detection

Enterprises and consumers face significant risks from fraudulent financial activities. Protecting financial transactions from fraud is crucial to ensuring the security and trustworthiness of global financial systems.

Increasingly, AI is being used to enhance fraud detection systems, identifying suspicious activities in real time. By leveraging advanced neural networks, these systems can analyse vast amounts of transaction data, detect anomalies, and flag potential fraud, safeguarding both consumers and financial institutions.

These systems often employ neural networks to scrutinise transaction data for patterns indicative of fraudulent behaviour.

Advanced Neural Networks

Neural networks are particularly effective in analysing complex transaction data. They can examine numerous variables, such as transaction amounts, locations, and times, to identify patterns that deviate from normal behaviour. These networks continuously learn from new data, improving their accuracy and ability to detect emerging fraud vectors.

As fraudsters evolve their tactics, these AI systems incorporate new data to refine their algorithms. This continuous learning process ensures that the fraud detection system remains effective, even as new types of fraud emerge.

Safer Financial Ecosystems

A neural network might flag a transaction as potentially fraudulent if it detects that a credit card, typically used in one country, is suddenly used for a high-value purchase in another country. By recognising this anomaly, the system can alert the cardholder and financial institution to verify the transaction's legitimacy. This can happen at a vast scale, processing huge numbers of transactions per second.

Such systems benefit from a dynamic approach, allowing them to respond swiftly to potential threats. Real-time monitoring and adaptive learning enhance the system's capability to prevent fraud before it occurs, reducing financial losses and maintaining consumer trust.

Outcome

The use of advanced neural networks in fraud detection is a powerful tool for enhancing the security of financial transactions. By continuously analysing and learning from transaction data, these systems provide robust alerting and defence mechanisms against evolving fraud tactics. This application of connected AI highlights the significant role neural networks play in underpinning our digital world.

Healthcare Image Diagnostics

The integration of neural networks, particularly convolutional neural networks, into healthcare has transformed the analysis of medical images.

These AI systems can efficiently scan X-rays, MRIs, and CT scans to detect abnormalities such as tumours, fractures, or signs of diseases with remarkable accuracy. Increasingly, they are able to spot early indicators or slight symptoms that may have been missed by human eyes.

These systems often employ convolutional neural networks to scrutinise medical images for patterns indicative of various health conditions.

Convolutional Image Analysis

CNNs utilise multiple layers of filters to detect patterns within medical images. The initial layers focus on identifying basic features like edges and textures, such as the outlines of bones in X-rays or the contrast between different tissue types in MRI scans. The deeper layers are designed to recognise more complex structures, such as organs or tumours.

This hierarchical approach allows CNNs to build a detailed understanding of the image content, improving the accuracy of their analyses. By mimicking the visual processing mechanisms of the human brain, CNNs can identify subtle anomalies and intricate patterns that are crucial for accurate diagnostics.

Early Diagnosis of Critical Conditions

CNNs are widely used to identify early signs of cancer in mammograms and detect neurological disorders in brain scans. These systems often spot issues that might be missed by the human eye, providing a second layer of scrutiny that enhances diagnostic accuracy.

For instance, detecting early-stage tumours in mammograms can significantly improve patient outcomes through timely intervention. The ability to diagnose conditions at an early stage is critical, as it allows for prompt treatment and can potentially save lives.

To be effective, these systems require vast amounts of labelled data for training, which is representative free of bias. This data must be meticulously annotated by medical professionals to ensure the system learns accurately. The quality and diversity of the training data are crucial in enabling CNNs to generalise well to new, unseen data, thus improving their reliability and robustness in real-world clinical settings.

Outcome

The application of CNNs in healthcare represents a significant advancement, improving diagnostic accuracy and patient outcomes. The ability of CNNs to analyse medical images with high precision offers a powerful tool for healthcare professionals, potentially transforming diagnostic processes and enhancing patient care. CNNs demonstrate how interconnected AI technologies can assist in solving complex and vital human problems.

Autonomous Driving

The development of autonomous vehicles heavily relies on connected AI, particularly recurrent neural networks. These advanced AI systems process vast amounts of sensory data in real time to navigate safely and efficiently.

These systems employ recurrent neural networks to handle the continuous streams of data needed for autonomous driving.

Recurrent Sequential Data Processing

RNNs are especially adept at managing sequential data, making them ideal for processing continuous information from various sensors, such as cameras, LiDAR, and radar. These networks can retain a memory of previous inputs, which helps in understanding the context and making more informed decisions. This capability is crucial for predicting future events based on past data, such as anticipating the flow of traffic or pedestrian movements, allowing the vehicle to react proactively rather than just reactively.

Safer Roads and Safer Journeys

RNNs enable autonomous vehicles to understand and predict the behaviour of vehicles, pedestrians, and other road users. By processing data in real time, they can provide vital context to wider systems which make timely decisions about steering, speed, and route planning. For example, if a pedestrian suddenly steps into the street, the RNN can quickly analyse this change and trigger signals which cause the vehicle to stop or swerve to avoid an accident.

The integration of RNNs into autonomous vehicles significantly enhances their ability to navigate complex environments safely and efficiently. These AI systems continuously learn and adapt from new data, improving their accuracy and reliability over time. As they process vast amounts of sensory data, they help vehicles anticipate and react to dynamic driving conditions, minimising the risk of accidents.

Outcome

The use of RNNs in autonomous vehicles highlights the advanced capabilities of connected AI, showcasing its potential to transform transportation by enhancing safety, efficiency, and autonomy. As research and development continue, these systems will become increasingly sophisticated, paving the way for fully autonomous driving solutions.

Conclusion

Connected AI—and especially neural networks—marked a pivotal advancement in AI research, significantly influencing the development of the modern technologies we use today. This breakthrough in connectivity allowed researchers to explore a diverse range of real-world applications. The versatility of neural networks enabled them to handle tasks once thought to belong exclusively to the domain of human intelligence.

However, this advancement has not come without challenges. One major concern is the immense power consumption required to train and operate large neural networks. Training a single large-scale model can consume as much energy as a sizable neighbourhood uses in a year—raising serious questions about the environmental impact and long-term sustainability of AI technologies.

Another challenge is the vast amount of data required to train neural networks effectively. This has led to issues around data privacy and security, as well as concerns about bias. Bias in training data can produce skewed outcomes, reinforcing existing societal inequalities and presenting ethical dilemmas—topics we will explore further in the next chapter, "Learning AI."

As neural networks grow in complexity, understanding how they make decisions is becoming increasingly difficult. This lack of interpretability and explainability can be a critical issue—particularly in fields like healthcare and criminal justice, where understanding *why* a decision was made is as important as the decision itself. Transparency is becoming essential for building trust in AI-powered systems.

Despite these challenges, the impact of connected AI cannot be overstated. Neural networks have enabled significant advances across fields by providing powerful tools for pattern recognition, decision-making, and predictive analytics. Their success has paved the way for new AI architectures tailored to highly specialised data types and tasks.

The legacy of connected AI—particularly through the development and refinement of neural networks—represents a breakthrough moment in AI history. These technologies are now the cornerstone of many advanced AI systems, driving innovation and solving complex problems across industries.

As we continue to refine and expand these technologies, the potential for further progress remains vast—promising a future in which AI can meaningfully improve quality of life and help address some of the world's most pressing challenges.

CHAPTER

5

Learning AI

From the moment we are born, humans—and indeed all higher-order animals—are not equipped with all the knowledge, skills, and behaviours needed to live and thrive. The vast majority of what is required must be learnt over time. This learning is fundamentally experiential, involving processes such as trial-and-error, making mistakes, and gradually adapting to the environment. It is through these costly and sometimes error-prone processes that individuals acquire the abilities necessary for survival and success.

Just as infant children cannot begin life with all the knowledge, rules, and processes they will need, early AI researchers soon recognised that developing complete, preprogrammed systems was too ambitious a goal for most practical use cases. The demands of early approaches, such as symbolic AI, proved too difficult to meet in practice, as encoding every possible rule and piece of knowledge was both time-consuming and inherently limited.

Instead, researchers began to look towards the paradigm of adaptation through learning. Rather than attempting to specify everything in advance, they explored ways for AI systems to acquire knowledge, skills, and behaviours by interacting with data and their environment—mirroring the way living beings learn and adapt over time.

This shift laid the groundwork for learning AI, algorithms, and models that could improve themselves through "experience," opening the door to more flexible and capable systems. The goal was AI that could adapt autonomously, without explicit direction from their creators, instead following the natural structure and patterns present in the data itself.

Overview

Let's begin with a concise overview of the core ideas, techniques, and motivations behind learning AI. We'll introduce how learning-based approaches enable systems to adapt and improve by finding patterns in data, using algorithms that adjust their internal models through experience. This overview gives you a clear sense of what learning AI is and why it matters, without diving into the technical details.

Machine Learning

Learning AI, or machine learning as it is more commonly known, grew out of the bedrock of *inductive systems*—which we described in Chapter 3, "Statistical AI." Such systems are data driven and use approaches like *statistical analysis* and *probability theory* to allow the data to reveal its own story. These mathematical tools provided a systematic approach to uncovering patterns in data, making predictions, and assessing uncertainties. With these techniques, researchers enabled computers to autonomously "learn" from past "experiences" and extrapolate to future scenarios.

Early pioneers included Frank Rosenblatt, whose perceptron work launched early neural network research, and Marvin Minsky and Seymour Papert, who later critiqued and helped define the field's limitations. The term *machine learning* was popularised by Tom Mitchell, who contributed to many influential early projects and helped formalise the field with a widely cited definition.

Machine learning coalesced as a distinct area of study in the 1980s, building upon the foundations of early neural networks and symbolic AI. Researchers realised that these algorithms could be employed beyond simple calculations to tackle intricate problems that had eluded earlier approaches to AI.

The essence of machine learning lies in its capacity to uncover complex relationships *hidden* within data. Algorithms learn from examples, gradually refining their understanding and predictive abilities. A pivotal aspect is the iterative process of training, testing, and fine-tuning, allowing them to enhance their performance over time.

Key figures such as Geoffrey Hinton, David Rumelhart, and Ronald Williams played a pivotal role in reviving interest in neural networks, particularly through their work on backpropagation—a breakthrough that enabled deeper, more capable architectures.

Around the same period, researchers like Yann LeCun developed convolutional neural networks (CNNs), a foundational technology for modern image recognition. More recently, Yoshua Bengio has been central to advances in deep learning. Researchers such as Ian Goodfellow and Andrew Ng have further popularised and applied these methods across many domains.

Despite these early advances, progress in machine learning—and AI more broadly—slowed in the late 1980s and early '90s. Limited practical results and hardware constraints led to a decline in funding, marking a period often referred to as the "Second AI Winter." In hindsight, the ambition of the field had outpaced the available data and compute resources.

Momentum returned in the late 1990s and early 2000s, as the growing availability of digital datasets and improved hardware made a bigger and better canvas for learning-based systems. Additionally researchers such as Vladimir Vapnik, Leo Breiman, Judea Pearl, and others advanced both theory and application by developing new approaches and more sophisticated algorithms, often more focused on specific use cases.

These contributions, combined with the explosive growth of digital data and computational capacity, helped machine learning evolve into one of the most dynamic and influential areas in modern computing.

Contrasts with Human Learning

As with neural networks, advocates of machine learning also drew inspiration from human experience. However, unlike its counterpart, machine learning did not attempt to directly mimic how humans learn. While both aim to extract knowledge from data, they fundamentally diverge in their approaches.

Human learning, honed by evolution, involves a complex interplay of cognition, emotion, and experience. It draws from sensory perception, reasoning, and abstract thinking—allowing us to grasp nuanced concepts, adapt to new situations, and generalise across diverse domains.

Machine learning, by contrast, is a systematic process in which algorithms autonomously detect patterns in data and optimise their performance against predefined objectives. While human learning is guided by intuition and context, machine learning relies on mathematical models and statistical methods.

Human learning is not confined to a single topic at a time. For example, when learning to swim a person is also developing physical coordination, building confidence, and learning to manage emotions such as fear or excitement. At the same time, they may be navigating social dynamics, like taking turns or encouraging others. Human minds are complex, intertwined systems where each part has a bearing on the others, and learning in one area often influences growth in many others.

In contrast, machines typically learn in narrow domains. For example, a machine trained to spot cancers in medical images will not apply its learning to unrelated areas, such as recognising emotions or understanding social cues. When researchers want AI to achieve a degree of cross-domain skill, they must apply specific, complex techniques like *transfer learning* to enable this kind of generalisation.

This narrowness can sometimes be an advantage, as such algorithms can be highly focused and less prone to certain types of human bias or distraction. However, it also limits their flexibility and ability to generalise beyond their training domain—a key reason why human oversight remains essential in many applications.

For many people, the technical differences between human and machine learning are not obvious because the terms share a common word. It is unfortunate that AI researchers often borrow terms from everyday, colloquial vocabulary. This practice frequently leads to confusion and inflated expectations, as people naturally carry over their everyday interpretations of these terms into the technical domain of AI.

The Learning Process

To illustrate how machines can "learn," consider a simple hierarchical algorithm used to diagnose a car fault. The nodes represent questions, and the links are possible answers. Traversing this decision tree leads to a fault diagnosis and suggested fix.

When a human is first entering their career, they might follow such a process in rote fashion, step-by-step from beginning to end. However, after a time, as experience is gained, they will learn to prioritise certain questions, focusing first on the most likely causes. Here, they will use what are often described in very human terms like "hunches" or "intuition"—rapid, experience-based judgements that draw on patterns recognised subconsciously from prior cases, even if the person cannot always articulate the reasoning explicitly.

Similarly, though perhaps more prosaically, a learning AI can adjust the internal parameters of its decision tree based on previous runs. Over time, it will learn to follow the most successful paths—where success might be measured by factors like time to complete, cost, customer satisfaction, or accuracy of diagnosis.

This adaptive process doesn't need to be explicitly programmed; the system learns and adjusts automatically based on accumulated experience. By refining its internal model through feedback and past encounters, the AI becomes more accurate and efficient in its decision-making—applying learning strategies to improve performance and adapt to new challenges.

It should be noted that, while a simple decision tree is used here as an example, most modern machine learning happens through the adjustment of neural network weights—a topic we will explore further in the "In-depth" section.

Core Concepts and Mechanisms

Learning AI consists of several key methodologies that collectively define its *learning from data* approach. Starting with techniques such as supervised, unsupervised, and reinforcement learning, the field emphasises the importance of identifying patterns and making predictions to drive improved outcomes. The development of more advanced techniques—including deep learning—has significantly enhanced functionality. In this section, we outline a handful of these approaches in broad terms, to give you a working sense of the toolkit and where each method fits.

note **Each of the concepts covered in this section—along with several others—is covered in much more detail in the "In-depth" section.**

Supervised learning is a core machine learning approach where algorithms are trained on *labelled data*—each example in the dataset is paired with a known correct answer. The model learns to map inputs to outputs by identifying patterns and relationships in the data, aiming to generalise its knowledge to make accurate predictions on new, unseen examples. This process typically involves splitting the data into training and validation sets, allowing the model to learn from one portion and be tested on another to ensure it can generalise beyond what it has already seen.

The effectiveness of supervised learning depends heavily on the quality and quantity of labelled data, which can be costly and time-consuming to obtain. *Feature selection*—choosing the most relevant attributes for prediction—is also critical, as it helps the model focus on meaningful patterns and avoid noise. When done well, supervised learning enables systems to perform tasks like spam detection, medical diagnosis, and more, by leveraging human-provided examples to guide their predictions.

While supervised learning can be applied to many types of algorithms, neural networks have become the most prominent tool for this approach. Neural networks are made up of potentially billions of interconnected nodes, with each connection assigned a weight and bias. These weights determine how information flows through the network and are crucial to the learning process.

During training, the network adjusts its weights to minimise prediction errors and improve accuracy. This is achieved through a process called *backpropagation*, where the network learns from its mistakes by comparing its predictions to the correct answers and updating the weights accordingly. Over many iterations, this allows the system to refine its internal model and enhance its performance.

Ensuring the quality and accuracy of supervised learning models goes beyond simple right–wrong measures. Researchers use a range of metrics—such as *precision*, *recall*, and *F1 score*—to gain a deeper understanding of a model's strengths and weaknesses. These metrics help balance the trade-offs between *false positives* and *false negatives*, and they are chosen based on the specific goals and risks of the application. For example, in spam detection high precision ensures legitimate emails aren't wrongly flagged, while high recall ensures most spam is caught.

Selecting the right evaluation criteria is crucial, as it shapes how models are developed and deployed in real-world scenarios. By using nuanced metrics and understanding the complexities of the problem domain, researchers can build AI systems that are not only accurate but also robust and dependable. This careful approach allows supervised learning to remain a cornerstone of AI, enabling machines to generalise from labelled data and make reliable predictions on new, unseen examples.

Unsupervised learning is a machine learning approach that does not rely on labelled data. Instead, it seeks to uncover patterns, structures, or relationships within raw data, allowing algorithms to group, cluster, or organise information without predefined answers. This makes unsupervised learning especially valuable when labelled data is scarce, expensive, or impractical to obtain.

By analysing the inherent structure of data, unsupervised learning can reveal hidden groupings, detect anomalies, and extract meaningful features that might not be obvious through manual inspection. This approach is widely used in applications such as customer segmentation, anomaly detection, and exploratory data analysis, helping researchers and businesses make sense of large, unlabelled datasets.

Clustering, a core unsupervised learning task, maps data points into *multidimensional space*, with each dimension representing a feature like genre or author in a book dataset. Clustering algorithms find compact regions of similar points, but while they efficiently detect these groupings, they do not understand their meaning. The outputs require human expertise to interpret their narrative or practical value. To make these findings more interpretable and efficient, techniques like *dimensionality reduction* are used to simplify complex, high-dimensional results while preserving key patterns.

Unsupervised learning excels at uncovering hidden relationships and patterns within data, notably through *association rule learning*, which finds correlations such as items frequently bought together in shopping basket analysis. By surfacing these associations, it enables deeper insights and more informed decisions. Another key application is *anomaly detection*, where the algorithm identifies outliers—data points that deviate from typical patterns—such as unusual purchases by a fraudster or abnormal network activity by a hacker, highlighting significant or unexpected real-world events.

Assessing the quality and accuracy of unsupervised learning models is challenging because there are no predefined labels or correct answers, making evaluation interpretative and probabilistic. Technical issues like *underfitting* and *overfitting* can affect model quality, but deeper concerns arise from biased input data, which can amplify societal imbalances if not carefully managed. To ensure positive outcomes, it is essential to incorporate ethical guidelines and consider the broader societal impact when deploying these models.

Reinforcement learning is a process where an agent learns by interacting with its environment, receiving rewards or penalties based on its actions. Imagine a lab rat in a maze searching for cheese: through trial-and-error, it discovers which paths lead to food and which to dead ends. This approach mirrors how animals and humans learn from feedback, gradually improving their strategies over time.

This concept is also similar to training a dog, where repeated interactions and consistent feedback help the animal associate certain behaviours with positive or negative outcomes. The agent must learn to balance *exploration* (trying new actions) with *exploitation* (using known good actions) to maximise its rewards. At the heart of reinforcement learning are the ideas of states, actions, and rewards: The agent observes its current state, takes an action, and receives feedback, which shapes its future decisions through a learned policy.

Reinforcement learning is widely used in areas where ongoing interaction with the environment is essential, such as robotics and game-playing AIs. Robots can learn tasks through repeated practice, while game-playing systems like those for chess or Go improve by playing many games, often against themselves.

Deep learning uses neural networks with many stacked layers to model complex patterns in data, enabling hierarchical representation learning across supervised, unsupervised, and reinforcement settings. These deep models automatically learn useful features from raw data, reducing the need for manual feature engineering, but require careful design, large amounts of data, and significant computational resources. While highly effective for tasks like image and speech recognition, deep networks can be difficult to interpret, and explaining their decisions remains a challenge.

In-depth

Building on the foundations of the overview, let's now dive deeper into the technologies and approaches of learning AI. This section explains how computers can be trained to learn from data—enabling them to make predictions or decisions without being explicitly programmed for each specific task. It explores how these capabilities form the foundation for AI systems that adapt to new challenges and solve complex problems.

Learning from Data

When you were a child, you had to go through the slow, difficult, but vital process of learning how to live and survive in the complex world around you. You had to learn new *physical* skills like walking and talking, *social* skills like interacting with friends and family, and *mental* skills like language and identifying objects.

Some abilities, like sensing, eating, and basic movements, were innate and didn't require learning. These came pre-wired as a direct inheritance from your parents. Evolution strikes a careful balance between nature and nurture, depending on the survival requirements of each species. Human children, born into deep social structures, can afford to take some time to learn and adapt before facing the world unaided.

We now understand that young children are "learning machines," absorbing knowledge at rates they will never achieve again as adults. Within just a few months, a human baby acquires more knowledge than many other species can hope to gain in a lifetime. What a casual miracle this is.

As children experience the world around them, they use different strategies to learn and adapt—such as observation, mimicry, trial-and-error, and play. They prioritise rewards, focusing most on things that satisfy their immediate needs or make them happy. As they grow older, their rewards can become more complex, involving long-term, interpersonal, and social outcomes.

Learning Strategies

While social and motor skills are vital in the human world, for AI we focus primarily on the acquisition of *mental skills*. We can recall several approaches that helped us build useful and accurate mental models of the world. Here are some common approaches that humans use to learn:

- **Direct**—Sometimes we were directly taught the correct answers to given knowledge. For example, we were shown flashcards with vivid images and bold text stating "Apple," "Ball," "Cat," etc.

- **Exploratory**—Other times we were allowed to explore a space and learn for ourselves how to categorise and use items—like pulling Lego bricks from a jumble of toys and using them as a building set.
- **Rewards**—In both cases, rewards played a strong role in reinforcing the right approach or correct answer—encouraging words and smiles from adults, fun play, or a tasty snack.

These natural learning processes are mirrored in AI systems, which also use various approaches to acquire knowledge to improve performance. In AI, there are three primary learning strategies that parallel human learning:

- **Direct—supervised learning:** Structured learning with clear instructions and feedback—models learn from examples with known outcomes.
- **Exploratory—unsupervised learning:** Exploration and discovery without explicit instructions—models independently discover hidden patterns within data.
- **Rewards—reinforcement learning:** Positive reinforcement shapes behaviour—models learn optimal actions through trial-and-error with feedback.

It is important to note that these are not exclusive approaches. A system might employ any or all of them in combination to achieve its goals. They are, however, the fundamental strategies that researchers have developed over time.

Each brings its own advantages and limitations, and each can be used to target use cases with specific characteristics and data dynamics. The choice of approach depends on the problem at hand, the nature of the data, and the desired outcomes.

Applying Digital Learning

However knowledge is acquired, how can it be applied in the digital world of computers?

The primary route for applying knowledge in a modern AI system is through the *weights* used within a neural network. In fact, machine learning has become so synonymous with neural networks that people in the industry often casually mix the two up. You will often see the term AI/ML used as a joint nomenclature for the area. Although neural networks are just one mechanism through which digital systems can adapt through learning, it is nonetheless the dominant paradigm.

In Chapter 4, "Connected AI," we outlined neural networks and how they are built and deployed to solve complex problems. In such networks, the fundamental building blocks are nodes, which process information. These nodes are connected by links, each carrying a weight that determines the strength and influence of the connection.

To understand weights more generally, think of each link between nodes as a pathway for information to flow. Some pathways may carry information that is much more important for the task at hand than others. In these cases, the network can assign a larger weight to that pathway, making its influence on the receiving node much stronger.

For example, if a particular input or signal is especially relevant, its pathway can be given a high weight, so it has a greater effect on the outcome. Conversely, less important pathways can be given smaller weights, reducing their impact. This ability to adjust the strength of connections allows the network to emphasise the most useful information and downplay the less relevant, helping it to make better decisions and predictions as it learns.

When digital learning is applied, it is the adjustment of these weights on the links between nodes that enables the network to learn from data, adapt, and improve its performance. These adjustments are most commonly made using a process called *backpropagation*, which we first introduced in Chapter 4. Backpropagation allows the network to learn from its mistakes and improve over time.

This structure of nodes and links with learnt weights is what allows neural networks to model complex relationships and solve challenging problems. However, when operating at large scale, this can introduce a further challenge of explainability.

Many advanced models, especially deep learning networks, make decisions in ways that are difficult for humans to understand or trace. Such models can operate as opaque "black boxes" whose internal reasoning is often hidden. This lack of transparency can be problematic, especially in critical fields like healthcare or law, where knowing how and why a decision was made is essential for trust and accountability.

Supervised Learning

Imagine you've been assigned the task of directing fans at a sports event, where your job is to guide them to the correct sections of the stadium. However, due to the rush of the day's activities, you haven't reviewed the task instructions or watched the training videos. You also know nothing about the sport or the teams involved, making your prospects seem daunting.

Fortunately, before your shift begins, you have the chance to observe another employee doing the very job you're about to take on. As you watch, you begin to notice patterns: Fans wearing blue are supporters of one team, while those in red support the other, and they are directed left or right based on their allegiances.

As you continue to *supervise* your colleague, you pick up more subtle details. Some fans wear neutral clothing, but clues like scarves, badges, and banners help reveal their loyalties. Over time, you learn that not all features are useful. You tune out irrelevant details—like age, height, or gender—and focus only on those items that help make the right decision.

Further observation reveals additional nuances: Fans with children are directed to a different stand, people using wheelchairs to another, and VIPs present extra identification and are met by attendants. The more you observe, the more you grasp the underlying logic.

Eventually, the shift change occurs, and you take over. Despite receiving no formal training, you're able to perform the task effectively based solely on your observations.

This simple analogy mirrors a technique in AI called *supervised learning*. Like all learning AI, this methodology relies on large volumes of training data—but what distinguishes it is the presence of *correct* answers in the training material. Just as you learnt by observing someone else, a supervised learning model learns from a dataset that includes both the inputs (known as *features*) and the correct outputs (known as *labels*).

The term *supervised* can be misleading. It might suggest a teacher guiding a student, but in AI there is no teacher in the traditional sense. This is one more example of AI researchers adopting everyday words, only to bend their meaning. Here, the data itself *is* the supervision—a structured set of examples that pairs inputs with correct answers.

Any system where both inputs and expected outputs are present, such that general patterns can be learnt, qualifies as supervised learning. This methodology typically involves the following steps:

- **Labelled data:** First, a training dataset is gathered, consisting of input–output pairs. For example, in a spam detection system, emails (inputs) are labelled as "spam" or "not spam" (outputs).
- **Model training:** A portion of the data is used to train the algorithm. It learns to map inputs to outputs by adjusting the weights of the network's internal connections to minimise prediction errors.
- **Output validation:** The trained model is then tested against a separate portion of the dataset that wasn't used during training. This checks whether the model has genuinely learnt useful patterns, not just memorised specific examples.
- **Classifying and making predictions:** Once validated, the model is deployed to make predictions on new, unseen data—where the correct labels are no longer known. For example, it might classify fresh emails as "spam" or "not spam" based on patterns it learnt during training.

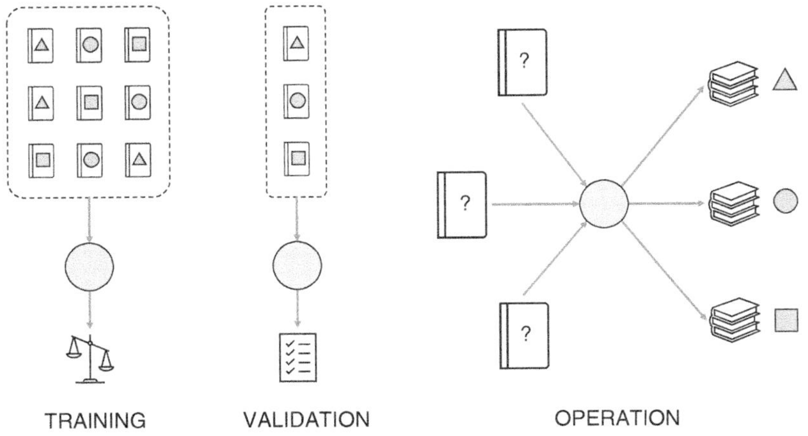

Figure 5.1: Supervised learning

Figure 5.1 illustrates the process of supervised learning. On the left is a training phase, where weights are adjusted in the light of observed labels. In the centre is a validation phase, where those learnt weights are tested with fresh labelled data. Finally, on the right is the model in operation, correctly classifying new data using the criteria learnt in the earlier steps.

Once training is complete and the model is deployed, it no longer has access to the correct answers—the labels are not present in the data being processed. At this stage, we rely on the model to apply the patterns it has learnt and make accurate determinations on our behalf.

Gathering Labelled Data

One of the biggest challenges in supervised learning is the collection and preparation of labelled data, which indicate to the AI the "correct" answer or expected outcome. This process can be time-consuming, labour-intensive, and expensive.

The challenge is further exacerbated by the need to collect a large and varied dataset for the supervised learning process to consume. The goal is to expose the machine learning algorithm to representative examples of all the types and classes it may encounter in operation—not just common or canonical cases, but also ambiguous, rare, or infrequent ones.

Take, for example, the spam detection use case mentioned earlier. An effective training dataset might consist of millions of emails labelled as "spam" or "not spam." This requires considerable resources to source and prepare before the learning process can even begin.

In practice, sometimes the labelling is already present in data from an alternative source. For example, by dragging messages in-and-out of their junk folders, over time email users indirectly create a labelled training set. The emails are being automatically classified through the actions of human users.

Another example might be in medical diagnosis, where existing libraries of images combined with known patient conditions can serve as a naturally labelled dataset. Scenarios such as this are the background to controversial discussions we often encounter when AI companies attempt to gain access to public health data.

When users are interacting with websites and apps, they may unknowingly be helping AI researchers label datasets. For example, when you rate a product, flag a comment as inappropriate, or provide feedback on whether a search result was helpful, your responses are used to label data for training AI systems.

Recently, large AI companies have been paying humans to label data directly. They often collect labels from multiple workers for the same data point, comparing answers to ensure accuracy and consistency. Both user-driven and paid labelling approaches are used to improve data quality and coverage. While paying people to label data is a practical approach, it can sometimes raise challenging questions about low-wage exploitation of people in less economically developed parts of the world.

Sometimes, other AI systems are used to create a *synthetic dataset*—machine-generated data designed to act as a labelled set for training on a given outcome. This might be used alongside, or instead of, naturally occurring data.

Say, for example, you needed a series of images to represent whether a railway crossing barrier was up or down, in order to train an algorithm to detect this. You could gather these from a real crossing—but what about infrequent situations like fog, snow, or obstructions? Instead of waiting for every possible event to occur in the real world, you might synthesise images of crossings in various scenarios using an image generation AI.

However, synthetic data can introduce artefacts and domain-gaps that cause models to learn unreal features, so their use must be carefully validated, blended with representative real examples, and the resulting models tested on genuine data to avoid poor real-world performance.

Regardless of how the labelled material is gathered, the quality of the dataset directly impacts the performance of the model. If poor, patchy, or unrepresentative data are fed in, a corresponding drop in quality will be reflected in the model's output. For example, in our earlier sports event analogy, if we had not witnessed rare events like fans in wheelchairs or a VIP, our understanding of the overall task would have been diminished, affecting our ability to complete the work correctly.

Neural Nets and Feature Selection

Supervised learning as a technique is not limited to use with neural networks. The ability to learn from labelled training material can be applied to many processes, both computational and otherwise. However, neural networks have become the most prominent tool for implementing this technique in recent times. Here, we will focus on that application.

In supervised learning, the choice of *features* in the input data is crucial. Features are the attributes or characteristics the model uses to make its determinations. In our sports event analogy, we identified features such as shirts, scarves, and banners to determine fan allegiances—while ignoring less relevant features like age, height, or hair colour. We focused on those traits that provided the most useful signals for the problem at hand.

Similarly, in a machine learning model, selecting the right features from the source material is essential. In a spam detection system, features might include the presence of certain keywords, the sender's email address, or the frequency of specific phrases. Choosing the right features helps the model learn the most relevant patterns and improve its accuracy.

It is important to note that choosing the wrong features, or including less relevant ones, can significantly impact the model's output. Sometimes, the resulting skewed outcomes are difficult to quantify, as the model might still perform well on the bulk of canonical or common cases while failing on edge cases or rare scenarios. We will explore more about the quality and accuracy of such systems later in this section.

As discussed in Chapter 4, these features can correspond to the *nodes* in a neural network. Each feature is represented as an input node, encapsulating a specific characteristic or piece of information from the data. The connections (links) between nodes are *weighted* based on their importance—just as we observed the significance of shirts, scarves, and banners when deciding where to direct fans.

In practice, each feature is usually encoded as a numerical value—for example, a colour histogram, a count, or a simple binary flag indicating presence—so the network works with numbers rather than raw objects. While the underlying principles are similar to other learning systems, it is the scale and automation in neural networks that enable their remarkable power and flexibility.

Weights and Biases in Neural Networks

Recapping Chapter 4, we recall that neural networks are complex systems consisting of potentially billions of nodes and links, each with its own weights and biases.

The *weights* determine the strength and importance of connections between nodes and are crucial for the learning process. They are adjusted during training to minimise errors in predictions. This adjustment is performed through a process whereby the network learns from its mistakes by modifying the weights to improve future performance.

A *bias*, on the other hand, is a learnt constant added to a node's input before its activation—it lets a node fire even when its inputs are small or zero, effectively shifting the decision boundary. In short, weights scale inputs and biases shift them, and together they let the network represent a much richer set of functions.

In a neural network, the structure of the network can be thought of as its innate capability—similar to senses and movement in humans. Conversely, the weights and biases can be considered as learnt behaviour, like language or object recognition. This loose analogy helps separate the static elements of the network from the parts that adapt to signals and experience.

The sheer complexity of neural networks, with their vast number of nodes and links, makes their learning operate beyond direct human cognition. While the underlying principles are similar to simpler systems like decision trees—adjusting weights based on feedback—the scale and intricacy are exponentially greater. Managing and fine-tuning billions of weights and biases manually is not feasible, so the process relies on automated algorithms to handle this complexity.

As a loose analogy, this resembles how the human brain learns. In the brain, learning involves strengthening or weakening the synaptic connections between neurons based on experience and feedback. Similarly, in a neural network, the weights and biases are adjusted to reflect learnt patterns and improve accuracy.

While this comparison is illustrative and helps convey the concept, it is important to remember that the mechanisms are fundamentally different. Both systems learn through experience, using feedback to refine their internal models. However, while the brain's learning processes involve numerous biochemical and electrical interactions, neural networks use mathematical models and algorithms to achieve similar outcomes.

Even though the learning process in neural networks is based on the same simple principles as smaller systems, it happens on a size and scale that cannot be managed or adjusted manually by humans. This is what enables neural networks to perform incredibly complex tasks—such as image recognition, natural language processing, and game playing—often surpassing human capabilities in specific domains.

Backpropagation—Learning from Mistakes

Whenever we learn a new skill or area of knowledge, we inevitably make mistakes. This is not a negative thing; it's an integral part of the learning process. As long as we recognise that a mistake has been made, understand how it happened, and adjust our behaviour for next time, the mistake can bring great value to our overall learning goal.

Let's think back to our earlier analogy of directing fans at a sports event. Suppose you've been directing fans based on their team colours, but make a few mistakes early on—sending some fans to the wrong sections. This might have happened because some fans were wearing alternative or away kits for their team. When the mistake is brought to your attention, you reflect on why it happened and modify your approach to achieve better accuracy for later arriving fans.

In AI, a similar mechanism called *backpropagation* is often used in supervised learning. Here a model adapts its behaviour when errors are discovered and highlighted. Such errors are used to further improve the model.

The concept of backpropagation was popularised in the 1980s, largely due to the influential work of David Rumelhart, Geoffrey Hinton, and Ronald Williams. Their 1986 paper provided a practical and accessible framework for applying backpropagation to neural networks, allowing them to learn from earlier mistakes. This work revitalised the field of neural networks by making it feasible to train multilayer models—a breakthrough that underpins many of the complex AI tasks tackled today.

Whenever a supervised learning model makes a prediction, each output can be compared to the correct answer to calculate the error. Backpropagation computes gradients—measures of how much each weight contributed to the error—and traces these signals back through the network's layers, indicating how much each parameter contributed to the discrepancy. Metaphorically, the mistake is "dragged backward" through the network, assigning "blame" values to the nodes that led to its genesis. An optimiser then uses those gradients to update the weights and reduce future error.

After adjustments are applied, more predictions are made, and further mistakes identified and backpropagated. Eventually, the model becomes increasingly refined and accurate, and error counts are diminished. In a real-world system, this training happens over many cycles, or *epochs*, with the network processing thousands or millions of examples—each time adjusting the weights slightly to reduce error.

Due to its complexity, the process requires substantial computational power, especially as the size and scale of the data and networks increase.

In practical applications, backpropagation enables neural networks to perform high-level tasks such as image and speech recognition, continually learning and improving through each iteration.

Quality and Accuracy

Given that ensuring the quality and accuracy of a supervised learning model is paramount, what processes exist to measure how well such a model is performing? While a simple right–wrong accuracy assessment is a useful starting point, it doesn't always provide the full picture. To gain deeper insight, we need to consider other, more nuanced metrics.

An important concept to understand is that of *false positives* and *false negatives*. A false positive occurs when the model incorrectly identifies something as belonging to a category when it does not—for example, marking a legitimate email as spam. A false negative is when the model fails to identify something that does belong to a category—for example, letting a spam email through as if it were legitimate. These concepts are illustrated in Figure 5.2. Minimising both types of errors is important for building reliable AI systems, as each can have different consequences depending on the application.

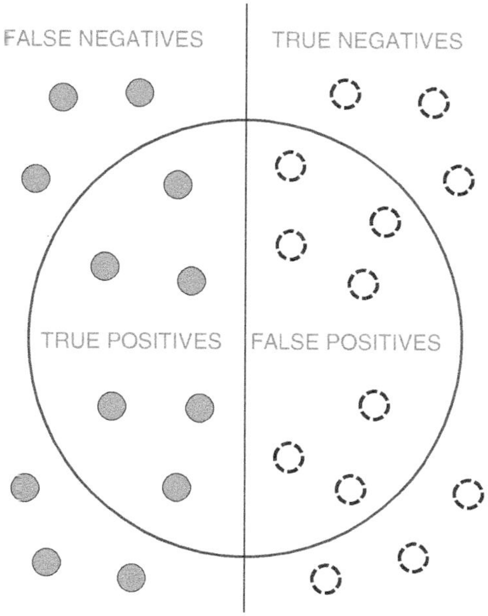

Figure 5.2: True and false positives

When AI researchers evaluate models, they typically use a few standardised metrics to measure and gauge performance:

- **Accuracy:** The ratio of correctly predicted instances to the total number of instances. While useful, it can be misleading with imbalanced datasets, where one class significantly outweighs the others. For example, in a medical diagnosis system, an accuracy of 95 percent might seem impressive—but if the disease being tested for is rare, this figure may not reflect meaningful performance.
- **Precision:** The proportion of predicted positive instances that are actually positive. High precision indicates a low false-positive rate. In a medical diagnosis context, precision tells us how many of the patients identified as having the disease truly have it—helping to reduce the number of healthy people wrongly diagnosed as ill.
- **Recall:** The proportion of actual positive instances that were correctly identified by the model. High recall means a low false-negative rate. In medical diagnosis, recall tells us how many of the patients who actually have the disease were successfully detected—ensuring fewer cases are missed.
- **F1 score:** The harmonic mean of precision and recall. This balanced metric considers both false positives and false negatives. It is especially valuable with imbalanced datasets, where accuracy alone can be deceptive. In medical diagnosis, the F1 score helps balance catching true cases (recall) with minimising unnecessary treatment of healthy individuals (precision).

By focusing on metrics such as these—and applying them thoughtfully to the domain in question—supervised models can be made more reliable and effective. High precision, recall, and F1 scores are key to building robust AI systems that make dependable and impactful predictions.

Unsupervised Learning

One of the fundamental challenges of supervised learning is its reliance on large volumes of labelled data, which is used to teach the AI the "correct" answer or best outcome. These labels are essential to how supervised learning operates. However, obtaining such data can be both costly and time-consuming, as it often requires extensive human effort to label each item accurately. In fields like medical imaging, the level of expertise needed to provide correct labels adds significant cost and complexity.

The quality of the training data is also directly tied to the accuracy of the labels. Since labels are usually generated by human annotators or derived from other digital processes, they are prone to error and inconsistency. In many real-world scenarios, the sheer volume and speed of incoming data make the labelling process impractical. The rapid accumulation of data can overwhelm traditional methods, leaving large datasets unlabelled and underutilised.

In response to these challenges, AI researchers have another option in their toolbox: *unsupervised learning*. This approach does not rely on labelled data and provides a viable alternative in situations where acquiring labels is difficult or infeasible.

Uncovering Patterns in Data

Chapter 3 presents a good example of *unsupervised learning* on statistical AI is presented. There, we discussed a new bookshop where the owner had to organise a myriad of books that arrived mostly unlabelled and unordered.

While some books might have cursory labels—such as genre stickers or author names—these would only allow for a basic, surface-level categorisation. In a supervised sense, these labels could be used to sort books into broad groups like "fiction" or "nonfiction." However, to create a truly meaningful and useful organisation, the owner would need to go beyond these simple labels and delve into the content itself—examining themes, writing styles, and deeper connections between works.

As the owner explored further, subtle groupings could begin to emerge. Books by the same author or within the same literary tradition might start clustering together, and thematic similarities could link otherwise diverse works, creating an intuitive organisation system. For example, the owner might discover that the works of J.R.R. Tolkien and J.K. Rowling, though written decades apart, share motifs and narrative structures with ancient Norse myths—connections that are not stated on any label but become apparent through deeper analysis.

This is analogous to what algorithms in unsupervised learning do: They group data based on discovered similarities without relying solely on predefined categories. In the bookshop scenario, such a method would not only make the shop easier to navigate but could also reveal unexpected connections between different works—enhancing customers' browsing and buying experiences by surfacing relationships that labels alone would never capture.

This analogy illustrates how unsupervised learning works in practice. In the absence of labels and explicit clues from humans, AI can still forge ahead to interpret and organise the data it is given. This is because the data itself contains inherent structures that can be mined to uncover patterns and relationships—often revealing insights not initially apparent to humans.

Figure 5.3 illustrates the process of unsupervised learning. On the left is a training phase, where unannotated data is examined and clusters are identified and tagged. In the centre is a validation phase where domain experts and AIs work together using ground truth data is test the clustering. Finally, on the right, is the model in operation, correctly tagging new data into the clusters it learned during earlier steps.

A crucial difference between AI and the human owner of a bookshop is that the latter possesses a semantic understanding of the domain—they comprehend *what books are*. Concepts such as authors, genres, and settings have intrinsic meaning for humans, but for AI, data is just a numeric landscape to be navigated.

When a machine identifies a grouping or relationship within a dataset, it interprets this purely as a mathematical structure. For example, it might recognise a cluster of points in a multidimensional space that are "close" to each other. It has no understanding of the real-world implications of this discovery.

An AI processing data about books might feasibly find similarities between the works of Rowling, Tolkien, and ancient mythology. For the AI, this is simply because the numerical representations of these works reside in a compact part of its mathematical landscape—not because the works produced similar "experiences" when it "read" them.

Hence, the outputs of unsupervised learning often require human domain experts to interpret them, assign meaning, and leverage the insights in the real world.

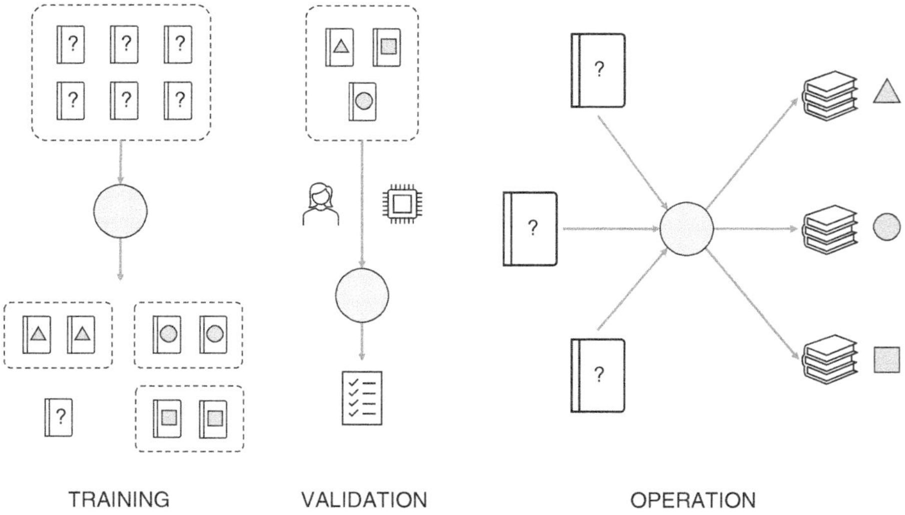

Figure 5.3: Unsupervised learning

Working in Multidimensions

Imagine you're presented with a line graph without any title, axes, or labels and asked to interpret it. You might initially be puzzled by the lack of context. However, even with limited information, you could still describe some characteristics: flat sections where the value appears static, parts where it suddenly increases or decreases, the highest peak, and the lowest trough.

This type of analysis holds, whether the graph represents temperature or stock prices. The structure of the line tells a story that is separable from its context. If I had instead given you a table of numbers, you would have struggled to form the same instant judgments. Humans are not accustomed to interpreting tables of numbers, as we did not evolve needing this skill, but we can certainly read and understand lines. Graphical representations align better with the skills we have developed for survival throughout the millennia.

Now, suppose this line represents a financial chart, with time on the horizontal axis and share price on the vertical. This would be much easier for you to read and interpret. But if I were to introduce a third dimension, representing foreign exchange exposure, what was once a line would become a surface in three dimensions. This is a significant leap for most humans, as such surfaces are harder to interpret instantly. However, with some effort and careful analysis, they too are comprehensible.

Now imagine I introduced a fourth dimension, perhaps exposure to interest rates. At this point, you would struggle to even visualise it. Humans cannot think in four dimensions—it's simply beyond our cognitive capability, although some physicists, like Richard Feynman, have seemingly bucked this trend.

Now what about a fifth, a sixth, or even hundreds of dimensions? Clearly, we have moved beyond the ability of humans to conceptualise such representations. But what about machines?

In fact, all of the scenarios I described are just normal behaviour for machines—the line, the table of numbers, the surface, or even the 100-dimensional graph. A computer does not care because mathematics doesn't care, and computers are simply mathematical devices.

In mathematics, the coordinates of a point in two dimensions might be (2, 3); in three dimensions, it might be (2, 3, 6); in four dimensions, (2, 3, 6, 9). The math still works, the algorithms still function, and the data is no less computable.

AI routinely operates in multi-dimensional space. This simple sentence might take a moment to sink in. AI works in a domain beyond human comprehension in terms of visualisation, but AI doesn't visualise things the way we do. Rather, things function at a mathematical level using a device called a matrix.

A matrix is simply an array of numbers arranged in rows and columns. As dimensions grow, so do the columns of a matrix—but it still maintains its row–column structure. Here's how matrices grow with dimensions:

- The corners of a **square** in **2D** space: 2 columns, 4 rows.
  - Columns are directions (left–right and up–down).
  - Each row is a corner of the square.
- The corners of a **cube** in **3D** space: 3 columns, 8 rows.
  - Columns are directions (left–right, up–down, forward–back).
  - Each row is a corner of the cube.
- The corners of a **hypercube** in **4D** space: 4 columns, 16 rows.
  - Columns are four directions.
  - Each row is a corner of the four-dimensional shape (even though we can't easily describe or picture it).

Matrices are an efficient way to represent complex data, making it easy to store and process. One of their greatest advantages is that many matrix operations can be performed in parallel, rather than serially. In serial (or sequential) computation, each operation is carried out one after another, which can be slow for large datasets. In contrast, parallel computation allows many operations to be executed simultaneously, dramatically speeding up processing.

Matrices are also a fundamental tool for drawing real-world gaming environments. In computer graphics, matrices are used to represent and transform objects, positions, and perspectives, making it possible to render complex, immersive worlds. To process these matrix operations at high speed, special hardware called graphical processing units (GPUs) was developed. GPUs were originally designed to accelerate the rendering of graphics for smooth gaming experiences on consoles and computers.

Lately, GPUs have found tremendous utility in the AI world because the same matrix mathematics used in graphics is also at the heart of modern AI algorithms. Training and running AI models—especially deep learning networks—requires vast numbers of matrix calculations, which GPUs are exceptionally well suited to perform. As a result, the global supply of GPUs is under strain, since these devices have become essential for a wide range of AI deployments and research, in addition to their ongoing role in gaming and graphics.

For AI, each row or column in a matrix represents a different feature of the data. For example, a simple two-dimensional matrix might represent data with only two features, while a higher-dimensional matrix can represent data with many more features.

AI uses matrix operations to manipulate data, and these basic operations form the foundation of more complex calculations used in machine learning algorithms to analyse and interpret data. In fact, three types of representation are commonly used:

- **Vectors:** A vector is a one-dimensional array of numbers, either a single row or column (but not both). It can represent quantities like velocity, which have both magnitude and direction. In machine learning, vectors might represent features of an input, such as pixel values in an image or weights in a neural network.
- **Matrices:** A matrix is a two-dimensional array of numbers, consisting of rows and columns. It extends vectors to two dimensions and is often used to represent data with two axes of analysis, such as greyscale images (where each pixel is an element in the matrix) or the weights in a neural network layer.
- **Tensors:** A tensor generalises vectors and matrices to higher dimensions. A tensor can be thought of as an n-dimensional array of numbers, where "n" can be 1 (vector), 2 (matrix), or more. For instance, a 3D tensor might be a cube of numbers, with height, width, and depth. Tensors are used in deep learning models, where data is often multidimensional.

We will revisit the concept of high-dimensional space in Chapter 6, "Generative AI," where we'll explore the workings of a key methodology known as autoencoders.

Clustering

In Chapter 3, we outlined the concepts of classification and clustering. Classification involves applying predefined labels to data, whereas clustering is a method for discovering patterns within the data. For example, classification might label books by their well-known genres, whereas clustering might identify two authors with a similar writing style. Having now covered both supervised and unsupervised learning, it should be clearer that supervised learning aligns with classification, while unsupervised learning is typically used for clustering.

Clustering is a key application of unsupervised learning, useful not only for organising book collections but also for more critical applications like medical diagnosis and climate change analysis. Clustering involves mapping data points into a multidimensional space where each dimension represents a feature of the data. For example, in a dataset of books, dimensions might include genre, author, length, and publication year. The clustering algorithm then identifies compact areas where data points are "close" to one another, indicating similarity.

It's important not to try and imagine "closeness in multidimensional space" in a spatial sense. Instead, think of it as a mathematical proximity. Once the points are mapped, the algorithm looks for clusters—areas of points that are close to each other. The closer the points, the more similar they are considered to be.

Clustering usually happens in four main steps:

Step 1: Pick starting points. The computer chooses some points to act as the first "centres" of the groups. This can be done randomly or by following a simple rule.

Step 2: Group the data. Each item in the dataset is put into the group with the nearest centre.

Step 3: Move the centres. The centre of each group is moved to the average position of all the items in that group.

Step 4: Repeat. Steps 2 and 3 are repeated until the groups stop changing much, or a set number of rounds is reached. This helps make the groups as clear and separate as possible.

Once the process is completed, the strongest *centroids* are revealed, representing the central points of the clusters. Common clustering algorithms include:

- **K-Means clustering:** Partitions data into a predefined number of clusters by minimising variance within clusters. It is widely used for customer segmentation, image compression, and pattern recognition.
- **Hierarchical clustering:** Builds a family tree of groups by either joining small groups together or splitting big groups apart. This helps show how data points are related at different levels, from small clusters up to larger ones. It is often used to find patterns in things like social networks or market research.
- **Density-based (DBSCAN):** Finds groups by looking for areas where data points are packed closely together. Points that are far away from any group are marked as "noise" or outliers. This method is good for finding clusters of unusual shapes and for spotting points that don't fit in anywhere, such as in maps or when looking for rare events.

- **Mean shift clustering:** Finds clusters by searching for the most crowded, or densest areas in the data. It does not need to know the number of groups in advance. This method is often used in image processing and for tracking moving objects.

These algorithms can identify clusters that may not be immediately obvious to human analysts. However, the computer does not inherently understand the real-world meaning of these clusters. For the machine, a cluster is just a mathematical pattern. But each of these patterns can have a real-world interpretation—such as authors sharing a similar writing style, or a patient showing characteristics of a specific disease.

That's why, in unsupervised learning, human expertise is needed to interpret these clusters, understand the stories they reveal, and apply the insights in practical ways. The machine finds the clusters; human experts give them meaning and use them.

Dimensionality Reduction

If human experts and AI are to work together effectively, they must be able to share an interpretation of the data space. But since AI operates in high-dimensional space, its findings need to be simplified for human understanding while keeping the essential patterns and relationships. This process is crucial for several reasons:

- **Interpretability:** High-dimensional data can be difficult to interpret and understand. By reducing the number of dimensions, the data becomes more manageable and easier to visualise, helping human analysts grasp the underlying patterns and relationships more effectively.
- **Efficiency:** High-dimensional datasets can be computationally intensive to process. Reducing the number of dimensions significantly decreases the computational load, making algorithms run faster and more efficiently.
- **Noise reduction:** Not all dimensions (or data features) are equally important. Some may contain noise or irrelevant information that can obscure the true patterns in the data. Dimensionality reduction helps filter out this noise, improving the quality and clarity of the results.
- **Avoiding overfitting:** High-dimensional data can lead to overfitting, where a model learns the noise in the training data rather than the actual patterns. Reducing the number of dimensions minimises the risk of overfitting, leading to better generalisation to new data.

Obviously, there's a balance to be struck—reducing dimensionality has significant advantages, but it carries the risk that important patterns and relationships could be lost or diminished. Choosing the right algorithm for dimensionality reduction is key. Several methodologies can be applied, some of the most common ones being:

- **Principal component analysis (PCA):** PCA finds the directions in the data where the differences are biggest, and uses those to create a simpler version of the data. It helps show the most important patterns while ignoring less important details.
- **t-Distributed stochastic neighbour embedding (t-SNE):** t-SNE is mainly used to make complex data easier to see on a 2D or 3D plot. It groups similar things together so patterns are easier to spot, but is mostly for visualisation, not for further analysis.
- **Linear discriminant analysis (LDA):** LDA looks for the best way to separate different groups in the data. It uses the known categories to find the features that make each group stand out, and is often used for classification as well as reducing dimensions.

Don't worry if these algorithms are hard to understand. The key takeaway is that high-dimensional data is a "compute space," and low-dimensional data is an "application space." By employing dimensionality reduction techniques, AI can transform complex data into a more interpretable and usable form, facilitating better analysis and more practical applications.

We will return to the topic of dimensionality reduction in Chapter 6, where we will explore the workings of a key methodology called autoencoders.

Relationships and Associations

Another critical aspect of unsupervised learning is detecting relationships and associations within the data. In our bookstore example, while clustering helps us find books with a similar style, relationship detection can uncover connections between different books, such as those set in the same historical time period. This approach, known as *association rule learning*, helps identify hidden patterns and correlations within the data that may not be immediately obvious.

Be aware that association rules show co-occurrence, not causation. Just because two states often occur together this does not necessarily mean one *caused* the other. For example, you might find that customers who buy exam revision guides also often buy dictionaries. This does not mean that buying a revision guide causes someone to buy a dictionary—just that these purchases tend to happen together more often than by chance.

Association rules are commonly used in shopping basket analysis to discover sets of items that frequently co-occur in transactions. For example, customers who buy books by a particular author might often go on to purchase other books of the same genre. Once identified, these associations can be used to power features such as purchase recommendations.

Continuing with this example, here's a brief overview of how association rule learning works:

- **Data preparation:** The process begins with a dataset of transactions. Each transaction records the items purchased together. For instance, in a bookstore, a transaction could be a list of books bought by a customer during a single visit.
- **Generating itemsets:** The algorithm scans the dataset to generate all possible combinations of items (called itemsets). For example, it might find all pairs of books that have been purchased together.
- **Support calculation:** Support measures how frequently an itemset appears in the dataset. It is calculated as the proportion of transactions that include the itemset. For example, if the pair *Harry Potter* and *The Hobbit* appears in 30 out of 100 transactions, the support is 0.3.
- **Confidence calculation:** Confidence measures the likelihood that a transaction containing one item will also contain the other item in the itemset. It is calculated as the ratio of the support of the itemset to the support of the antecedent. For example, if *Harry Potter* appears in 50 transactions and the pair *Harry Potter* and *The Hobbit* appears in 30 transactions, the confidence is 0.6 (30/50).
- **Lift calculation:** Lift measures the strength of an association rule compared to the expected co-occurrence of the items if they were independent. It is calculated as the ratio of observed support to the expected support if the items were independent. A lift greater than 1 indicates a positive association.

By uncovering these relationships, unsupervised learning enables businesses and researchers to gain deeper insights into their data, leading to more informed decisions and innovative solutions.

Anomaly Detection

Earlier in this chapter, we discussed the importance of finding clusters of closely associated values in datasets. In many ways, the opposite of finding clusters is identifying anomalies and outliers. These are data points that do not fit the pattern of the overall dataset. Detecting anomalies is another key use case for unsupervised learning, as such anomalies often represent significant events in the real world.

For example, your spending habits over time might follow a predictable pattern: the same shops, services, and products. If you suddenly start purchasing different items, this would appear as an anomalous data point in your purchase history. Such anomalies stand out clearly against the normal landscape of your spending behaviour.

This might indicate that your credit card has been stolen and misused. Similarly, anomalies in other datasets might indicate events such as network intrusions by hackers, dramatic shifts in climate, or the sudden onset of a health condition.

There are many algorithms by which unsupervised learning can detect and flag anomalous data points:

- **Statistical methods:** These identify data points that deviate significantly from expected statistical patterns or distributions. These methods assume that normal data points follow a certain distribution, and any point that deviates from this pattern is considered an anomaly.
- **Clustering-based methods:** Here, clustering algorithms group data points into clusters and then identify points that don't fit well into any cluster. These outliers, located far from any cluster centroid, are flagged as anomalies.
- **Density-based methods:** This technique examines the density of data points in the feature space. It identifies clusters in high-density regions and labels points in low-density or isolated regions as anomalies.
- **Isolation forests:** This tree-based method isolates observations by randomly selecting features and splitting the data along these chosen features. Points requiring fewer splits to isolate are considered anomalies, as they are more likely to be outliers.

Anomaly detectors often need carefully chosen thresholds because improving sensitivity typically reduces specificity, and vice versa. A low threshold catches more true anomalies but produces many false positives, while a high threshold cuts false positives at the cost of missed events. This trade-off can overload downstream systems and erode trust, so thresholds need to be validated on representative data, and include some human review when possible.

Finding clusters and detecting anomalies are both equally important, though they are statistical opposites—they are two sides of the same coin. Each plays a crucial role in understanding and interpreting data. In practice, both clustering and anomaly detection uncover meaningful insights and help drive informed decision-making.

Quality and Accuracy

When we discussed verifying techniques for supervised learning, we highlighted a significant advantage: the presence of "correct" values or expected outcomes in the training material. However, as we've seen, such definitive labels are not available to unsupervised learning. Just as unsupervised learning must discover and describe the data without human direction, it must also verify its outputs independently.

The absence of predefined labels presents a challenge in verifying the accuracy and quality of unsupervised learning models. Instead of labels, researchers need to use other metrics to assess the model's value:

- **Silhouette score:** This score measures how similar an object is to its own cluster compared to other clusters. Values range from –1 to +1, with higher values indicating better clustering quality, where objects are well matched to their own cluster and poorly matched to neighbouring clusters.
- **Davies–Bouldin index:** This index calculates the average similarity ratio of each cluster with its most similar cluster. Lower values indicate better clustering, as it signifies that clusters are compact and well separated from each other.
- **Within-cluster sum of squares:** This metric measures the variance within each cluster by summing the squared distances between each point and the centroid of its cluster. Lower values indicate more compact clusters, suggesting that the clustering algorithm has effectively minimised intra-cluster variance.
- **Adjusted Rand Index:** This method compares the similarity between the clustering results and a ground truth, adjusting for chance. Higher values indicate a higher degree of agreement between the clustering and the ground truth, with adjustments made to account for random clustering assignments.

Here you will see that the Adjusted Rand Index uses "ground truth" data—which is just a technical term for a set of correct answers determined by an external source, typically human experts. A small number of such labels can provide a benchmark for evaluating algorithm results.

One mitigating factor here is that the outputs of unsupervised models are often interpreted probabilistically, rather than as definitive, deterministic answers. If a supervised model were to miscategorise a book—say, as history rather than fantasy—we would rightly be concerned about its outputs, since these models are expected to return "right" answers.

However, users should understand that unsupervised model outputs are best presented in probabilistic terms. Intelligent applications do not treat the results of unsupervised learning as absolute truths. Instead, statements are typically framed probabilistically, such as "There is an 86 percent chance that ..." This approach helps set appropriate expectations and reflects the inherent uncertainty in unsupervised analysis.

Challenges and Considerations

Unsupervised learning faces a range of challenges, from technical issues like underfitting and overfitting to broader concerns about bias, model drift, and the lack of explicit feedback on prediction accuracy. These models can inadvertently perpetuate or even amplify societal biases present in their training data, and their autonomous nature means they may continue to operate on outdated assumptions as real-world conditions change.

Addressing these challenges requires ongoing vigilance: regular assessment of model performance, robust mechanisms for detecting issues, and a commitment to ethical guidelines and societal impact. These themes—along with strategies for mitigation—will be explored further in the Conclusion section at the end of this chapter.

Reinforcement Learning

Imagine a lab rat in a maze, navigating its way to find a tasty piece of cheese. The rat explores different paths, sometimes hitting dead ends and sometimes finding its way to the reward. Through trial-and-error, the rat learns which routes lead to the cheese and which do not. This process of learning from interaction with the environment, adjusting behaviour based on rewards and penalties, is at the heart of reinforcement learning.

Reinforcement learning is similar to training a dog. Initially, the dog doesn't know which behaviours will result in treats (rewards) and which will result in scolding (penalties). Over time, through repeated interactions and consistent feedback, the dog learns to associate certain actions with positive outcomes and adjusts its behaviour accordingly.

Figure 5.4 shows a typical reinforcement learning process, where a lab rat experiences both rewards and penalties and using these to build a policy for how to navigate a space.

Additionally, an agent using reinforcement learning must also learn to balance exploration (trying new actions) and exploitation (using known

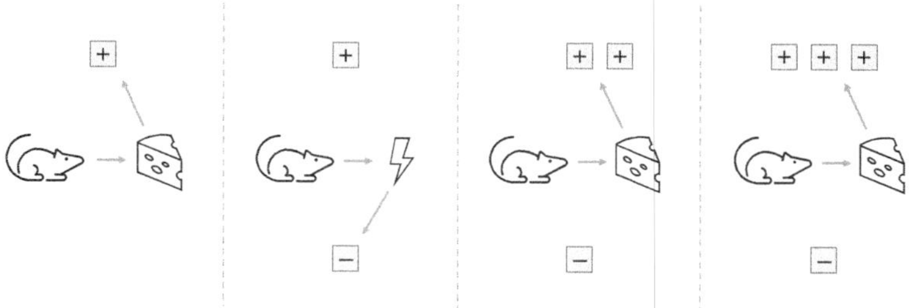

Figure 5.4: Reinforcement learning

good actions). This balance is a central challenge in reinforcement learning. Exploration involves trying new or less certain actions to discover potentially better rewards, while exploitation means choosing actions that are already known to yield good results. Too much exploration can waste resources on poor choices, while too much exploitation can cause the agent to miss out on better strategies. Effective reinforcement learning requires a careful balance between these two approaches to achieve the best long-term outcomes.

At the core of reinforcement learning is the concept of an agent interacting with the environment through states, actions, and rewards:

- **State:** The current state of a system, such as the position of a rat in the maze.
- **Actions:** A set of possible actions that can be taken, such as turning left or right in the maze.
- **Rewards:** Payoffs in terms of rewards or penalties, such as finding cheese (reward) or hitting a dead end (penalty).

Through this model of continuous feedback in the form of rewards and penalties, an agent develops a *policy*. This policy enables the agent to understand the best action to take in any given state to maximise the total rewards over time.

Reinforcement learning is a good fit for systems that have scope to try, test, and adapt their behaviour based on experience. For example, consider an AI tasked with optimising website layout to maximise user engagement. The AI can experiment with different arrangements of content and features, observe how users interact, and receive feedback in the form of engagement metrics (such as click-through rates or time spent on the site). By treating these metrics as rewards, the AI can learn which layouts are most effective, continually adapting its strategy to improve outcomes—all by learning from feedback, not from labelled examples or explicit human instruction for each decision.

This method can also be applied in scenarios with complex rulesets, such as game-playing AIs. These AIs can play rule-based games like chess and Go many times over (often against themselves), developing adaptive behaviour and improving their performance with each iteration.

However, reinforcement learning shows its greatest utility in scenarios where an AI can move and navigate within a physical environment, much like the lab rat. Classic examples include robotics and autonomous driving.

In robotics, an AI-controlled robot uses its sensors to gather signals from the world—such as distance measurements, images, or touch feedback. It then takes actions, like moving an arm or navigating a room, and receives payoffs in the form of rewards or penalties (for example, successfully picking up an object or colliding with an obstacle). Similarly, in autonomous driving, the vehicle's AI senses its surroundings through cameras, radar, and lidar, makes driving decisions, and receives feedback based on safety, efficiency, and passenger comfort.

In both cases, the AI adapts its behaviour over time, learning to make better decisions by linking sensory input, actions, and outcomes. This cycle of sensing, acting, and learning from payoffs is at the heart of reinforcement learning's power in real-world applications.

Before deploying reinforcement learning in real-world environments, it is common to use simulation. Simulated environments allow agents to experiment, learn, and make mistakes without real-world risks or costs. For example, robots and autonomous vehicles can be trained in virtual worlds that accurately mimic physical conditions, enabling them to develop effective strategies safely and efficiently. Once the agent performs well in simulation, it can be transferred to the real world, where further fine-tuning may occur.

It is important to note that reinforcement learning works only in environments where things can be tried and mistakes can be tolerated as part of the learning process. This makes it a powerful approach for domains like robotics, gaming, and autonomous vehicles, where experimentation and gradual improvement are possible.

However, it is a poor choice for safety-critical applications—such as controlling a power station or managing critical medical devices—where mistakes could have severe or catastrophic consequences. In such cases, the risks of trial-and-error learning outweigh the potential benefits, and more conservative, rule-based, or supervised approaches are preferred.

Like most things in machine learning, reinforcement learning often finds expression in neural networks, where it can be used to adjust weights and biases in the network to maximise outcomes. This is especially true in complex, high-dimensional environments.

It is also important to note that reinforcement learning can be computationally demanding and may require many trials to learn effective strategies, especially in complex scenarios. This can be a costly endeavour in terms of time and energy consumption. The expense of continuous experimentation is a key consideration when applying reinforcement learning to real-world problems.

Neural networks are not the only place where reinforcement methodologies can be applied. Traditional techniques such as linear models and decision trees can also make use of reinforcement approaches. The choice of method depends on the specific problem, the complexity of the state and action spaces, and the computational resources available.

Contrasting Machine Learning Approaches

Supervised learning (SL), unsupervised learning (UL), and reinforcement learning (RL) are all distinct and essential tools within the domain of learning AI, each with its own goals and applications. Here's a summary contrasting these approaches:

- **Learning:**
  - **SL:** Via a labelled dataset.
  - **UL:** Via the inherent structure of the data.
  - **RL:** Via environmental interaction with trial-and-error.
- **Feedback:**
  - **SL:** Direct feedback with correct labels.
  - **UL:** Limited explicit feedback, only inherent patterns.
  - **RL:** Feedback in the form of rewards and penalties.
- **Objective:**
  - **SL:** Minimise error between predicted and actual labels.
  - **UL:** Discover hidden patterns or structures.
  - **RL:** Maximise cumulative reward over time.

Each of these learning methods serves different purposes and is suited to different types of tasks, reflecting the diverse and dynamic nature of artificial intelligence and the use cases it serves. Picking the right approach is key to achieving the best outcomes.

It is not necessarily an either-or choice. Many AI systems combine two or more of these learning methods to achieve effective results. For example, an autonomous driving system will likely include sub-systems that use supervised, unsupervised, and reinforcement learning, each addressing different aspects of the overall task.

Advanced Learning Techniques

While supervised, unsupervised, and reinforcement learning form the foundation of AI, there are also more advanced techniques that extend these methods. These approaches are rapidly advancing, so let's look at some of the current key innovations.

Deep Learning

Deep learning is a powerful subfield of machine learning that uses neural networks with many layers to model complex patterns in data. It can be applied across supervised, unsupervised, and reinforcement learning—it is a deeper, more expressive approach to solving problems that require hierarchical representations.

Unlike traditional methods that break a problem into a sequence of separate, hand-designed steps, deep learning organises processing into stacked layers. Each layer transforms its inputs into a slightly different representation, with successive layers building on the outputs of earlier ones.

Lower layers therefore learn simple, local features—edges in an image, short phonetic patterns in audio, or word embeddings in text—while deeper (higher) layers compose those elementary features into progressively broader, more abstract concepts. In this way the network forms a hierarchy of representations, from local detail to global structure.

The advance of deep learning has been made possible by the abundance of digital data that has become available in the last decade—though it is important to note that deep learning models are also highly data-hungry and often require vast datasets to perform well. Along with this, the availability of affordable, high-performance hardware required for such complex and data-intensive approaches has enabled rapid progress. Advances in algorithms—such as improved optimisers, regularisation techniques, and open source frameworks—have also played a crucial role in making deep learning practical and effective.

One major advantage of deep learning is that it greatly reduces the need for manual feature engineering—models learn useful representations from raw or lightly pre-processed inputs. That said, human choices remain important: architecture, optimisation, data pre-processing, and regularisation still shape what the model can learn, and practitioners must tune these aspects carefully.

This capacity for automatic feature learning makes deep learning especially effective for tasks such as:

- Image recognition (e.g. identifying objects in photos)
- Speech recognition (e.g. turning voice commands into actions)
- Natural language processing (e.g., translating languages)

Take *convolutional neural networks* as an example—a subject we covered in detail in Chapter 3. This is a canonical example of a deep learning structure. Early convolutional layers have small receptive fields that detect local patterns, while deeper layers aggregate these responses over larger spatial regions, yielding higher-level features that can represent textures, parts, or whole objects.

Another example of a deep learning system we covered in chapter 3 on connected AI is the *recurrent neural network*. An important such system we will cover in detail in the next chapter on generative AI is the *transformer* model, which lies at the heart of humanlike chatbots.

Deep learning powers many of today's most capable AI systems, but because these models consist of many interacting layers, their internal representations can be hard to interpret—a complexity that both enables their power and makes them challenging to understand.

Transfer Learning

Transfer learning is a powerful technique that allows a model trained on one task to be repurposed for another, related task. This approach significantly reduces the time and data needed for training. Rather than starting from scratch, the model leverages the knowledge gained from the first task to improve performance on the new one.

For example, imagine a model trained to understand general language patterns in English text. This model can then be fine-tuned—a process where a pre-trained model is further trained on a smaller, task-specific dataset, like analysing the sentiment of customer reviews. Similarly, a model trained on a large dataset of everyday objects can be adapted to identify specific types of tumours in medical images.

Transfer learning is especially valuable when labelled data is scarce, but related data is plentiful. In practice, such transfers works best when source and target domains are closely related, and where dataset biases or mismatched labels are not present.

This method is effective because it allows models to build on pre-existing knowledge, enabling faster and more efficient training, and leading to high performance in specialised tasks.

Ensemble Learning

Ensemble learning brings together several different models and asks them to agree, so the final decision is usually more reliable than that of any single model. Common approaches include:

- **Boosting:** Models are trained one after another, with each new model learning from the mistakes of the earlier ones so the group improves over time.
- **Bagging:** Many models are trained independently on different subsets of the data, and their answers are combined to reduce random mistakes.
- **Stacking:** Several models make predictions, and a second-level model learns the best way to combine those predictions into a final answer.

Used together, these techniques often give more dependable and accurate results than a lone model, though they are not a guaranteed fix for every problem.

Meta-Learning

Meta-learning, sometimes called "learning to learn," trains systems so they can adapt quickly to new tasks from only a few examples. It is especially useful where situations change often, or in few-shot and zero-shot learning scenarios, because the model learns how to learn new problems rather than learning just one fixed task.

For instance, in personalised medicine a meta-learning system might use experience from many previous cases to adapt more swiftly to a new patient's data, helping clinicians explore tailored treatment options faster.

Meta-learning enhances the flexibility and scalability of AI systems, enabling them to perform well even in situations with limited data and dynamic environments.

Federated Learning

Federated learning is a technique that allows AI models to be trained across many devices or locations without pooling the raw data in one place. Instead of sending personal data to a central server, the learning happens locally—on phones, hospitals, or other institutions—and only the model updates are shared and combined.

This approach is particularly valuable for privacy-sensitive applications. For example, a smartphone keyboard might learn your typing patterns to improve predictions, but your actual messages never leave your device. Similarly, hospitals can collaborate to improve diagnostic models without sharing patient records, helping preserve confidentiality while still benefiting from collective learning.

Federated learning offers a way to build effective AI systems while respecting data ownership, privacy regulations, and the practical reality that sensitive information often cannot or should not be centralised.

Use Cases

In the previous sections, we have delved into the foundational elements of learning AI, exploring the concepts of supervised, unsupervised, and reinforcement learning. We examined how these methodologies enable machines to learn from data, uncover patterns, and make decisions based on experience.

As we move from theory to practical application, it's time to illustrate how these learning AI techniques are employed to solve real-world problems. In this section, we highlight the versatility and power of learning AI, demonstrating how these models process and analyse complex data to drive impactful outcomes.

The following use cases will showcase how learning AI models are applied across various domains, emphasising their role in advancing technology and enhancing decision-making processes. As we explore these applications, we will see how learning AI not only stands on its own but also serves as a crucial component in the broader AI landscape.

Real-world deployments involve much more than algorithms: human oversight, organisational processes, quality assurance, regulatory constraints, bias mitigation, and safety considerations all play critical roles. For simplicity and clarity, those elements are omitted here so that the examples can concentrate on illustrating how learning AI contributes to solving practical problems.

Email Spam Detection

Spam has become a constant annoyance in our lives. Every day, billions of emails are sent trying to persuade us to make unwanted purchases or trick us into allowing hackers to access our systems. Clearly, a system that can identify and mark spam is invaluable for busy email users.

For many years, there has been an ongoing arms race between spammers and spam detectors. Each side is becoming more sophisticated with advancements in technology. For detectors, false positives are especially harmful—marking a legitimate email as spam can lead to serious consequences for the recipient.

These systems often use supervised learning to identify and categorise spam emails.

Supervised Learning

Spam detection systems rely on a large dataset of labelled emails for training. Each email is tagged as either spam or legitimate, providing a clear guideline for the model.

Sometimes, datasets are generated through user behaviour. Over time, email users tag emails as spam or move them to the junk folder, which indirectly creates labelled data that can be used for training. Although labour-intensive and noisy, this labelling is crucial for model accuracy.

Using supervised learning-based neural networks, the AI analyses features such as email headers, content, and topics. It learns to identify common spam indicators like specific keywords, suspicious sender addresses, and unusual formatting. The system continually improves by learning from user actions.

Improved Email Experience and Security

By accurately identifying and filtering spam, these systems protect users from threats such as phishing attacks and malware. Emails that resemble known spam are redirected to the spam folder, reducing the risk to the user.

If the system makes a mistake, users may move an email back to the inbox. This feedback provides a learning opportunity for the model, which adjusts its weights to improve accuracy.

Outcome

Supervised learning significantly enhances email security and the user experience. By continuously learning from new data, spam detection systems adapt to emerging threats, offering robust protection against spam and malicious emails. This application highlights how supervised learning improves everyday digital interactions.

Customer Segmentation in Marketing

In marketing, understanding customer behaviour and preferences is crucial for creating effective campaigns. Traditional methods often rely on manual segmentation, which can be time-consuming and imprecise. Machine learning offers a powerful alternative by automatically identifying natural groupings within the customer base.

By analysing patterns in customer data, algorithms can discover hidden structures and relationships that human analysts might miss. These insights can be leveraged to deliver more targeted sales and promotions.

These systems often use unsupervised learning to segment customers based on purchasing behaviour, preferences, and other attributes.

Unsupervised Learning

Unsupervised learning doesn't require labelled data, making it ideal for tasks like customer segmentation, where predefined categories may not exist. Clustering algorithms group customers into segments by analysing features such as purchase history, browsing behaviour, and demographic information.

For example, a clustering algorithm might group together customers who frequently purchase high-end electronics or those who consistently buy health and wellness products.

The lack of predefined labels allows the model to uncover natural segments without prior assumptions. This approach can reveal unexpected insights, such as identifying new customer segments or discovering seasonal purchasing patterns.

Personalised Marketing Strategies

Once customers are segmented into clusters, businesses can tailor their marketing strategies to each group. Personalised campaigns can be created to target the unique preferences and behaviours of each segment.

For example, a segment identified as frequent buyers of outdoor gear might receive promotions for camping equipment, while a segment that prefers organic foods might be targeted with offers for health-related products.

By delivering more relevant content and offers, businesses can enhance customer satisfaction and loyalty, ultimately driving higher sales and engagement.

Outcome

The application of unsupervised learning in customer segmentation significantly boosts marketing strategies by providing deeper insights into customer behaviour. By automatically identifying natural groupings, these systems enable businesses to create more effective and personalised campaigns. This example demonstrates how unsupervised learning can improve customer interactions and business outcomes.

Game-Playing AI

AlphaGo, developed by DeepMind, is a groundbreaking example of how AI can achieve human-like performance in complex games. By training through numerous games and learning from the outcome of each move, AlphaGo demonstrated the immense potential of AI to master strategic thinking.

While game playing might seem trivial, it provides a bridge between the dry world of mathematics and the human-centric world we inhabit. Playing games against machines not only engages us but also helps us understand the capabilities and limitations of such technology.

These systems often use reinforcement learning to iteratively improve their performance through self-play and feedback.

Reinforcement Learning

AlphaGo's success was largely due to its ability to train through self-play. By playing millions of games against itself, it explored a vast number of possible moves and strategies. This extensive training enabled it to recognise effective patterns and tactics that might not be immediately apparent to human players.

The AI constantly adjusted its strategies based on the outcomes of these games, gradually improving its performance. Eventually, it played far more games than any human could hope to achieve in a lifetime.

The self-play mechanism allowed AlphaGo to learn and adapt without needing labelled data or human intervention. Instead, it relied on the rewards and penalties system inherent in reinforcement learning to guide its progress.

Achieving Strategic Mastery

Through reinforcement learning, AlphaGo achieved a level of mastery in Go that was previously thought unattainable for AI. It defeated top human players, showcasing its ability to handle the game's immense complexity and subtlety. The AI's capacity to learn from each game and continuously refine its strategies exemplifies the power of reinforcement learning in tackling intricate problems.

The impact of AlphaGo extended beyond the game itself. It demonstrated the potential of reinforcement learning to solve problems in various domains, from robotics to resource management, where decision-making in dynamic environments is crucial.

Outcome

The application of reinforcement learning in game playing highlights the powerful potential of this approach. By leveraging the principles of rewards and penalties, AlphaGo mastered one of the most challenging games, showcasing how reinforcement learning can achieve human-like performance. This example underscores the broader applicability of reinforcement learning in solving complex, real-world problems through continuous learning and adaptation.

Voice Recognition

Voice recognition and speech-to-text technologies have seen remarkable advancements, thanks to developments in AI. These systems have become integral to numerous applications, from virtual assistants to transcription services, transforming the way we interact with technology.

While the concept of voice recognition might seem straightforward, the underlying technology involves complex processing and learning to accurately transcribe spoken words into text. This task is particularly challenging due to the vast variability in human speech, including accents, intonations, and background noise.

These systems often use deep learning techniques to enhance their ability to accurately recognise and transcribe spoken language.

Deep Learning

Deep learning models, particularly recurrent neural networks (RNNs) and their variants like long short-term memory (LSTM) networks, are crucial in voice recognition. These models are designed to handle sequential data, making them well suited for processing spoken language.

Through extensive training on large datasets of recorded speech and their corresponding transcriptions, deep learning models learn to identify patterns in the audio signals. This training allows them to understand the nuances of different speech patterns and improve transcription accuracy over time.

Additionally, convolutional neural networks (CNNs) are often employed to process raw audio signals, extracting features that are then analysed by the other models. This combination of approaches creates a powerful system capable of handling the complexities of human speech.

Enhanced User Interaction

The use of deep learning in voice recognition has significantly enhanced user interaction with technology. Virtual assistants rely on these technologies to understand and respond to user commands. By accurately transcribing spoken language into text, these systems can execute a wide range of tasks, from setting reminders to providing weather updates.

In transcription services, deep learning models have greatly enhanced the process of converting spoken content into written text. This has applications in various fields, including legal, medical, and media industries, where accurate and efficient transcription is essential.

Outcome

The implementation of deep learning in voice recognition and speech-to-text technologies has greatly improved accuracy and usability. By leveraging advanced neural networks, these systems can understand and transcribe spoken language with remarkable precision. This application highlights the transformative power of deep learning in enhancing human-computer interaction and demonstrates its potential in a wide range of practical applications.

Conclusion

Machine learning has revolutionised the field of artificial intelligence, providing many of the foundational techniques that drive much of the AI technology we use today. This innovation has opened up new possibilities across a broad spectrum of applications, enabling machines to perform tasks that require human-like intelligence.

However, the journey of machine learning is not without significant challenges. One of the most persistent is the *explainability* of its models. Many advanced systems, especially deep learning networks, operate as "black boxes"—their internal logic is often opaque: inputs and outputs are known, but there is little to no explanation of their reasoning. This lack of transparency is especially problematic in critical domains like healthcare and legal systems, where understanding the reasoning process is essential.

Some mitigations, such as openly publishing information about the model, its training material and applied guardrails can offer more assurance and transparency, but much more work is required for true interpretability.

Another major challenge is bias. Machine learning models are only as good as the data they are trained on. Just as a child learns from the environment around them, a model learns from its data—if that environment is biased, so too will be the model's understanding. If the data contains biases, the model will likely perpetuate—or even amplify—them, leading to unfair or harmful outcomes.

This issue has significant ethical implications, as biased models can reinforce societal inequalities and lead to discriminatory practices. The field has seen active research into bias mitigation, with techniques such as data augmentation, reweighting, and fairness constraints. These have delivered some benefits, but more analysis and ongoing vigilance are needed for effective bias mitigation to become the norm.

Machine learning models also require vast amounts of data and computational power. The need for large datasets raises concerns about privacy and data security, while the high energy demands increase the environmental footprint. Training state-of-the-art models can consume as much energy as powering a small town, raising questions about sustainability much like the environmental impact of large-scale industrial processes. This is not a sustainable practice in the long term.

Another key challenge is the narrowness of machine learning models. Unlike humans, who can generalise across many domains, machine learning models are often highly specialised. A model trained to spot cancers in medical images will not apply its learning to unrelated areas, such as recognising emotions or understanding social cues. This narrowness makes them powerful but also limits their flexibility and ability to adapt to new challenges without explicit retraining.

As we know from our own lives, learning never stops. Things we believed to be true when we were young may no longer be so. In a dynamic society, attitudes, habits, language, and laws all evolve. If models are taught once and never updated, they can become outdated, irrelevant, or even dangerous. For example, if a model used in the justice system had been trained in the 1960s, would we still want to rely on its judgments today?

This challenge is known as *model drift*—the gradual process by which a model's predictions diverge from expected norms or outcomes. To address this, models need to be periodically—if not continuously—assessed and retrained, much like a person must continually adapt to a changing world.

Despite these challenges, the legacy of machine learning is profound. It has transformed industries by enabling sophisticated pattern recognition, predictive analytics, and decision-making capabilities. Advances in machine learning have paved the way for many new AI technologies that continue to push the boundaries of what machines can achieve. The success of machine learning underscores its importance in the AI landscape. It has provided the tools necessary for breakthroughs in a wide range of fields, driving innovation and offering solutions to complex problems. As we continue to address the challenges of explainability and bias, and work towards more sustainable practices, the future of machine learning holds immense potential for positive impact.

CHAPTER 6

Generative AI

For many years, AI researchers aimed to mimic human skills and behaviours in the widest sense. They dreamed of creating machines that could think, reason, and interact like humans across all domains. However, as the challenges mounted, the costs increased, and the need for funding grew, their focus shifted towards narrower, more specific outcomes. These targeted objectives were more likely to succeed and lead to commercially viable solutions.

AI was increasingly being employed effectively across a wide range of industries, delivering both practical utility and significant financial returns. The broader goal of emulating all aspects of humanity gradually and quietly receded into the background.

However, throughout the early part of this century, several factors combined to create new opportunities for exploration. Digital data abundance, computational availability, ubiquitous connectivity, and advanced algorithms all combined to create a perfect storm of opportunity.

Suddenly, and perhaps even to the surprise of the researchers themselves, this convergence led to breakthrough advances, enabling AI to achieve feats previously only dreamt of. The early goals of human-like intelligence came back into view. Now AI systems were creating outcomes previously thought in the realm of humans only.

Overview

Let's begin with a concise overview of the core ideas, techniques, and motivations behind generative AI. We'll introduce how generative approaches enable systems to create new text, images, audio, video, and other media by learning patterns from existing material and using those patterns to produce novel outputs. This gives you a clear sense of what generative AI is, why it has become so significant, and what makes it different from earlier forms of AI, without diving into the technical details.

Machine Creativity

One of the many characteristics that distinguish us from machines is creativity—the ability to produce something original, pleasing, and valuable. This trait is not confined to a single technique but encompasses a variety of approaches, each with its unique strengths and applications. Writers, artists, musicians, dancers, designers, poets, photographers, sculptors, chefs, software developers, comedians, and graffiti artists—there is no limit to human creativity.

As machine learning advances and algorithms consume more material generated by humans, an intriguing question arises: Can a machine generate new and original material consistent with the patterns identified from its training data?

Human creativity does not occur in a vacuum. When an artist creates a new work, while it may be original, it is still rooted in all the material that influenced them as they developed their skills. For example, a musician may have spent a lifetime listening to other musicians who inspired their musical style—in a very real sense, this is their training dataset.

Clearly, this homage to earlier artists falls on a spectrum. On the one end, you have direct mimicry, like an Elvis impersonator who belts out the same songs in the same style. On the other, you find artists like John Lennon, who, though influenced by Elvis, forged his own path and brought his unique style.

But let's set aside the broader discussion of creativity, as it will surely be debated now that machines can create original works. Instead, consider what happens when a machine has read all the books we've written, listened to all our music, and gazed at all our art.

When a machine "experiences" art, it does so differently from human cognition. It's not entirely valid to say that its consumption is less than ours; perhaps in a philosophical sense, but in a comprehension sense, it is considerably more granular and detailed.

When a machine "listens" to a concerto, it can process subtle variations in a much more fine-grained and precise manner than humans can. This doesn't make its "experience" better or worse, but it is different. Machines can detect subtle connections between works that human cognition may miss or only experience subconsciously.

On the other hand, humans can also be creative in ways machines would struggle with—such as weaving seemingly unrelated elements together, making complex analogies, writing "between the lines," and engineering long narrative arcs that give a work emotional coherence and cultural resonance.

The volume of previous art accessible to machines is vast compared to any human. If you read a book every day for 50 years, you would have read just over 18,000 books. In contrast, a computer can read thousands of books a second, instantly referencing every page.

As much as we celebrate artists who create new and novel works, we must acknowledge that most art fits within long-standing conventions and formulas. For example, a typical popular song structure might consist of two verses and choruses, an instrumental break, followed by a rousing final chorus. Similarly, in storytelling act one establishes characters and motivations, act two introduces a crisis, and act three resolves the story with consequences for the characters.

Clearly reducing an artist's influence to be analogous to a model's training data is reductive. Artists also draw on intention, lived experience, cultural context, and conscious selection—factors far richer than the statistical exposure a model receives. Nevertheless, artists routinely work *within* conventions—deliberately selecting and reshaping norms to create distinctive, context-sensitive work.

As we discussed in Chapter 3, "Statistical AI," machines thrive on patterns. They can independently identify, assess, and evaluate the prevalence and value of these patterns. Later AI approaches, such as those outlined in connected AI and learning AI, demonstrated how these patterns could be leveraged to produce valuable outcomes.

The humbling discovery of recent years is that patterns extend not just to non-human phenomena like weather or human behaviours like shopping, but also to human creative outputs. This led to the emergence of generative AI, where the objective shifted from simply learning patterns within data to generating new and novel outcomes aligned with those discovered patterns.

Emergence of Non-Human Methodologies

As AI delves deeper into domains traditionally reserved for human expertise, a paradox emerges. The methodologies used to achieve these remarkable feats are diverging from those understandable by everyday human cognition.

If you were to teach someone to play music, write stories, or paint, how would you start? Whatever method you choose, it likely wouldn't involve mathematical concepts like matrices, tensors, and vectors. Yet, these are the very elements forming the basis of modern generative models.

As we progress through the chapters of this book—from symbols, to statistics, to connections and learning—the concepts being described move away from our everyday experiences. This trend continues throughout this chapter.

As machines begin to interact like us, the means by which they do so become harder for us to comprehend. The more they replicate human behaviour, the further they seem to diverge from our methods.

Perhaps a better way to frame this is that these processes become deeper, rather than more complex. A poet might describe gazing upon a rose in eloquent words, whereas a physicist might describe rays of light hitting photoreceptors, which send electrical charges down the stem to the brain, stimulating neurons. Both descriptions are valid, but the latter is far removed from our everyday experiences.

The functionality of generative AI models hinges on techniques that elude our everyday intuition; they lack direct analogues to the actions driving human creativity. It's no surprise, then, that their inner workings don't always make immediate sense. We will describe the algorithms in detail in this chapter, but you should not be surprised if these explanations do not perfectly align with your experience of their outcomes.

Creativity Algorithms

Generative AI burst into public consciousness only a few years ago but has already come to define AI in many people's minds. Suddenly, instead of merely answering dry questions, AIs are writing original texts, drawing original images, and composing original music.

As we will explore in the coming pages, generative AI is driven by rapid and advanced changes in algorithms that operate under the hood. It also represents a significant advancement in the types and range of use cases for which we enlist technology's assistance.

In many respects, AI has matured, moving beyond its early years as a mere tool and joining the upper echelons of human-level creativity. AI is now among us, helping us create art, design architecture, draft laws, and educate children. The genie is out of the bottle, and we must all now come to terms with the creative energy these machines can unleash.

The emergence of generative AI is rooted in the historical progression of artificial intelligence, both technically and motivationally. The 1980s saw the rise of connectionist models, most notably neural networks, which were inspired by the human brain's structure. Key figures such as Geoffrey Hinton and Yann LeCun were instrumental in developing these models, although their true potential was not fully realised until decades later, when computational power caught up with the theoretical advancements.

The true breakthrough for generative AI came in the 2010s with the advent of deep learning. Algorithms like generative adversarial networks (GANs), introduced by Ian Goodfellow in 2014, and variational autoencoders (VAEs), developed by Diederik P. Kingma and Max Welling, enabled machines to create new data from learnt patterns. These advancements marked both a technical and motivational shift in AI development. Algorithms were no longer confined to identifying existing patterns but could now apply their learnings to generate new and original artefacts, such as images, music, and text, that mimicked human creativity.

In 2017, the introduction of the transformer model by researchers at Google, including Ashish Vaswani, Noam Shazeer, and others, marked another significant milestone. The transformer architecture, outlined in the paper *Attention Is All You Need*, revolutionised natural language processing and led to the development of powerful models like GPT (generative pretrained transformer) by Alec Radford, Ilya Sutskever, and others.

Natural language processing has evolved from simply manipulating symbols to understanding the meanings behind words and context. New generative models demonstrate an unprecedented ability to generate coherent and contextually relevant text. These models appear to have a level of understanding that goes beyond merely mimicking their training data.

As these creativity algorithms evolve, they have transitioned from novelties to powerful tools capable of producing high-quality, original content. Today, they continue to advance, driven by ongoing research and an ever-growing repository of human-generated data, pushing the boundaries of what machines can create and understand.

Core Concepts and Mechanisms

Generative AI encompasses several foundational methodologies that collectively define how machines generate new and innovative outcomes. These approaches enabled machines to not just learn patterns, but to generate novel data based on them, creating images, music, and text. In this overview section, a handful of these approaches are outlined in broad terms, to give you a working sense of the toolkit and where each method fits.

note **Each of the concepts covered in this section—along with several others—is covered in much more detail in the later "In-depth" section.**

To process information, computers must translate text, images, and sounds into numbers—a process known as *encoding*. Encoding is the essential step that transforms the rich variety of real-world data into a digital format that machines can understand and manipulate. By converting everything into numbers, encoding allows computers to treat all kinds of information in a consistent, computable way.

Building on the idea of encoding, *autoencoders* are neural networks that learn their own compressed internal representation of data and then reconstruct it again. In effect, they try to preserve the features that matter most while discarding redundancy, noise, or less useful detail. This makes them useful for tasks such as compression, denoising, and anomaly detection. An autoencoder trained on normal images, sounds, or sensor readings can learn what "usual" data looks like, help clean up noisy inputs, and flag unusual cases that do not fit the pattern.

Variational autoencoders (VAEs) extend autoencoders by making the compressed representation probabilistic rather than fixed. Instead of mapping an input to one exact point, they learn a range of likely internal representations, which makes it possible not only to compress data, but also to generate new examples that fit the overall pattern of the training material.

This makes VAEs useful wherever we want plausible variation rather than exact reconstruction alone. They can create synthetic images, propose new molecular structures, or generate training data that resembles the original dataset without simply copying it, making them an important bridge between compression and generative modelling.

Generative adversarial networks (GANs) generate new data through a contest between two neural networks: a generator, which tries to create convincing outputs, and a discriminator, which tries to tell generated data from real examples. As each improves in response to the other, the system can produce increasingly realistic results.

GANs became especially important for generating lifelike images, video, and audio, and helped show how AI could synthesise highly convincing media rather than merely analyse it. That same realism, however, also underpins more controversial uses such as deepfakes, making GANs both influential and ethically significant in the history of generative AI.

Transformers are the core architecture behind most modern *large language models (LLMs)*, including the chatbots and writing assistants that brought generative AI into everyday life. Their major advance was to handle language far more effectively than earlier systems, especially by looking across a broad span of text at once rather than working through it only step by step.

In simplified terms, transformers break text into parts of words called *tokens*, convert those tokens into mathematical representations called *embeddings*, and then predict what token is most likely to come next. A mechanism called *self-attention* helps the model weigh which earlier words matter most, allowing it to maintain context and generate more coherent responses.

This combination of scale and context-handling is what makes transformers so important. It allows LLMs to summarise, answer questions, draft prose, and hold remarkably fluent conversations. Yet beneath that fluency, they still operate as probabilistic token predictors rather than as systems with humanlike understanding in the full sense.

Diffusion models became especially important in modern image generation by learning how to reverse a process of gradual corruption. During training, images are progressively turned into noise, and the model learns how to denoise them step by step. At generation time, it starts with random noise and repeatedly refines it into a coherent image, which makes diffusion a powerful way to create detailed and often highly realistic visual outputs.

What made diffusion models especially influential was their ability to condition that denoising process on a prompt or other guidance, so the emerging image could be steered towards a requested scene, style, or subject. This is the basis of many text-to-image systems used today. They can generate portraits, illustrations, product concepts, and fantastical scenes with striking control, helping drive the recent public surge of interest in generative image tools.

Orchestration in generative AI means coordinating multiple models, tools, and workflow steps so that a system can pursue a broader goal rather than produce one isolated output at a time. Instead of just answering a single prompt, an orchestrated system may plan, retrieve information, generate drafts, check results, and pass context between stages, combining AI with more traditional software, rules, APIs, and data sources.

Agentic AI takes this further by giving a system some bounded autonomy in how it works towards a goal. An agent can retain context, use tools, make limited decisions, and continue acting until it either completes the task or needs human input. In practice, many so-called agentic systems are coordinated collections of specialised parts, which is why their usefulness depends not only on capability, but also on clear guardrails around permissions, oversight, and responsibility.

Multimodal AI extends generative systems beyond any single medium by allowing them to work across text, images, audio, video, and other forms of input within a shared process. By converting different kinds of data into compatible mathematical representations, these systems can increasingly connect media types that people naturally use together—for example, by describing an image, extracting text from a photograph, answering questions about a chart, or responding to spoken language with visual awareness. This makes generative AI feel less like a collection of separate tools and more like a flexible interface for everyday human communication.

In-depth

Building on the foundations of the overview, let's now look more closely at the technologies and approaches behind generative AI. This section explains how machines can be trained to generate new text, images, audio, video, and other media by learning patterns from existing material rather than being explicitly programmed for each individual output. It explores how these methods form the foundation of systems that can create, remix, extend, and respond across many forms of human expression, opening up powerful new creative and practical possibilities.

Mathematical Representations

In computer science, encoding is the process of transforming information into a digital format. Computers are mathematical machines, so any information we want them to store, process, analyse, or present must be in a digital format. Ultimately, within the machines, these are represented as binary digits—zeroes and ones. Transforming real-world information into numbers is called *encoding*, and converting those numbers back into a human-interpretable form is known as *decoding*.

A common type of encoding is text encoding, such as ASCII (pronounced ass-key). It was developed in 1963 to add uniformity to textual data representation, so that information could be transmitted between systems with shared expectations. In ASCII, every letter and punctuation mark is represented as a number. For example, A is 65, B is 66, C is 67, and so on. Therefore, HELLO becomes the numeric sequence [72, 69, 76, 76, 79].

There are many encoding schemes, each optimised for different purposes, such as size, accuracy, or speed. Just as with human languages, the same concepts can be represented in different forms, with each adding its own spin and nuances to the content being captured.

Encoding discrete data, like text, is the simplest case. A challenge arises with continuous data, such as images and audio, which aren't made up of distinct blocks. To handle this, they undergo a process called *sampling*, where continuous data is broken into small discrete blocks. For images, sampling involves converting the image into pixels, tiny coloured dots that make up the picture. For audio, the continuous wave is sampled thousands of times a second to turn it into a stream of numbers. We covered this topic in more detail in Chapter 2, "Symbolic AI."

However, sampling can lead to some loss of information—where more information is present in the original data than can be captured in the sample. This leads to a trade-off between information loss and file size—the more pixels in an image, or the higher the frequency of audio sampling, the less information is lost. However, there is a practical limit to this. Eventually, we reach a point where human senses can no longer detect a difference.

Digital data often contains redundant information. For example, in an image, large sections might have similar colours. This redundancy offers an opportunity for *compression*, which reduces the size of the data by removing unnecessary information.

Compression can be *lossy* or *lossless*. With lossless compression, the data can be fully restored to its original form, whereas with lossy compression, some details are permanently lost in exchange for smaller file sizes. Lossless compression is essential for text, where the removal of information would radically alter the perception of its value. But for images and audio, lossy compression can work well because small differences are often undetectable or unimportant.

In practice, you experience encoding day to day through file formats. For instance, an image might be stored as a JPEG, PNG, or WEBP file. Each file format defines a specific encoding scheme, allowing decoders to know what to expect from the stored data.

Once information is encoded digitally, mathematical operations can be applied to the data. These operations include identifying patterns using statistical and machine learning techniques. When the dataset is very large, consisting of billions of items, the computer can not only detect patterns but also model how those patterns are distributed across the corpus. With this probabilistic model, it can generate a new dataset that reflects the patterns identified in its training material while still differing in its specific details from the original data.

Autoencoders

Imagine you are the architect of a beautiful and well-respected building in your city. You are contacted by another architect from a distant place who wants to replicate your building in her own town.

To assist her, you create a schematic version of your building. On a large piece of paper, you meticulously draw out every wall, window, door, pipe, duct, joist, etc. Your diagrammatic representation is a form of encoding. You have transformed a real-world building into a series of lines on a plane. In doing so, you have indirectly decided to discard unimportant features such as the texture of the building's outer walls or its paint colour.

Since your diagram is a set of lines, it can be encoded further into a purely mathematical representation. Each line can be captured as the geometry of two points: the start point (x_1, y_1) and the end point (x_2, y_2).

Now your beautiful, grand, and ornate building has been expressed as a large set of numbers.

When you send your design to your colleague, she is not happy. The design is too detailed for her; she wanted a much simpler representation. On the telephone, you agree with her that some features of the building are not important for the purpose she will use it for. Perhaps she has her own ideas about where to put the ducts and pipes or the details of the windows and doors. Other parts, though, are integral and cannot be removed, such as the overall structure and the supporting joists.

Given the discussion and better understanding of her requirements, you reduce the diagram to a smaller set of lines. These lines represent only the features that are relevant to her needs. Correspondingly, the numerical representation shrinks in size.

Now your colleague can take your simplified representation of the building and use it in her own town to build a similar one. The simplified form allows for a building that is consistent with yours, but with scope for subtle differences and variations as well. The process she goes through here can be thought of as decoding the schematic representation.

This simple analogy, also illustrated in Figure 6.1, gives us a window into an important but complex AI methodology called *autoencoders*. Autoencoders are used to encode data into a compressed format and then decode it back, much like simplifying the building's schematic to meet specific needs.

In standard use cases, encoding is performed to smooth the relationship between the machine processing information and the human consuming it. Real-world human requirements such as "crop this image" or "increase the volume" can be achieved through mathematical manipulation of the encoded object. The data is then decoded for presentation as a smaller image or a louder song.

AI researchers have taken this process much further. Instead of encoding information as simple numbers alone, they map it into a multidimensional space, often called a latent space. You can think of this as a mathematical map in which different dimensions capture different features of the source data. In our building analogy, those features might include wall height,

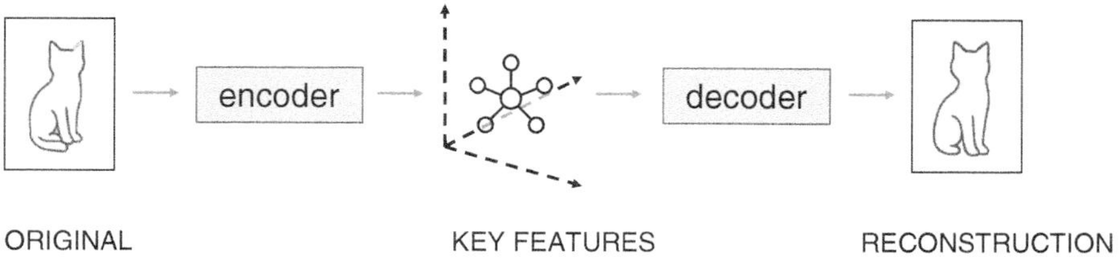

Figure 6.1: Autoencoder

window position, and duct length. A particular building would then appear as a point, or small cluster of points, within that map.

Humans cannot easily picture such spaces, but computers do not need to picture them in order to work with them. In this form, machines can compare examples, spot recurring patterns, detect outliers, and separate useful structure from noise. This is one of the reasons encoded data becomes so powerful in AI, and it connects directly to the ideas about pattern-finding discussed in the previous chapters on connected and learning AI.

But encoded data cannot stay in that abstract form forever. At some point, it has to be turned back into something people can use, see, or hear. That is fairly straightforward when the encoding is simple, such as cropping an image or increasing the volume of a sound file. With richer AI encodings, however, the task is harder: we need to simplify the data while still preserving the features that matter.

Just as the two architects agreed on simplifying the schematic to meet specific requirements, AI researchers often use techniques like dimensionality reduction to simplify encoded data while preserving essential features. This ensures that when the information is decoded, the critical attributes remain intact for practical use cases.

Autoencoders in AI work much like the architectural analogy. They compress a dataset into a smaller representation that keeps the most important features while leaving out less useful detail. In simple terms, an autoencoder is a neural network that learns how to make a compressed version and then how to rebuild the original data from it. It has two main parts: the encoder and the decoder.

The encoder takes the original data and reduces it to a compact internal representation, rather like turning the full building plan into a stripped-back schematic. This compressed form, often called a latent representation, keeps the features that matter most while dropping much of the rest. The decoder then works in the opposite direction, using that compact summary to rebuild the data, just as the second architect uses the simplified plan to produce her own version of the building.

The strength of autoencoders is that they learn what to keep and what to ignore. They can strip away noise and repeated detail while preserving the structure that matters. This makes them useful for tasks such as compression, denoising, and anomaly detection.

In practical terms, an autoencoder can clean up a noisy image without losing its important features, or learn what normal data looks like so unusual cases stand out more clearly. Used well, they offer a practical way to handle complex data without drowning in unnecessary detail.

You may now be wondering how encoding and autoencoders relate to generative AI. The link becomes clearer when we stop thinking of latent spaces as fixed maps and start thinking of them in probabilistic terms.

Variational Autoencoders

Imagine now that the process you went through to describe your building has been so successful that many people all around the world have done the same. Over time, a large database of such schematics has been developed, containing geometric descriptions of many buildings.

We now have a vast collection of encoded building descriptions arranged in a shared mathematical map, often called a *latent space*. Once we have enough examples, we can start to think about that map probabilistically. Instead of treating each building as a fixed set of points, we can ask how likely certain features are to appear in different parts of the mathematical map.

In the context of autoencoders, this probabilistic method is embodied by variational autoencoders (VAEs). A VAE doesn't just encode a building into a single set of numbers; it encodes it into a distribution of possible values. This distribution tells us how likely it is to find a building with certain features in different parts of that map. The VAE learns the underlying patterns and variations within the dataset of buildings.

Let's say we want to design a building with a roof but no walls. We can place that unusual design into the map and see how well it fits with the other buildings already there. Clearly, in this case the fit would be poor. However, we could imagine other designs that sit much more comfortably within the same map. This allows us to test how "expected" a design is based on the architectural conventions of earlier buildings.

But we can go one step further—a big step ...

Instead of encoding actual buildings, we can create entirely new points in the map that correspond to buildings which do not exist yet. These new points are probabilistic variations based on the earlier examples. Using this approach, we can generate buildings that never existed in the real world, but are still statistically similar to the ones in the dataset.

What happens when we turn those new points back into building designs? Surprisingly, the resulting buildings fit well within the architectural styles and structural norms of earlier designs. They look and feel familiar because they follow the learnt patterns, yet they are unique and original. This variational decoding is shown in Figure 6.2.

VAEs work by learning what tends to appear in different parts of the map and then using that knowledge to generate new examples that follow those patterns. The new buildings or designs do not copy any one original, but they do reflect the common features and relationships found in earlier examples.

Now, let's imagine we are no longer working with building designs, but with images of buildings, cats, or any other objects. The same basic process

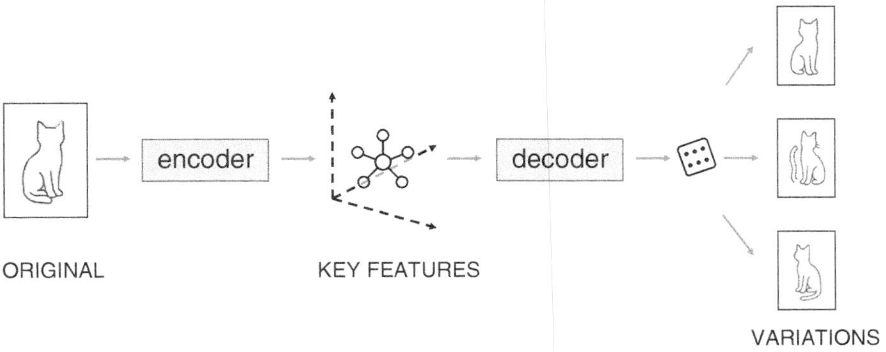

Figure 6.2: Variational autoencoders

still applies. We encode many examples into the map, learn the patterns of what usually appears there, and then generate new examples that fit those patterns. When we turn them back into images, we get pictures of buildings or cats that never actually existed, but look as though they could have.

It may seem like a large leap to expect mathematical manipulation of abstract numerical representations to generate novel and original images, especially ones that can trick our minds into thinking they are real-world objects. The outcomes can be surprising, even to the creators of these models. Yet, the generative creation of such assets is a very real result of these mathematical processes.

These techniques were not originally developed mainly as creative tools. Early work on VAEs focused more on learning useful internal representations of data and on generating plausible new examples for research and training. They were used for tasks such as producing variants of handwriting, filling gaps in incomplete datasets, and creating synthetic examples for model development.

Over time, however, the full potential of these techniques became clearer, and their outputs became valuable in their own right. Today, VAEs are used in areas such as drug discovery, medical imaging, and speech synthesis, where they can help propose new candidates, create synthetic data, or model complex patterns.

Generative Adversarial Networks

Imagine you are a master forger trying to create fake banknotes—please temporarily set aside any moral qualms for the sake of a useful analogy. You gather all the equipment you need: custom ink, specialised paper, and intricately engraved plates.

You begin making your fake notes, but once released, they are quickly identified as counterfeit and destroyed. Your adversary in the fraud department of the central bank spots them and prevents their circulation.

While you have a lot of specialised equipment, what you really need now is information. You need to understand what features your adversary has used to identify your fakes. Luckily, you obtain this information from his report and use it to make adjustments: a slightly different ink colour, improved paper, and tiny details on the engraving plate.

These version two notes are better, but they too get detected. Once again, you access the report on identifying features and make more improvements. Over time, this iterative process can lead to better and better fake notes. Eventually, with enough time and resources, your forgeries may become practically indistinguishable from the real ones.

The key driver of improvements in your forgeries is information—specifically, information coming from your adversary, whose goals are diametrically opposed to yours. Together, you are converging on a solution, meaning the fakes have become nearly impossible to identify.

This process is analogous to a fascinating development in generative AI called generative adversarial networks (GANs). GANs consist of two neural networks that are trained against each other to generate new, realistic outputs, such as images, sounds, or other digital content. This can be likened to a master forger and a fraud investigator, constantly trying to outwit each other.

The two components of GANs are the *generator* and the *discriminator.* The generator's job is to create fake data that looks as close to real data as possible. Initially, the generator might produce crude attempts, much like a novice forger making their first fake banknotes. The discriminator, on the other hand, is like the fraud investigator, whose role is to distinguish between the real data and the fakes produced by the generator.

The process begins with the generator creating a first batch of fake examples. The discriminator then compares them with real examples and tries to tell which is which. Its feedback helps the generator improve the next batch. This cycle repeats, with the generator getting better at producing convincing results and the discriminator getting better at spotting flaws.

Over time, like our forger refining their techniques based on the investigator's feedback, the generator in a GAN can learn to produce data that is nearly indistinguishable from the real thing. This adversarial relationship can drive both networks to improve, resulting in high-quality synthetic data. The process of GANs is illustrated in Figure 6.3.

GANs were introduced more broadly as a way for neural networks to learn how to model and generate realistic new examples from existing data, and researchers also explored them as a tool for learning useful

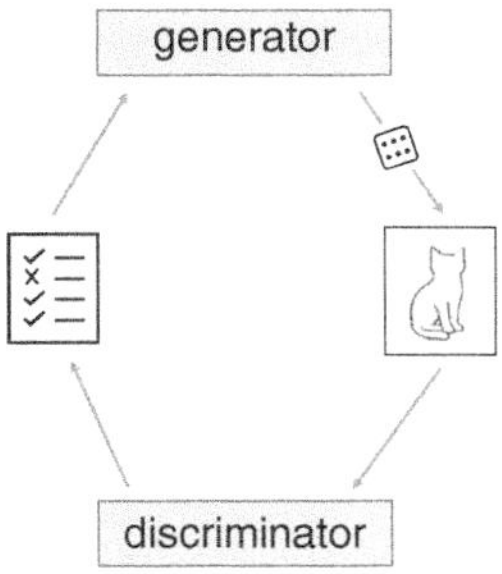

Figure 6.3: Generative adversarial network

internal representations. Today, they are used in a range of creative applications, such as generating realistic images and videos, creating art, and composing music.

The core idea behind GANs is that by pitting two networks against each other, we can achieve remarkable advancements in generating realistic and useful data. Even if the initial output of the generator is poor, as long as the discriminator provides useful feedback, the iterative process will lead to better and better results.

A key element here, as with much of AI, is that the discriminator has access to many real examples against which it can judge the generator's outputs. The generator then uses this feedback to refine its results.

GANs, like other generative AI methods, embody a simple process that leads to surprisingly pleasing results. These results can often astonish not just casual users, but also the very researchers who created the technology.

Transformers and Large Language Models

In recent years, we have all become accustomed to chatting with AI assistants. These digital helpers can converse with us on a wide range of topics, from quantum physics to cheesecake recipes.

The rise of AI-enabled chatbots did much to bring artificial intelligence into mainstream consciousness. Suddenly, computers were operating and behaving like humans, engaging in conversation as if there were a friendly human expert on the other end of a text discussion. It seems remarkable that these assistants can act so naturally in human terms and possess such a broad range of knowledge.

In the 1950s, computer pioneer Alan Turing, while contemplating the possibility of machine intelligence, designed a test he called *the Imitation Game*, which we now know as the Turing test. He posited that if a computer could engage in conversation indistinguishably from a human, then we might consider it an intelligent being.

Modern AI chatbots can sometimes appear to meet this benchmark—but are they truly intelligent? Let's dive into how they work under the hood to see if they truly understand the world, or whether, as some critics suggest, they are simply "statistical parrots."

Imagine I take a random book from a library shelf, turn to a page somewhere in the middle, and read you the following sentence out loud: "Alice turned to see who was speaking and realised it was the ..." What word could come next?

Clearly, there is a long list of words that could follow such a sentence opener. Now suppose I continue and say, "... rabbit." Talking rabbits aren't normal; this sentence would be highly unlikely—unless, of course, we're reading Lewis Carroll's *Alice in Wonderland*.

A piece of language in isolation is just an arbitrary sequence of words that could take many directions or capture a wide spectrum of meanings. However, the more context we add, the more the meaning is narrowed, and our expectations of what comes next become more focused.

For example:

- The classroom was crowded with students. Alice turned to see who was speaking and realised it was the ...
- Someone broke the silence in the courtroom. Alice turned to see who was speaking and realised it was the ...
- Wonderland was proving to be a puzzling and unexpected place. Alice turned to see who was speaking and realised it was the ...

This principle—context shaping meaning—is central to how *transformers*, a type of generative AI model, process and generate text. By using wider context, transformers can predict and produce more accurate and coherent sentences.

Transformers are a revolutionary new technology in AI, powering chatbots like OpenAI's ChatGPT, Google's Gemini, Meta's LLaMA3, and others. These AI assistants, often called large language models (LLMs), have taken the world by storm—surprising and sometimes worrying their human counterparts. Perhaps they are part of the reason you chose to read this book.

Let's now dig a little deeper into how transformers work. This is an important topic that deserves detailed coverage, because interacting with language models has become commonplace, yet many users have little sense of how a machine can converse so naturally in human terms.

Before we begin, however, a word of warning may be useful. As we noted at the beginning of this chapter, many of the internal techniques used in generative AI do not resemble anything familiar from everyday human experience, even when their outputs feel very familiar indeed. So if some of the detail presented on transformers do not immediately click, do not worry too much. The subject is intricate, and even many AI practitioners can be hazy on parts of it.

Despite first appearances, AI chatbots do not speak in sentences in the same way that humans do. What they output is a "statistically plausible sequence of tokens" based on a given context. This might sound like a confusing statement, but let's break it down to explain how they actually operate.

Transformers, which underpin most modern LLMs, work in three main steps:

- **Chunking:** A corpus of text is broken down into small units called tokens. These tokens could be words, parts of words, or even punctuation marks, depending on the system.
- **Embedding:** The tokens are then converted into vectors, which are lists of numbers in high-dimensional space. This helps the model represent the tokens in a way that captures their meaning in context.
- **Generation:** Given a sequence of tokens, the model uses the context so far to predict the most likely next token. This prediction is informed by nearby vectors in the abstract embedding space created in the earlier step, where related patterns of language tend to sit close together. This allows the model to continue generating text that aligns with the context of the conversation.

This overview, also illustrated in Figure 6.4, might seem a bit abstract, especially if you've experienced the rich output of AI assistants. The development of transformers represents a significant leap in AI model performance. Despite being grounded in mathematical processes, these models appear to exhibit a surprising level of comprehension about the text they process.

The quality of output from transformers has astounded many people, including the researchers who designed, built, and trained them. The fact

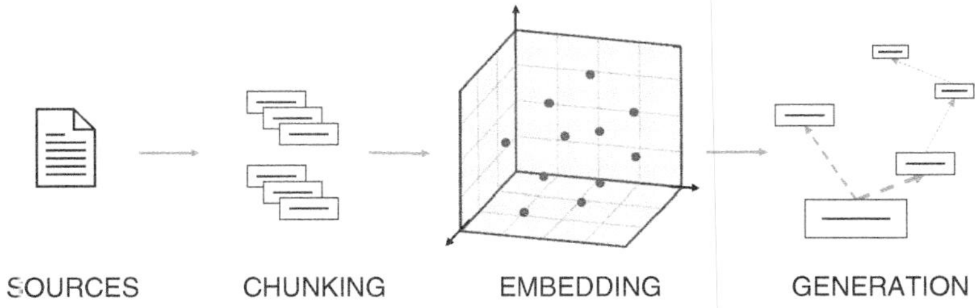

Figure 6.4: Transformer processes

that such reductive methods can produce seemingly intelligent behaviour has sparked an ongoing debate in both the tech industry and wider society. This topic, as well as the tantalising concept of artificial general intelligence, will be explored further in the Afterword of this book.

While GPT models have dominated discussions on transformers, they are not the only implementation of this technology. Three prominent approaches are outlined below, each with distinct characteristics:

- **BERT:** Bidirectional encoder representations from transformers are designed to capture the context of words in a sentence by considering the text from both directions. BERT excels at tasks like question answering and sentiment analysis, where understanding the full context of a sentence is key.
- **GPT:** Generative pretrained transformers are designed to generate coherent and contextually relevant text by predicting the next word in a sequence. They are widely used in text generation, chatbots, and creative writing.
- **T5:** Text-to-text transfer transformers frame every task as a text-to-text problem, which makes them versatile for various tasks such as translation, summarisation, and classification.

For the remainder of this section, we'll focus on GPTs as the main framework for understanding this pivotal technology.

Chunking

Natural language processing (NLP) is a long-standing branch of artificial intelligence, with its roots stretching back to the Dartmouth Conference. Teaching computers to "understand" human discourse has been a goal of AI researchers for many decades. After all, what can be more natural than human conversation?

The first step in these approaches has generally been to break text down into small units, a process called *chunking* or *tokenisation*. The output of this process is a list of small units of text, typically called *tokens*.

The process usually begins with a cleaning step, where extraneous elements are normalised—things like punctuation, capitalisation, multiple spaces, or accented characters are removed or changed to a standardised form. Once the text is cleaned, it is broken down into smaller units for efficient processing as an ordered set of tokens. The simplest method of chunking is based on word boundaries. In this case, a sentence is broken up into recognisable words:

Alice, turned, to, see, who, was, speaking, and, realised, it, was, the

Another method might break the text into finer units, such as syllables:

Al, ice, turn, ed, to, see, who, was, speak, ing, and, real, ised, it, was, the

In transformers, chunking is a critical step in handling and processing text. Many chunking techniques exist, each suited for different purposes:

- **Word boundaries:** Breaks text into individual words based on spaces and punctuation. This method is simple and intuitive, but may not handle compound words or languages with complex structures effectively.
- **Byte pair encoding:** Starts with individual characters and iteratively merges the most frequent pairs of characters to form subwords, balancing between word-level and character-level tokenisation.
- **WordPiece:** Breaks down words into subwords or characters, optimising for a fixed vocabulary size. This method is commonly used in models like BERT.
- **SentencePiece:** Treats text as raw text rather than relying on pre-tokenisation by spaces, enabling language-independent tokenisation across different scripts and languages.
- **Character tokenisation:** Splits text into individual characters, providing fine-grained tokenisation. This can capture morphological variations but may increase sequence length and complexity.

Over decades of research in natural language processing, many other approaches to chunking have been developed. Don't worry if these are hard to understand; just take away that language can be broken down and processed as small units.

The tokenisation technique most commonly used in GPT models is byte-pair encoding (BPE). Here, text is initially split into individual bytes. Then, frequently occurring pairs of bytes are merged iteratively to form subwords. This process continues until a predefined vocabulary size is reached.

For example, the character *a* is often followed by *l*, but less often by another *a*. Similarly, *al* is more often followed by *i* than by *x*. During this one-time training process, vast amounts of text are processed to identify frequent byte pairs, which effectively compress the text into meaningful subwords. This method ensures that common patterns in text are efficiently captured while maintaining a manageable vocabulary size.

BPE is free of semantics—in that it does not try to "understand" the text as a high-level description of real-world entities. For example, it doesn't comprehend that Alice is a person or that Alice has identified someone speaking. BPE is a purely statistical, frequency-based approach to chunking text.

Nevertheless, by using chunking and tokenisation techniques, GPT models can efficiently process and generate text. Even complex and lengthy documents are handled effectively as sets of smaller, manageable units. Even without a semantic understanding of the text, the previous tokens provide the context that steers generation towards increasingly plausible continuations.

Embedding

After text has been chunked into tokens, the next critical step is to convert these tokens into a format that the machine can process effectively.

Embedding is the process of converting tokens (the chunks of text) into vectors (lists of numbers). This methodology transforms words into a mathematical form that computers can directly manipulate. These vectors are designed to represent tokens in a way that captures patterns of usage, relationships, and context within language.

We mentioned earlier that chunking is devoid of semantics or meaning; it is purely statistical analysis. So, how can we capture meaning in a way that a machine can understand? After all, how can we expect a machine to assist in our tasks if it has no real-world understanding?

In the early days of AI, this issue was tackled head-on. Schemas were developed that aimed to map out parts of human knowledge in rigid and interconnected ways. In these schemas, real-world entities were represented in ways that humans could relate to: dogs have properties, they are mammals with further properties, and cats are mammals too.

However, as we saw in Chapter 2, this approach ultimately proved inadequate for capturing the full spectrum and complexity of our world. It was most effective in narrow domains, like a database of users or a catalogue of products.

So where is meaning, and how can we bring it to the machine?

Language turned out to offer a practical route forward. Language has structure, vocabulary, and grammar, and patterns in how these elements are used carry useful information about context and meaning. Once again, statistical AI came to the rescue, particularly with the wealth of human language now available in digital form. When large corpora of text were analysed by algorithms, the natural patterns and distributions within them revealed useful relationships between the concepts they were describing.

Take the sentence "Alice saw a rabbit." When you think about rabbits, what words come to mind? Perhaps bunny, meadow, hopping, ears, or carrots. If you were to read all of the human discourse available digitally and tally the words that most commonly appear close to rabbit, you'd likely form a concise list of words that frequently co-occur with it. There are many other words that would not feature in such a set, words that are much less closely related to rabbits—such as nuclear, printer, classroom, or engine.

This common co-occurrence of words is at the heart of how embeddings surface meaning indirectly: not by encoding explicit semantics, but by capturing statistical patterns of use.

Embeddings encode chunks into vectors such that common co-occurring words and phrases are placed "close to each other" in vector space. Think of a vector as a point in a multidimensional space, where points close to each other represent words that commonly co-occur and hence are likely to have similar meanings. By using this approach, embeddings provide a statistical yet powerful way to represent the context and semantics of language, making it easier for AI models to process and understand language.

Let's consider how relationships between words are represented in vector space. After reading vast amounts of language data, we identify that two frequently co-occurring tokens with bunny are *rabbit* and *Easter*. This frequency analysis helps us understand that these concepts are closely related in specific contexts.

When we talk about co-occurrence, we mean the appearance of words within a certain window of text—a specified number of words before and/or after bunny. Ideally, these words might appear next to each other, forming a bi-gram, such as *bunny rabbit* or *Easter bunny*. They might also appear at a distance, such as in the sentence, "He wanted a rabbit, so his parents bought him a little bunny." The size of the surrounding text used for such analysis is called the *context window*.

Initially, each token is assigned a random vector with many elements. During training, those vectors are adjusted as the model processes more and more text, so tokens used in similar ways tend to end up closer together. Earlier techniques such as Word2Vec or GloVe helped show how this kind of statistical learning could work. Over time, the vectors settle into a more useful arrangement.

For instance, the vector for bunny might be adjusted to be similar to rabbit, cute, fluffy, and hop, but also close to Easter, chocolate, and basket. However, while bunny is linked to both sets of words, basket and hop will not share close proximity.

After processing billions of documents, we create a multidimensional space filled with points. When points are adjacent, they tend to reflect similar patterns of usage and often related meanings. The distance between vectors is calculated using mathematical methods like *cosine similarity*, where closer vectors generally represent more closely related meanings.

Embeddings are often learnt during a model's training on a vast corpus of text. When you type into an AI assistant, your words are chunked, and those chunks are converted into vectors using the embedding layer the model has already learnt.

This example illustrates how embeddings encode semantic relationships between words based on their usage and contexts in large text corpora. The distances in the embedding space effectively capture these relationships, enabling models to process and manipulate language in a way that reflects some aspects of meaning.

This ability to capture meaning through vector proximity has practical applications beyond language generation. *Semantic search* uses these embeddings to find information based on meaning rather than exact keyword matches. For example, searching for "cardiovascular health" might surface documents about "heart disease" and "blood pressure" even if those exact words don't appear in your query, because their vectors sit close together in the embedding space. This approach powers many modern search systems, recommendation engines, and the retrieval mechanisms in AI assistants.

Text Generation

Building on the foundational processes of chunking and embedding, the text generation phase in GPT models represents the culmination of these initial steps into coherent, actionable text output. This process showcases the true power of the generative pretrained transformer (GPT), as it uses these prepared representations to generate new, coherent text sequences.

GPT models operate with a decoder-only architecture that predicts the next token in a sequence based on the input it receives. The model follows an autoregressive approach, meaning it generates one token at a time and feeds each prediction back into the model as input for the next prediction.

This sequential processing allows the model to consider the previous tokens available within its context window when predicting each new token. This is why AI assistants appear to type out text piece by piece, much like an old-style teleprinter.

Here's how the process works:

1. **Input**
   User: The process begins with an input, which could be a user-provided prompt or text accumulated from earlier interactions. This input sets the initial context for the model's operation.
   System: There may also be a *system prompt*, set by the developer or service, which gives higher-level instructions about the model's role, tone, boundaries, or priorities.
2. **Chunking:** The input text undergoes a chunking phase, where it is *broken* down into manageable pieces, or tokens. These tokens are the basic processing units of the model and capture the essential elements of the input text.

3. **Embeddings:** Each token produced during chunking is transformed into a dense vector through the embedding process. These embeddings provide a numerical starting representation that the model can refine using the surrounding context.
4. **Attention:** With the embeddings in place, the GPT model uses its self-attention mechanism to evaluate the importance of each token within the sequence. This mechanism helps the model weigh how each token relates to others, factoring in the context built up across the sequence.
5. **Prediction:** Based on the contextual map refined by attention, the model predicts the next most appropriate token. The prediction is made using probability distributions learnt during training, ensuring that each new token fits within the overall context. Users can adjust settings such as *temperature* to control how predictable or creative the output is—lower values mean more focus and consistency, while higher values lead to variety and surprise.
6. **Output:** The predicted tokens are compiled into a complete output sequence. This sequence flows logically, simulating human text production with a natural rhythm and coherence.
7. **Respin:** Each new token is added to the output and reintroduced into the input for the next prediction. This dynamic updating ensures that the model continues to refine its predictions, maintaining contextual relevance and linguistic coherence throughout the process.

One remarkable capability of transformer-based models is that the input step can contain minimal instruction. In *zero-shot learning*, the model tackles a task without any examples—guided only by the prompt. In *one-shot learning*, it learns from a single example, while in *few-shot learning*, it learns from a handful of examples provided in the conversation. This versatility distinguishes modern LLMs from earlier AI systems that required extensive retraining for each new task.

Self-attention lies at the heart of the transformer model and is a key innovation that allows it to generate language with remarkable accuracy. Unlike older models that processed text sequentially, transformers can capture long-range dependencies between tokens, regardless of their position in the sequence. In GPT-style models, each token is weighed in relation to the earlier tokens available to it, helping the model weigh context more effectively.

This structured process demonstrates how GPT models handle text generation, from initial input to final output. It highlights the sophistication and iterative nature of modern AI language models, which combine statistical learning with contextual awareness to simulate understanding.

The result is text that often reads as if it were written by a human, reflecting the model's ability to learn nuances of language, style, and even subject-specific patterns. This is especially true of models that have been trained on a vast corpus of digitally encoded knowledge. This capability makes GPT models incredibly useful for tasks like writing assistance, summarising documents, creating content, and engaging in natural conversations.

In summary, text generation in GPT models is a sophisticated orchestration of chunking, embedding, attention-driven focus, and predictive output. Together, these elements enable the creation of contextually relevant text that can closely resemble human writing.

Challenges and Limitations

In recent times, a common social media trend has involved people demonstrating language AIs making comical mistakes. In a typical example, they show how AIs cannot always accurately answer simple questions like "How many Rs are there in strawberry?" After decades of thinking about computers as the bastions of correctness, it feels odd and even perhaps unsettling to find them slipping up on a question that even very young children could answer. But if you read the previous section with care, it should be clear why such mistakes are possible.

Transformer-based language models are probabilistic token predictors. They are not directly concerned with correctness in the way a calculator or database is. Their goal is to predict which token is most likely to come next in a sequence—that is the core of what they do. The meaning, the implications, and the impact of the chosen token are not directly assessed by the model itself. For a large language model, what appears true is strongly shaped by the statistical co-occurrence of terms in its training data.

We have seen time and again AI researchers loosely borrowing terms from human cognition to apply them to AI. Continuing this trend, the term *hallucination* is often used to describe the situation where a language model confidently talks about events that never happened, people who never existed, or places that were never real. The term is not technically correct, as the model is not hallucinating in a human sense. It is merely talking about events, people, and places that could have existed with statistical plausibility.

While researchers are looking for ways to minimise such errors, their occurrence is nonetheless woven into the fabric of how the transformer architecture works. It will take a while to rewire our brains to the concept of hallucinating AIs. So far we have seen many debacles: lawyers citing made-up case law, scientists referencing made-up papers, and so on.

Rather than dwelling on their occasional missteps, we might instead marvel at how astonishingly capable they are, given what we know about how they work under the hood. It remains genuinely surprising, even to many in the AI community, that something built to predict tokens can produce outputs of such enormous value. Whether some kind of emergent understanding has grown from these simple roots remains an open question. We will return to this topic in the closing Afterword.

Generally, we can say that such models are best used for questions needing judgement but are less useful for questions demanding correctness. One way to understand the difference is to test whether your question can comfortably follow the sentence opener "With the balance of probabilities ..." This works well for "Summarise this text," "Prioritise these items," or "Identify the main point." But it doesn't work well for "What's the date tomorrow?," "Calculate the tax," or "How many Rs are there in strawberry?"

We said earlier that for many AIs, truth is simply the statistical structure of their training material. But what if that material was itself flawed? Very often, data used to train models contains biases or inaccuracies. These might be the result of earlier processes or the human biases present in the data generation. But once captured in an embedding space, these biases are baked into the responses of a language model. Those biases and inaccuracies can perpetuate or even amplify problems for already marginalised and victimised groups.

When you were young and learning how to hold conversations, you were no doubt scolded when you said things that were inappropriate or rude. Living in groups, we all learn the art of self-censorship in language, restricting our words to things that are broadly accepted in our society. Language models inherit much of this from the training material too, but nonetheless they do not themselves have an independent moral framework.

For this reason, responsible AI systems are rarely left to operate on raw model output alone. Developers typically add external safeguards, often called guardrails, such as content filters, system rules, reinforcement from human feedback, retrieval checks, and human review for high-stakes tasks. These measures can improve reliability and reduce harm, but they do not change the underlying nature of the model itself. At base, it remains a statistical generator of plausible continuations, which is why caution and oversight remain essential.

Large language models can be remarkably useful, helping us write, summarise, research, and communicate more efficiently. But they are built on a technology that brings many challenges, constraints, and trade-offs of its own. If we are to benefit from them fully, we must learn to use them with caution, awareness, and a clear understanding of both their strengths and their limitations.

Diffusion Models and Image Generation

One of the most remarkable aspects of generative AI use cases is that they don't just replace tasks traditionally handled by humans; they inspire us to explore new and inventive applications that we may not have thought of in the past.

Take text-to-image generation as an example. Here, users can input a simple prompt and have an AI generate an image based on that prompt.

For instance, imagine you need a picture for a presentation, like one of three people in a meeting, where one person is presenting and the others appear confused. You can now simply ask for exactly that. Specify the genders, attire, hairstyles, artistic style, colour palette—whatever you desire, the computer can create it. A chimpanzee riding a unicorn, wearing a spacesuit on the moon, in the style of Van Gogh? No problem.

A common approach for creating such art is through diffusion models. These models represent a cutting-edge development in generative AI, known for their ability to produce high-quality, visually striking images that can at times appear remarkably realistic. Diffusion models work on a fascinating concept, starting with a pattern of random noise and gradually refining it into a detailed, coherent image.

Imagine, for a moment, you visit the beautiful Italian city of Florence, home to many incredible attractions, including Michelangelo's remarkable statue of David. Created over 500 years ago, it's rightfully considered a masterpiece of Renaissance art.

If we could wind the clock back to the early 16th century, we might find Michelangelo standing in front of a solid block of marble. Armed with mallet and chisel, he would have begun his work. At first, crude strokes would form a vague shape. As time went on, the tools became more precise, and the sculpture began to resemble a human figure. After three long years, chisels gave way to files and sandpaper, and the finishing touches were applied to this masterpiece.

While this may seem a distant analogy, the process of generating art with a diffusion model mirrors the methods of master sculptors. The process, shown in Figure 6.5, is both iterative and transformative—starting with a formless beginning and, through gradual refinement, arriving at a refined and intentional end.

Just as Michelangelo revealed David from the marble, diffusion models sculpt lifelike images from the chaos of visual noise. Each iteration brings the digital canvas closer to an artistic vision, gradually refining the image from random noise to clarity.

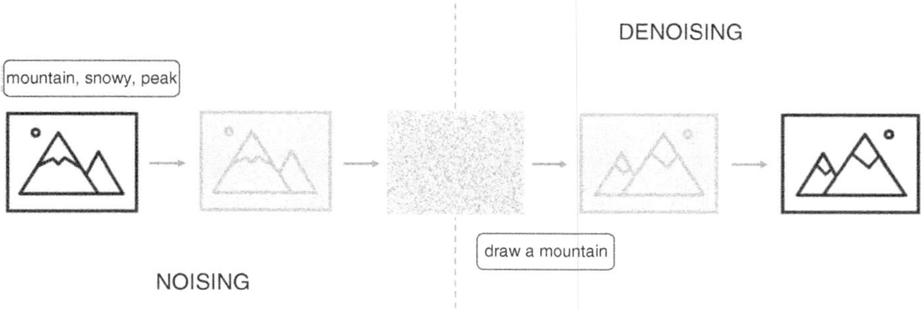

Figure 6.5: Diffusion processes

What makes these models particularly fascinating is their ability to generate images based on specific user prompts. This is possible thanks to the integration of conditional information during both the training and generation phases. Let's break down the steps.

The Forward Process: Adding Noise

The model begins with a dataset of training images, each labelled with descriptive text (such as *grass*, *lawn*, or *a cat playing on a lawn*).

In the forward process, noise is gradually added to the images across several steps, guided by a predefined noise schedule. By *noise*, we mean random perturbation spread across the image, which progressively transforms the original image into pure visual chaos.

During training, the model is shown many such noised images together with their descriptive labels. In this way, it learns how certain visual features are linked to certain words. For example, when the label is *grass*, the model gradually learns to associate features such as green textures and outdoor surfaces with the corresponding words. This relationship between the visual data and the descriptive labels is crucial for conditioning the model later on.

By the end of the forward process, the original images have been completely obscured by noise. Across many training examples, however, the model has learnt relationships that will later help it generate coherent images during the reverse process.

The Reverse Process: Learning to Denoise with Conditions

Once the forward process is complete, the model begins the reverse process. It learns to predict and remove the noise, step by step, gradually restoring the image.

Here's the key: During training, the model doesn't just learn how to remove noise in a general sense—it learns how to predict and remove noise in a way that aligns with the descriptive labels. For example, if training examples are labelled *grass*, the model gradually learns denoising patterns that correspond to outdoor scenes, such as green textures, blades of grass, and other natural elements.

This process is crucial because it allows the model to generate images based on user input later on, ensuring that the final image reflects not just the structural form but also the visual features tied to the specific labels.

Generating Images from User Prompts

When a user provides a prompt, such as *a dog sleeping on the lawn*, the model uses this text to guide the image generation process. Here's how it works:

1. **Encoding the prompt:** The user's text prompt is converted into a high-dimensional vector using a text encoder. As described in the earlier section on transformers, this vector captures the essence of the prompt and is fed into the model as conditional information.
2. **Starting with noise:** The image generation process begins with a field of random visual noise, much like a blank digital canvas.
3. **Guided denoising:** As the model progresses through the reverse diffusion process, it uses the encoded prompt to guide each step. The denoising process is conditioned on the user's input, ensuring that the emerging image gradually aligns with the elements described in the prompt. Because the model has been trained to associate specific features with certain labels, it can use this learnt knowledge to produce images that match the user's request.
4. **Iterative refinement:** With each step, the model refines the image, continuously adjusting it based on both the removal of noise and the user's prompt. This ensures that the image not only becomes clearer but also reflects the visual characteristics requested. The process continues until the final image is a detailed, coherent representation of the prompt.

This ability to generate customised images from prompts makes diffusion models exceptionally powerful for creative tasks. While this process might seem different from how humans approach creation, it can still be likened to Michelangelo's sculpting—iteratively refining the marble slab while keeping the patron's vision in mind.

In practical applications, diffusion models have quickly found their niche. In the arts, they create complex, detailed pieces that could be mistaken for human-made artwork. In design and fashion, they help develop new patterns and styles that push the boundaries of traditional aesthetics. In entertainment and media production, these models generate textures and backgrounds for animations and video games, enhancing visual storytelling with their nuanced outputs.

The potential of diffusion models extends beyond just image generation. Their underlying principles suggest possible applications in other creative domains, such as music, video, and even sculpture. As these models evolve, they are likely to redefine what machines can achieve in the creative industries, further blurring the lines between human-made and machine-generated art.

In essence, diffusion models do not just replicate the process of creation—they reimagine it, offering tools that enhance human creativity with computational power and algorithmic innovation.

Orchestration and Agentic AI

In the early days of generative AI, people mainly used it for discrete tasks—write an email, summarise a document, draw an image, and so on. But as understanding and acceptance have grown, we are increasingly seeing larger generative AI systems that coordinate many such tasks in pursuit of broader goals.

For example, while a diffusion model might help us make a single image, how might we go about creating a video? A video is not just a sequence of images; those images must maintain a spatial relationship to one another. Elements within the scene must position themselves across that sequence in a way that is consistent with their movement through the film. If the camera is moving too, that must also be accounted for. Then there is music, lighting, and dialogue.

Making a movie is an example of orchestration—the controlled coordination of multiple systems that work in concert, share context, and pursue a common goal. Many real-world scenarios fit this pattern of orchestration—booking a holiday, organising an event, or planning a house move.

AI Orchestration

Fully orchestrated systems sit on a spectrum of activity that humans and AI can share. At one end, the AI helps with isolated tasks. In the middle, it works alongside the user on a broader objective. At the far end, it can be given more freedom to act within boundaries set by the user. Broadly, we can think of that spectrum as follows:

- **Assistance:** The user gives occasional one-off tasks to the AI, but the AI is not aware of the wider goal or overall picture. It responds to the instruction in front of it—drafting a paragraph, summarising a note, or generating an image—without taking responsibility for what comes next.

- **Augmentation:** The user and the AI work together on a shared task, with the AI aware of the broader goal. The user still leads, but the AI adds value in a co-pilot style by filling gaps, proposing options, carrying out sub-tasks, and helping the overall process move forward.
- **Autonomy:** The user sets a broader goal, ideally including a definition of done, and then allows the AI more latitude in how it achieves that outcome. Here the system may plan steps, choose between options, use tools, recover from minor setbacks, and continue working with less moment-to-moment direction, though still within the constraints and permissions the user has defined.

Assistance has already become commonplace and largely mainstream. People now use generative AI for drafting, summarising, brainstorming, searching, and similar one-off tasks. Augmentation is also spreading quickly, especially in areas such as software development, office productivity, research, and customer service, where AI can work alongside people across a broader thread of activity.

Full orchestration around large tasks or broad goals is still emerging. Moving further along this spectrum depends on growing confidence in AI systems acting with greater independence, using tools, making bounded decisions, and continuing a process without constant supervision. That confidence is still being built across organisations, professions, and regulators, particularly where the outcomes are consequential, costly, or high-risk.

Typically, an orchestrated AI system brings together several distinct aspects:

- **An end-user goal:** The system is not merely trying to generate a single output, but to achieve a broader outcome defined by the user, ideally with a clear sense of what counts as success or completion, such as planning a trip, producing a report, or carrying a multistep task through to completion.
- **A workflow:** The work is broken into stages or steps, with some actions happening in sequence because they rely on one another, and others running in parallel, rather than everything happening at once. The workflow gives the system shape, helping it know what should happen first, what can happen together, and what must wait until earlier steps are complete.
- **Conditions and decisions:** The system must respond to circumstances as they arise—if a flight is full, try another; if a summary is

unclear, revise it; if a result fails a check, try a different route; and if one path proves unworkable, backtrack and pursue another.

- **Context management:** Information gathered in one step must remain available in later steps so that the system can stay coherent and avoid conflicts, repetition, or repeatedly starting from scratch. At the same time, not every step needs every detail, so part of the orchestration is selecting the right context for the right stage.
- **Artefacts:** Intermediate outputs are often created and reused along the way—notes, plans, drafts, images, schedules, or other working materials that help carry the process forward. These artefacts also need managing, since some may be temporary or time-sensitive, or become outdated or overridden as the process unfolds.
- **Coordination across components:** Different models, tools, or services may each handle part of the task, with the orchestration layer keeping them aligned with the same objective. In practice, each step often proceeds on a need-to-know basis rather than exposing every component to the entire goal.
- **Memory and feedback:** The system may need to remember earlier choices, assess whether progress is being made, and adjust its behaviour when something is not working. Gathering feedback is vital to ensure the process has not drifted off course and still aligns with the user's goal.

Orchestration systems are a complex endeavour and are at the cutting edge of current AI adoption. In practice, they are rarely built from generative AI alone, or even from AI alone more generally. They usually combine traditional software, workflow logic, data systems, APIs, search, rules, and one or more AI models, using each where it is strongest in order to achieve the desired outcome.

In bounded domains, however, the problem becomes more manageable. Workflow engines are beginning to emerge for specific tasks, such as making a movie, processing a claim, or booking a holiday, where the objective is more clearly defined and the decision space is more constrained. In some respects, this echoes the expert systems we encountered in Chapter 2, but with a crucial difference: Rather than relying on a single rigid rule set, these newer systems can operate through a more fluid workflow that blends rules, models, tools, and context.

But to realise such operations fully, we must grant the AI some autonomy—enough scope to get on with things without constant feedback or direction. In human terms, we often do something similar when we ask another person to solve a problem on our behalf.

This is what happens when you ask a contractor to build an extension to your home, a mechanic to fix a fault in your car, or a surgeon to perform an operation. Your role is to set clear expectations around the requirements, constraints, budget, and desired outcome, and then allow them to carry out the work using their own judgement. In such cases, we can say they are acting as your agent.

Agentic AI

Agentic AI emerged as confidence grew in using AI for specific tasks and people began to want systems that could achieve broader goals. Users increasingly found themselves carrying work from one AI to another, or from one session to the next, and inevitably wanted a more streamlined way to use multiple AIs together.

In this sense, an agent is best understood as a system that has a role, a goal, and some latitude in how it pursues that goal. Rather than merely responding once and stopping, an agent can take in information, make bounded decisions, use available tools, and continue acting until it has either completed the task or reached a point where it needs further instruction. An agent may itself consist of a collection of smaller agents, each taking on an aspect of the goal with tighter constraints and a more focused scope.

Such agents rarely work in isolation. In practice, they are usually orchestrated as part of a broader system, and that orchestration layer may itself behave rather like a higher-level agent with a wider objective. One part of the system may plan, another may retrieve information, another may generate content, another may check whether the result is acceptable, and another may communicate with the user. What we call an *agentic system* is therefore often a coordinated structure of specialised parts rather than a single monolithic machine.

In more advanced arrangements, some agents may even critique or evaluate the work of other agents, echoing the way the discriminator improves the generator in a GAN. Overall, the whole system is not entirely unlike the dynamics of a human team, where different members contribute different skills while still working towards a shared outcome.

A typical agent might have:

- **A role:** A defined responsibility within the wider system, such as researcher, planner, writer, reviewer, or coordinator
- **A goal:** A clear objective or subobjective that tells it what outcome it is trying to achieve
- **Tools:** Access to the functions it needs, such as search, retrieval, calculators, APIs, databases, or generation models

- **Context:** The information, instructions, and memory required for it to act coherently and consistently
- **Checks:** Some way to assess progress, detect failure, and decide whether to continue, revise, escalate, or stop.

A critical question is just how much autonomy a user wants to grant an AI agent to operate on its behalf. Can the AI book appointments, make purchases, or contact other people without approval? Suppose you ask an agentic system to respond to your emails. You might be content for it to draft replies, but not to message a particular person, discuss a sensitive subject, or attach a document from your files. In practice, useful autonomy depends not only on capability, but on carefully defined boundaries.

Agentic systems are powerful, and with that power comes risk and responsibility. Traditional permission models in software are often narrow and limited, focusing mainly on access to files, systems, and networks. Agentic AI pushes us to think more carefully about the division of labour, authority, and accountability between people and machines. If an AI can act in the world rather than merely advise, then questions of oversight, control, and responsibility become central rather than optional.

Multimodal Generative AI

For much of AI's history, text received special attention. Compared with images, audio, or video, text is relatively easy to store, structure, search, and label. That made it a natural starting point for many early systems, and it helps explain why language has played such a prominent role in the public rise of generative AI.

But human activity is not confined to text alone. Most real-world tasks span several forms of information at once. A meeting may involve spoken words, slides, diagrams, facial expressions, and a written follow-up. A web page may combine text, images, menus, and video. A photograph may contain objects, locations, emotions, and also embedded text on signs or labels. If AI is to operate more naturally in human settings, it cannot remain limited to just one medium at a time.

This has led to the growing importance of multimodal AI – systems that can work across text, images, audio, and video together. In broad terms, the boundaries between these media are beginning to blur. A modern system may be able to look at a picture and describe it in words, extract text from a photograph, answer questions about a chart, generate an image from a written prompt, or respond to spoken language while also taking visual context into account. Tasks that once felt unusual, such as selecting text from an image or asking questions about the contents of a screenshot, are now becoming commonplace.

Under the hood, this does not mean that every kind of data is suddenly the same. Images, sound, and language still have different structures and require different handling. But by converting these inputs into compatible mathematical representations, AI systems can increasingly connect them within a shared process. This is one of the clearest signs that generative AI is moving beyond isolated outputs towards more flexible, humanlike interaction with the mixed media of everyday life.

Combined with orchestration, agentic systems, and growing autonomy, this points towards a future in which AI does not merely generate isolated outputs, but engages more fluidly with the full mixture of media, context, and goals that shape everyday human activity.

Use Cases

In earlier sections, we explored the innovative realm of generative AI, examining various architectures like autoencoders, VAEs, GANs, transformers, and diffusion models. These technologies form the foundation of machines' ability to create and innovate, generating everything from images and text to music and synthetic data.

Now, as we shift from the theoretical underpinnings to real-world applications, let's explore how these technologies are employed to transform creative processes. In this section, we'll highlight the versatility and power of generative AI, demonstrating how these models synthesise complex data to produce novel and valuable outputs.

Medical Image Synthesis

The generation of medical images marks a significant advancement in healthcare technology. These synthetic images are particularly valuable in situations where medical data is scarce, or where patient privacy concerns limit access to real datasets. They provide realistic medical images that support training and research without compromising patient confidentiality.

The generation of synthetic medical data is often powered by variational autoencoders (VAEs).

Variational Autoencoders

Variational autoencoders are a type of generative model that efficiently learns the underlying probability distribution of a given dataset. After processing large amounts of training data, VAEs learn how elements of that data are probabilistically arranged. They can then generate new items that align with the probabilities identified during training.

In medical imaging, VAEs are trained on real patient data to generate synthetic images that realistically represent various medical conditions and anomalies, helping to create diverse datasets for training and research.

Enhanced Patient Outcomes

The use of VAEs in medical image synthesis offers several key benefits. They can generate additional training data for machine learning models, particularly in fields like radiology, where annotated images may be limited.

By generating synthetic images that do not correspond to real patients, VAEs ensure patient privacy is maintained. Furthermore, medical researchers and students can study a wide range of medical conditions and scenarios without the need for extensive real-world clinical trials or data collections.

Outcome

Variational autoencoders are transforming medical imaging and research. By facilitating the generation of realistic and diverse medical images, VAEs enable better machine learning model training, enhance educational opportunities, and support medical research while safeguarding patient privacy. This application of AI underscores the pivotal role of VAEs in advancing medical technology, showing their potential to contribute meaningfully to healthcare, research, and patient care.

AI Assistants

AI assistants, powered by sophisticated language models, have revolutionised how we interact with technology. These virtual helpers can understand and process human language to perform a wide range of tasks—from simple actions like setting reminders to more complex ones like comparing scientific papers. They also engage with us through open-ended and natural conversations.

These systems use transformer technology to power their interactive conversations.

Transformers

Transformers are a type of neural network architecture that has dramatically improved the performance of language models. Designed to handle sequential data, such as text, they excel at maintaining context over long distances within the text. This ability is crucial for understanding the nuances and complexities of human discourse.

Models like OpenAI's ChatGPT, Google's Gemini, and Facebook's Llama are all built on the transformer architecture. They process input text by understanding the context and generating responses that are contextually appropriate. This is achieved through mechanisms like self-attention, which enables the model to assess the importance of each word in a sentence, regardless of its position.

Assistance via Natural Language

AI assistants based on transformers provide a seamless and intuitive way for users to interact with technology using natural language. The ability to ask questions, receive answers, and execute commands without navigating complex menus or interfaces significantly lowers the barrier to technology use for a wide range of users.

These systems can be integrated into various platforms, enhancing user experiences across services such as customer support, personal planning, and educational tutoring. They integrate into daily tasks, offering improved outcomes like completing sentences, suggesting improvements, or pointing out errors. The adaptability and continuous learning from interactions ensure that they remain relevant and improve over time.

Outcome

The implementation of transformers in AI assistants has significantly advanced how we interact with machines. These systems provide not only convenience but also a deeper, more personalised interaction, making technology more accessible and user-friendly.

AI assistants exemplify how transformers can be applied effectively, transforming vast amounts of language data into meaningful communication. They make digital services more engaging and responsive to human needs. This illustrates the profound impact of generative AI on our everyday lives, blending technical sophistication with practical utility.

Images from Text

The ability to generate detailed and realistic images from simple text descriptions represents an exciting advancement in generative AI. This use case allows individuals to bring their visual ideas to life without the need for traditional artistic skills. It empowers the democratisation of creative arts and has the potential to revolutionise visual art generation on a large scale.

This process uses diffusion models to create artistic representations from human prompts.

Diffusion Models

Diffusion models are a class of generative models that begin with a pattern of random noise and gradually refine this noise into detailed images. These models achieve this transformation through a structured process that reverses the addition of noise, guided by a user's prompt, and powered by advanced deep learning techniques. They excel at capturing and reproducing the complexity and variety of visual data, making them well-suited for generating high-quality images from text descriptions.

Diffusion models use conditional training, where the model is trained on images paired with descriptive text. This process teaches the model to associate specific textual cues with visual features, allowing it to generate relevant images based on textual inputs.

Enabling Visual Communication

The ability to generate images from text offers significant benefits across many industries. Filmmakers and content creators can visualise scenes and characters directly from scripts, enhancing pre-production planning and creative storytelling. Companies can generate custom visuals for marketing campaigns based on descriptive inputs, creating more tailored and impactful marketing strategies. Academics and scientists can visualise complex data and simulate scientific phenomena, making them easier to understand and more accessible.

Across all sectors, creative individuals are empowered to use visual means to express themselves and communicate with audiences, accessing a rich stream of human cognition previously only available to those with specific artistic talents.

Outcome

The use of diffusion models to generate images from text marks a remarkable leap in AI capabilities, bridging the gap between textual descriptions and visual representations. By transforming written language into detailed visuals, these models not only enhance creative processes but also push the boundaries of how we interact with and utilise AI in content creation. This highlights the profound impact of generative AI, showcasing its ability to merge technical sophistication with practical utility and creative freedom.

Digital Actor Resurrection and De-aging

The digital resurrection of actors and the portrayal of younger versions of living actors have opened new creative avenues in the film industry. This use case involves the application of generative AI to re-create realistic and expressive versions of actors, regardless of their current age or whether they are, in fact, deceased. Such technology not only preserves the legacy of past cinema icons but also ensures narrative continuity in sequels and prequels.

These movies use GANs to seamlessly insert actors into stories.

Generative Adversarial Networks (GANs)

GANs are particularly suited for this task due to their ability to generate photorealistic images. In the context of film, these models are trained on a dataset of the actor's past performances and appearances, capturing nuances from different angles, expressions, and emotions.

Once projected on large cinema screens, even minor imperfections can become immediately obvious to discerning audiences. The adversarial nature of GANs, involving a generator and a discriminator working together, pushes the quality of the output to be indistinguishable from real footage of the actors, allowing audiences to remain immersed in the story without distraction.

Epic Sagas with Consistent Actors

Using GANs for digital resurrection and de-aging offers significant benefits to filmmakers. Now, they can tell stories without being constrained by the physical age or availability of actors, allowing narratives to span long timeframes. Epic sagas that span generations can be created without compromising the portrayal of characters.

This technology also reduces the need for expensive makeup, prosthetics, or hiring look-alike actors for younger or older versions of a character. These factors help maintain the integrity and continuity of the original films or broader story arcs.

Outcome

The implementation of GANs to digitally recreate actors has significantly transformed narrative filmmaking. By enabling the realistic portrayal of characters at any age, or even after an actor's death, GANs enhance storytelling, allowing filmmakers to explore narratives that were previously constrained by the physical limitations of human actors.

This technology not only pushes the boundaries of what's possible in film production but also raises important ethical considerations regarding the posthumous use of an actor's likeness. This use case highlights the profound capabilities and potential impacts of generative AI in the creative industries, illustrating both its practical utility and the broader cultural implications.

Conclusion

Generative AI is opening up genuinely new opportunities. It is expanding what individuals, small teams, schools, charities, and start-ups can create, often without the budgets, training, equipment, or production infrastructure that older creative industries demanded. People who could not previously afford specialist software, studio time, instruments, cameras, or film crews can now experiment with a wider range of media in ways that were once far less accessible.

But that opportunity arrives with serious challenges that should not be downplayed. One is bias and fairness: Models learn from historical data and can therefore reproduce or amplify social biases in harmful ways. Another is the factual unreliability of text generation, often described as *hallucination*, where systems produce fluent but false statements. When these outputs appear in search summaries or other trusted contexts, they can spread misinformation, weaken public trust, and make truth harder to distinguish from confident error.

There are also major questions regarding ownership, copyright, and artistic identity. If a model generates music, images, or prose from patterns learnt from vast bodies of existing work, it is not always clear how creators' rights should be protected or who should own the result. Creative people need new tools, but they also need an economy in which original work can still be recognised, valued, and rewarded.

Related concerns appear in deepfakes, where AI can convincingly imitate real people, resurrect deceased actors, or generate music in the style of existing artists. These developments may be creatively powerful, but they also create risks for reputation, consent, legacy, and public trust, especially when synthetic media is used to deceive, spread disinformation, or target individuals whose image or voice is used without permission.

Bad actors can also use generative AI to scale fraud, cybercrime, and manipulation. Scam emails, fake customer-service messages, cloned voices, fabricated documents, and highly personalised social-engineering attacks can all become cheaper and more convincing when generated at speed. This means the challenge is not only what well-meaning users do with these tools, but also how criminals, propagandists, and other malicious actors may exploit them.

Another challenge is dependency and skill degradation. If AI becomes the default route to creativity, writing, or decision-making, some people may stop developing the very skills that make those activities valuable. That is why regulation, governance, transparency, and practical guardrails will matter so much as the technology spreads.

Used carelessly, generative AI could deepen inequity, confusion, and over-reliance. Used well, however, it can become a deeply empowering technology: widening access to creativity, lowering barriers to entry, and helping many more people turn ideas into music, images, films, writing, and new forms of expression than ever before. The future could be bright because these tools can expand human capability rather than replace it, giving ordinary people, not just large companies or well-funded professionals, more chances to learn, experiment, communicate, and create work that would once have required far greater money, equipment, or institutional support.

Afterword

We began this book by recounting Mary Shelley's *Frankenstein*—not because we wanted to frighten you with monsters, but because it is a valuable cautionary tale about the *dangers of overreaching ambition*, and the *responsibility that comes with innovation*.

Here, in the closing words of the book, you have an advantage over us: Some time has passed since we penned these pages, so you will be more aware of developments in AI capability and use. The pace of change is so rapid that, even while we were writing, events were unfolding quickly. Do you now find yourself in a world of AI monsters, in an AI utopia, or—more likely—somewhere in the middle?

Shelley's monster made a dramatic and violent impact on the people in her story. Whilst this makes for compelling prose, in real life less dramatic outcomes can occur, which may still have profound impacts on the everyday lives of people and society.

In this Afterword, we briefly shift from explanation to reflection as we explore the opportunities and challenges that AI may bring as it becomes ever more woven into the fabric of our lives.

AI will play a crucial role in solving many of the challenges that shape our future—from tackling climate change to developing new forms of clean energy, and from managing resources in an increasingly depopulating world to supporting healthcare for ageing populations. These possibilities underline the enormous potential of AI to improve lives and strengthen societies.

Yet even as this optimism is well founded, we must also confront the difficult questions that may arise in our ongoing relationship with the evolving AI landscape.

The Winding Road of AI

To understand how we arrived here, let's briefly recount the winding road that brought us to this point. In the first chapter of the book, we took a comprehensive sweep through the history of AI. From its inception in the aftermath of war, to today where it plays an increasingly impactful role in all our lives, the journey of AI has been long, winding, and erratic—peppered with over-promises, false hopes, long periods of stagnation, and unexpected breakthroughs.

All the while, the dream of what AI could become was kept alive in films, books, and comics. The vision of an overarching technology that could help us in our everyday lives and solve our most pressing problems, was often presented as if it would inevitably arise. But until very recently, our dreams *of* AI outstripped our achievements *in* AI.

In the last few years a shift has occurred, and now AI capability has begun to outpace our expectations. AI-driven outcomes now surprise, delight, and concern us in equal measure. Yet these outcomes do not neatly align with the expectations of earlier writers and film-makers.

Today's AI is mainly in the form of disembodied intelligences. These can help us with cerebral tasks such as researching, planning, and analysing. But notably, embodied AI such as robots has failed to develop at the pace we expected. It turned out that writing a Shakespearean sonnet was an easier ask than unloading a dishwasher. We will all have to wait a while longer for such practical help.

The emergence of AI in our lives, societies, and workplaces has proved difficult to anticipate and prepare for. In the years ahead, this evolving technology may reshape many of the social structures, norms, and practices that have shaped our lives for centuries.

In this book, we broke down AI into five realms. These were designed to give you a non-technical, gentle, and structured introduction to the key elements of the technology. This is not a conventional computer science taxonomy, and some specialists may well object to it.

Unlike physics and chemistry, AI has not progressed as a neatly organised set of principles, with foundational aspects sitting at the bottom of a stable pyramid of understanding. Rather, it is more like that dirty toolbox you keep under the stairs: a practical set of methods that can be adapted, bent, or improvised to solve any number of requirements. This is not a flaw—it's a strength. AI helps us make sense of the messy and disorganised things that surround us: climate, economies, health, markets, language, etc.

Risking the wrath of purists, let's once again recap the five realms this book has outlined:

Symbolic AI Symbolic systems underpinned the earliest progress in AI, forming the bedrock on which our modern systems still rest. Built on explicit rules, symbols, and logic, this traditional approach behaves much like a classic computer program, following clear instructions to produce predictable and consistent outcomes.

Symbolic AI reminds us that not every problem requires mountains of data—sometimes clarity, logic, and careful reasoning still provide the most dependable route to an answer. It remains essential in areas where reliability and transparency are paramount. Yet, as we noted within Chapter 2, "Symbolic AI," rule-based systems often struggle to cope with the messy realities of human data, where ambiguity, inconsistency, and sheer complexity make rigid rules difficult to sustain.

Statistical AI Statistical methods transformed the field by learning from data rather than relying on fixed rules. Using statistical techniques to uncover patterns in large and often messy datasets, this approach helps AI make sense of information that could never be neatly arranged into ordered, rule-based systems—directly incorporating the outliers and exceptions that inevitably occur.

In Chapter 3, "Statistical AI," we discussed how techniques such as clustering and classification help uncover structure in data, and how more advanced methods like Bayesian approaches and regression enable models to make informed predictions. This data-driven perspective has become a major force behind progress in areas such as language processing, image recognition, and predictive analytics.

Connected AI Connected AI—including neural networks—mirrors aspects of the human brain's structure. These systems processed information by adjusting millions of interconnected weights, allowing them to recognise subtle patterns and relationships within data.

In Chapter 4, "Connected AI," we showed how this approach supports complex capabilities such as speech recognition, image analysis, and natural language understanding, and why neural networks have become central to the modern AI landscape. We also explored how specialised architectures, such as convolutional neural networks for vision and recurrent neural networks for sequence-based tasks, enabled major leaps in fields like image classification, translation, and time-series analysis.

Learning AI Learning AI, or machine learning, improves through experience rather than fixed instructions. These models refine their performance as they encounter more data, allowing them to adapt to new conditions and shifting patterns.

We discussed in Chapter 5, "Learning AI," the main learning styles—supervised, unsupervised, and reinforcement learning—and how each offered different ways for systems to discover structure, respond to feedback, or learn through trial-and-error. We also outlined key techniques and showed how they enabled AI to classify information, make decisions, and anticipate future outcomes. This adaptive capability marked a step-change in how computers respond to the world, moving from static tools to systems that could evolve alongside their tasks.

Generative AI Large language models, embodied in applications such as ChatGPT, brought the realm of generative AI into the public imagination. They showed how AI could generate convincing and original content at scale, expanding the boundaries of what machines could achieve.

In Chapter 6, "Generative AI," we showed how, by learning from vast amounts of data, such systems could produce new text, images, music, and video. We also outlined the core techniques and approaches that enabled these advances. These included variational autoencoders, which learned compact representations of data; generative adversarial networks, which used competing models to create realistic outputs; transformers, whose ability to capture long-range relationships revolutionised language and multimodal tasks; diffusion models, which refined random noise into coherent images; and orchestration and agentic AI, which coordinated tools and models towards broader goals.

When covering each of these realms, we provided both historic context and technical background to ground the discussion. Critically, we also included use cases, showing practical examples of where the methodologies are applied in everyday life. Finally, each concluded by placing the technology in broader context and outlining the key issues and challenges it raises.

Charting the Road Ahead

Making predictions about technology is historically very difficult, and about AI even more so. Nevertheless, we can still look ahead in a disciplined way, informed by earlier waves of technical change and by the signals already visible around us.

In this section, we do not attempt to predict the future with confidence, nor indulge every grand claim made on AI's behalf. Instead, we consider the more likely paths ahead: how current scaling trends may evolve, where practical applications may create the deepest impact, which emerging systems may matter most, how different parts of the world may respond, and what all this may mean for ordinary people.

Scaling and Applying AI

It is likely that the current surge in AI capability will slow down and stabilise. We are already seeing early signs that simply consuming ever more data and compute may produce useful advances, but not always the kind of radical leap that earlier breakthroughs seemed to promise. Among the most prominent recent families of language models, each new generation has not always represented as large a step as the one before it.

That does not mean progress has stopped, but it may suggest that some of the easiest gains from simple scaling have already been achieved. Beyond a certain point, adding ever more data and compute may yield smaller improvements, higher costs, and a more incremental pattern of advance. The challenge then becomes not merely building larger models, but finding better ways to apply the capability already in hand.

A further constraint may lie not in the quantity of training data, but in its quality and origin. For the first time, a substantial portion of the material used to train new models appears to have been machine-generated rather than human-produced. There is emerging evidence that repeatedly recycling such synthetic data can gradually erode model quality, reinforcing errors, flattening variation, and narrowing the originality of what later systems produce. In that light, data produced prior to 2022 may come to seem unusually valuable, not because it was perfect, but because it was overwhelmingly human in origin.

Earlier waves of technology have often followed a familiar pattern: early optimism colliding with the practical difficulties of application, scale, and cost, leading to disillusionment and, at times, backlash. This is typically followed by a slower, steadier rise as people come to terms with the technology, understand its real value, and apply it more intelligently and thoughtfully to specific domains. This is, of course, the classic *Gartner Hype Curve* in action. In other words, the story may turn out to be less about endless dramatic jumps in raw capability and more about the long work of refinement and deployment.

Whether or not AI scaling is reaching its limits, we are still likely to see a gradual but decisive shift—from an era defined by capability breakthroughs to one defined by applied use cases. Looking back at the rise of the

Internet and the web, those technologies were undeniably transformative. But it was only when they intersected with ubiquitous connectivity and mobile devices that they unleashed the applications that truly reshaped our world: Uber, Netflix, Amazon, Kindle, Spotify, Instagram, and many more. The infrastructural components were foundational, but it was the applications they enabled that created the real impact.

The application landscape for AI is still at a very early stage. Beyond obvious uses like chatbots and workflow augmentation, the deeper value of this new platform has yet to reveal itself. Predicting what will emerge today is as difficult as forecasting social media or real-time navigation at the dawn of the web, but that uncertainty should not obscure the broader direction of travel: Even if raw scaling slows, the practical impact of AI may only just be beginning.

AGI and Superintelligence

Some believe that the tech giants—invested as they are in large-scale AI rollouts—will continue scaling these systems far beyond their current capabilities. In that view, they may eventually become super-capable, beyond any human measure, perhaps even self-aware. There is a popular narrative that, if current systems are scaled far enough, they will suddenly spark, "wake up," and cross some unspecified threshold into *artificial general intelligence* (AGI).

But in reality, there is no tangible evidence that the algorithmic approaches used today will necessarily lead to such outcomes. By loosely reusing terms from our own existence, such as *neural* and *learning*, we risk mistaking resemblance in language for resemblance in kind. Indeed, as we deepen our understanding of the human mind, the gulf between our own internal states and that of AI becomes ever more stark.

AI development does not mirror human evolution, and current AI algorithms do not resemble the human mind closely enough for us to assume they are travelling the same road. The core difficulty is that we still have only a limited understanding of the basis of biological intelligence, and very little understanding of consciousness itself. What we do know points to stark differences between biological and technological approaches. Therefore, no practical reason exists to assume that AGI will simply spark into existence from the current technological track.

None of this is to deny that such systems may work faster than us, identify patterns or anomalies we would miss, and outperform us on many bounded tasks. This is a trend we have been living with and adapting to for many decades. But impressive performance should not be confused too quickly with understanding, consciousness, or anything like human inner experience.

Part of the difficulty here is that terms like *AGI* and *superintelligence* are used very loosely. Different players use contrasting meanings to pursue individual aims—policy, funding, entertainment, and so on. We can enumerate a spectrum of interpretations, each with different implications.

When people speak of *AGI*, some mean a system with broad competence across many domains rather than narrow excellence in one. Others mean human-level versatility: a machine that can learn new tasks, transfer knowledge between domains, reason in unfamiliar situations, plan over long horizons, and operate with relatively little specialisation. Still others use the term for something stronger: a system that is superhuman across most cognitive tasks, or one that behaves like a person not only in capability but in agency, emotion, self-awareness, or even consciousness.

The term *superintelligence* carries similar ambiguity. In its most literal sense, it might simply mean systems capable of computational tasks that exceed human scale or speed—processing vast datasets, simulating complex phenomena, or identifying patterns across millions of variables in ways no person could match. This kind of performance is already routine in fields like weather modelling, genomic analysis, and particle physics, and has been for decades. But in popular discourse, especially among some technology advocates, superintelligence often carries a more dramatic meaning: a system that transcends not just human *capacity* but human *intelligence itself*, surpassing us in general reasoning, creativity, and understanding. These are not the same claim, and they do not imply the same technical path.

Until people are clearer about what they mean, debate about AGI and superintelligence can become a pointless discourse, generating more heat than light. Better terms need to emerge to allow meaningful analysis. As an example, in autonomous driving we see an enumeration of clearly defined levels—from Level 0 (no automation) through to Level 5 (full autonomy)—that allow engineers, regulators, and the public to discuss capability with precision. Similar clarity would serve the discussion of AI capability far better than vague promises of systems that will "wake up" or become "conscious."

Closely related is the idea of an *AI singularity*: a hypothetical point at which AI systems begin improving so rapidly that change accelerates beyond normal human control or comprehension. The proposed mechanism is *recursive self-improvement*—where an AI becomes capable of redesigning and enhancing its own architecture, leading each generation to create an even more capable successor in an accelerating cycle. Some treat this as a possible existential risk to humankind. Such possibilities should not be dismissed out of hand, but nor is there good reason to project specifically human traits such as malice, ambition, or domination onto AI systems. The more immediate risks are likely to be less cinematic and more familiar: disruption to work, erosion of skills, concentration of power, misuse, and failures of oversight. Those are the concerns we will return to later in this Afterword.

This whole area requires a measure of caution. Grand claims about AGI or superintelligence can be culturally powerful, commercially useful, and politically influential long before they are scientifically justified. If we are not careful, such language can distract us from the more immediate questions we actually face: how these systems work, where they fail, who controls them, and how they should be used responsibly.

Emerging Directions

AI does not stand still. Existing approaches are constantly being refined, extended, and combined, while new ones emerge in response to the limitations of what came before. Predicting which direction will matter most is difficult, but a few broad lines of development are already beginning to come into view: some near-term, some more clearly taking shape, and some more speculative further out.

One of the clearest is the continued rise of *agentic systems*. As confidence grows, AIs are increasingly being trusted to "get on with things" within clearly defined boundaries. Rather than helping only with isolated prompts, they may be asked to carry out broader goals on our behalf, handling multistep tasks that unfold over longer periods, involve larger bodies of information, and require some degree of planning, memory, and adjustment along the way.

This is the agentic direction we discussed at the end of Chapter 6 on generative AI, and it is likely to widen and deepen as the surrounding tools, safeguards, and workflows improve. In practice, that may mean systems that do more than generate an answer: They may coordinate tools, revisit earlier steps, recover from minor errors, and continue working towards a defined outcome with less moment-to-moment direction from the user.

Today's explosion of AI is driven by general-purpose models with a broad understanding of the world, enabled by the consumption of vast quantities of human data. These large general-purpose systems are increasingly being called *foundation models* or *base models* in the AI community—reflecting their role as broad platforms that can be adapted to many tasks. The term *frontier models* is also emerging to describe the most advanced and capable systems at the leading edge of development.

Increasingly, foundation models are typically being adapted for specific use cases through a process called *fine-tuning*, where the pre-trained model is further trained on a smaller, task-specific dataset. Here these models are truly foundational as layers are built on top of them, allowing organisations to specialise general-purpose systems for their particular needs.

Alongside this trend, a quieter but potentially very important direction is the continued rise of *domain-specific AI*. In this less publicised area, narrower systems are also achieving remarkable outcomes by focusing on tightly defined problems where the data is better curated, the concepts are more stable, and the results can be checked more rigorously.

DeepMind's AlphaFold, for example, revolutionised protein structure prediction. It was able to predict three-dimensional protein structures from amino acid sequences with accuracy comparable to experimental laboratory methods, solving a challenge that had occupied biological researchers for more than 50 years. What might have taken months or years of painstaking laboratory work per protein could now be accomplished in hours across hundreds of thousands of structures. We are likely to see more such systems emerge in fields such as medicine, chemistry, engineering, law, and logistics, where depth, precision, and verification may matter more than breadth alone.

Another important direction is the growing interest in *neuro-symbolic AI*. Neural networks have long borrowed loose inspiration from the human brain, while symbolic systems offered more explicit logic, rules, and structure. Neuro-symbolic approaches try to bring some of these strengths together, combining the pattern-recognition power and flexibility of neural systems with the clarity, reasoning, and compositional structure of more traditional symbolic methods.

The appeal is straightforward. Today's neural systems can be remarkably powerful, but they can also be opaque, hard to verify, and unreliable in tasks that demand consistent reasoning or explicit rule-following. A more hybrid approach may therefore prove useful in domains such as science, law, engineering, and medicine, where pattern recognition alone is not enough and where traceable reasoning still matters.

Alongside this, there is growing interest in *brain–computer interfaces*, such as Neuralink, which aim to create more direct links between minds and machines. In the near term, their most important uses may be medical, helping restore communication, movement, or independence to people with severe injuries or neurological conditions. But over time they may also raise deeper questions about privacy, agency, augmentation, and just how closely human cognition should be intertwined with digital systems.

At the more speculative edge of the current discussion sits *cognitive computing*. This is another term that borrows loosely from human language, and it should therefore be handled with some care. At its broadest, it points towards systems that do more than classify, predict, or generate—systems that can maintain context, reason across multiple steps, adapt to changing conditions, and operate in ways that feel more cognitively organised.

Whether this becomes a distinct technical path, a label applied to the convergence of several existing trends, or simply a marketing term remains to be seen. Even so, it reflects a wider ambition in AI research: not merely to make models bigger, but to make them more capable of sustained, structured, and useful thought-like behaviour, grounded less in metaphor and more in practical performance across complex tasks.

International Perspectives

Different countries and cultures bring different priorities to technology, and AI will be no exception. This is not new. Across history, societies have adopted and governed powerful technologies in ways that reflect their own institutions, values, economic interests, and political traditions. The future of AI is therefore unlikely to unfold as one single global story.

One useful way to think about this comes from Dame Wendy Hall and Kieron O'Hara's idea of the *Four Internets*. Their argument is that the internet did not evolve into one uniform global space, but into several overlapping models shaped by different centres of power and different assumptions about freedom, markets, rights, security, and state control. Something similar may happen with AI:

- In *Silicon Valley*, AI is likely to be shaped mainly by commercial innovation, speed, venture capital, and platform competition.
- In *Washington*, it is more likely to be viewed through the lenses of national power, strategic advantage, security, and geopolitical rivalry.
- In *Brussels*, the emphasis falls more heavily on regulation, privacy, individual rights, accountability, and the protection of citizens from harm.
- In *Beijing*, AI is more readily drawn into state planning, industrial strategy, surveillance, and social control.

Yet ordinary users will not necessarily experience these worlds as neatly separated. A person using AI in everyday life, for example, may rely on tools, platforms, devices, and services shaped by several of these traditions at once, often without any clear awareness of where the underlying models, rules, or assumptions originated.

These differences will affect not only how AI is built and deployed, but also what kinds of systems are permitted, what risks are tolerated, and whose interests are placed first. They may also create pressure to adopt systems developed within very different political or cultural settings simply because their capabilities are too useful, efficient, or economically significant to ignore. In that sense, AI may increasingly resemble a competitive race, with states and firms feeling compelled to keep up even when they are uneasy about the values, dependencies, or strategic consequences that come with adoption.

For all these reasons, we should be cautious about speaking of "the future of AI" as if it were singular. There may instead be several AI futures, emerging in parallel across different regions of the world, each reflecting a different balance between innovation, control, openness, safety, and power.

Even so, complete fragmentation would carry serious risks. Over time, there may be growing pressure for some degree of global harmonisation, especially around safety, accountability, security, and the use of AI in high-stakes domains. International institutions such as the UN may therefore have an important role to play in the pursuit of global governance of AI for the good of society, helping to establish shared principles and frameworks that protect human interests while enabling beneficial innovation across borders.

The AI Experience

How might we be using AI in the years ahead? For the moment, chatbots dominate the public experience of AI, but that is unlikely to remain the case indefinitely. Modes of interaction are notoriously difficult to predict, especially during periods of technological change. Even so, a number of trends are now beginning to come into focus:

Natural modes of communication: Future applications will rely on less rigid forms of interaction—traditional interfaces and web-forms will give way to natural modes of communication such as speech, images, and video. The sharp division between data modalities will gradually erode, with users moving seamlessly between words, pictures, and sound.

Moving beyond applications: Indeed, the very concept of an application will likely drift away. The notion of having different apps for different purposes will seem quaint to future users. Instead of opening one tool to write, another to search, and another to organise, users may increasingly define a desired outcome and let systems assemble the necessary tools and steps in the background.

Humanlike interactions and personas: As communication becomes more natural, an allied trend is inevitable: anthropomorphisation. Increasingly, we will encounter AIs with human-like personas, tone, and style, and even simulated emotional empathy. In some settings, especially at a distance, it may become less immediately obvious whether you are interacting with a person or an AI.

Hyper-personalised systems: Again drawing on emerging trends, we can predict that AIs will become more personal. They will develop a deeper understanding of us as individuals—our preferences, our needs, our lifestyles, our friends, our appointments, and more. As this knowledge deepens, users will enjoy more relevant outputs, smoother interactions, and AIs that anticipate their needs and feel increasingly companion-like.

More autonomy and flexibility: As AIs become more established, capable, and trusted, it is likely they will gain more autonomy and be allowed greater flexibility in achieving the goals we give them. Already we are seeing the emergence of agentic systems that act as our representatives and counterparts, helping to accomplish complex workflows or negotiate multistep tasks on our behalf. Alongside this we will see parallel advances in governance and permissions models to ensure appropriate boundaries and oversight.

Environment and context awareness: AI systems will increasingly draw on contextual signals from our surroundings—location, environment, activity, schedule, even subtle behavioural cues. Rather than operating in isolation, they will integrate information from devices, sensors, and ambient systems to offer timely, situationally relevant assistance. This will shift interactions from explicit commands to implicit understanding, with AIs responding to where we are, what we are doing, and what we are likely to need next.

Robots and embodied AI: As models become more grounded in the physical world, we will see a closer coupling between AI and robotics. Improvements in perception, planning, and manipulation will allow robots to move beyond controlled industrial environments and into more fluid, everyday settings. Domestic helpers, warehouse automation, and assistive healthcare robots will become increasingly viable. Language-based interfaces will act as a universal control layer, enabling people to instruct machines using ordinary conversation rather than specialised commands.

The future of AI will remain uncertain, and no set of predictions will ever be fully reliable. Even so, attempting to anticipate what might lie ahead is both wise and useful—it helps us prepare for emerging opportunities, guard against potential risks, and navigate the years to come with a clearer sense of direction.

Opportunities and Challenges

Our relationship with AI has only just begun. Despite its rich history, this is still a young technology. It will rapidly evolve and adapt in the coming years and decades, likely becoming not only extraordinarily useful, but also a source of significant new challenges in its own right.

Indispensable Intelligence

Humanity faces a number of profound challenges in the years ahead: climate change, energy sufficiency, food and water security, biodiversity loss, and others. As if this were not enough, the world is also entering a period of population decline, ageing demographics, and shrinking workforces.

We have faced challenges before and won through by employing a range of skills and resources—principal among these being science, technology, and innovation. We cannot yet be sure how we will build our future, but we can be certain that AI will play a crucial role.

A characteristic of the major challenges ahead is that they are *big-system* problems—multilayered, complex, interdependent issues that display chaotic behaviour and feedback loops. We will need to rely increasingly on complex computational models whose nature mirrors the complexity of the problem space.

Demographic shifts mean that we must also rely more on automation to sustain our social systems, with machines taking on roles beyond manufacturing and into areas traditionally associated with human capability, such as nursing and teaching.

The more we deploy AI into critical areas, the more carefully we may need to reconsider the constraints that currently hold it back, such as strict demands for explainability and tightly limited autonomy. To get the most out of this technology, we may sometimes need to grant it greater freedom to explore the problem domain and develop its own solutions, though this will require proportionate oversight and judgement. Requiring it to explain every nuance of its process in fully human terms may, in some cases, become a stumbling block to progress.

Part of the difficulty is that strict explanations are inherently harder to achieve in the data-driven approaches that now dominate AI. Earlier in the book, we charted the gradual transition from symbolic, rules-based AI to statistical, data-driven AI. We outlined the difference between deductive systems, which start with structure and place data *within it*, and inductive systems, which start with data and mine structure *from it*. This latter approach is remarkably effective at finding patterns and making predictions, but it often lacks the clear causal pathways and explicit reasoning steps that make traditional systems easy to explain. Increasingly, we will see this trade-off between explainability and capability play out with far greater impact in a wide range of areas. "AI-first medicine" will explore treatments by examining huge datasets and iterating through countless simulations—unlocking breakthroughs that might have taken decades through conventional research alone. "AI-first science" will do the same for physics, chemistry, cosmology, and more—potentially opening entirely new frontiers of understanding and revealing phenomena that have eluded human investigation for centuries.

This will require a cultural shift in many disciplines—traditionally built on the slow accumulation of knowledge from first principles, and the pursuit of consistent and elegant models. Instead, AIs may pluck answers from the chaos and present them as is. This might be more practical, but it will be less satisfying. Yet, if the new medicine works, does it matter?

Nonetheless, AI will be a vital tool for future generations—deployed intelligently and thoughtfully, it will help humanity progress through the turbulent challenges in the years ahead.

Transformational Impact

The impact of AI will be felt widely and deeply across many domains and sectors. It is not possible to enumerate all of these, so let us point to just three example areas where the impact is likely to be truly transformational—education, healthcare, and defence.

Education

Many of the educational models we use today grew out of institutional traditions established a few hundred years ago. The notion that students of roughly the same age, who happen to live close to one another, should gather in a classroom to be taught domain-specific knowledge by a teacher is so ingrained that we tend not to question it.

In fact, these systems are already under pressure post-COVID and will be under greater pressure as AI advances. We model education this way because it has historically been the most effective route to scaling teachers to students. But does this requirement still hold in the future?

What will be the impact of AI in teaching?

In principle, every student could have access to a personal tutor attuned to their progress, their strengths and weaknesses, and their preferred learning modality. For all but the wealthiest students, this could represent a significant levelling of opportunity.

But a teacher is not only a teacher—what about the pastoral aspects of their role? Teachers also mentor, guide, and safeguard their pupils. Can AI fulfil these functions too? In the future, do we separate pastoral care from instruction?

Education is not a solitary affair. Much of what students gain from school and university comes not only from instruction, but from learning alongside other people—through friendship, peer mentoring, debate, collaboration, and healthy competition. Just as important is the slow social process of encountering difference, misunderstanding, growth, and mutual understanding. If AI becomes more central to teaching, how will these shared and deeply human aspects of education be preserved?

Much of the way we teach students today is geared towards demonstrating memory and (hopefully) understanding in an end-of-year examination. But if AI can provide instant answers, is this still the best skillset to prioritise? Should teaching focus more on soft skills, problem-solving, argumentation, creativity, and critical thinking? Ironically, might this signal a return to an ancient, more Socratic curriculum?

It is too early to say precisely how education will adapt to AI-driven change. But it is not too early to say that the transformation will be deep, and that the pressures on learners, teachers, and institutions will make it unavoidable.

Healthcare

Healthcare systems worldwide are founded on models developed in the 19th and early 20th centuries. They were designed for populations that were younger, smaller, and afflicted by a narrower range of conditions than we face today. Yet the basic structure endures: A patient travels to a clinic or hospital, consults a doctor with limited time and imperfect information, and receives treatment shaped by professional judgement and available resources.

These systems are now under profound strain. Populations are ageing, chronic conditions are rising, and in many countries there are simply too few younger people entering the workforce to sustain an expanding demand for care. The core assumption that human clinicians must perform almost every cognitive and procedural task deserves fresh scrutiny.

What will be the impact of AI in healthcare?

Every patient could have a continuously updated, AI-driven health model that monitors their vital signs, detects anomalies early, and recommends personalised interventions. Diagnostics might be performed by systems that never tire and never overlook rare conditions. For many, this could amount to a level of equitable access far beyond anything previously imagined.

But clinicians do more than diagnose and prescribe—what about the human dimensions of care? Doctors and nurses comfort, counsel, and advocate for their patients. Can AI, or even robots, meaningfully provide these forms of support? Do we envisage a future in which the technical and emotional components of care are increasingly separated?

As robotics advance, will machines take on roles in eldercare, rehabilitation, and everyday assistance that once relied entirely on human staff? If a society has far fewer young people to look after its elderly, is the greater use of robotic caregivers a choice or a necessity? And if robots can safely lift, move, and monitor patients, how might this reshape hospitals, homes, and the wider care ecosystem?

Drug development and medical research may also transform. AI systems can explore biochemical spaces far beyond human capacity, proposing treatments that emerge from patterns too complex for traditional scientific methods. If AI-designed drugs prove effective, does it matter that their origins are not rooted in elegant theories but in large-scale computational exploration?

It is too early to say precisely how healthcare will adapt to AI-driven change. But it is not too early to say that the transformation will be deep, and that the pressures of demography and demand will make it unavoidable.

Defence

Modern defence systems are largely built on 20th-century assumptions: large standing armies, human-piloted aircraft, crews operating ships and armoured vehicles, and command structures that rely on human judgement at every stage. These models emerged from an era when nations could field vast numbers of young people and when technological cycles moved slowly enough for doctrines to stabilise.

But these assumptions are rapidly eroding. Many countries now face shrinking populations, ageing demographics, and insufficient younger citizens to sustain traditional defence forces. At the same time, AI is advancing at a pace that challenges long-held ideas about how militaries are organised and how conflicts unfold. If armed forces cannot be staffed at previous levels, what must be reimagined?

What will be the impact of AI in defence?

Surveillance and intelligence analysis can be performed continuously, at a scale no human organisation could match. Defensive systems may identify threats faster and respond more precisely. Low-cost AI-enabled drones and battlefield systems may also shift the balance of capability, placing persistence, coordination, and strike capacity into the hands of actors that once lacked them. Decision-support tools could help commanders navigate vast information spaces that previously overwhelmed human cognition. In a world with fewer personnel, autonomous systems may be required simply to maintain basic operational readiness.

Yet defence is not only a matter of capability—it is also a matter of ethics, judgement, and accountability. Soldiers and officers interpret intent, understand context, and make moral decisions under pressure. Whether AI, or autonomous platforms, can meaningfully replicate this remains doubtful.

If machines take on more operational roles, responsibility when things go wrong becomes harder to define, and the prospect of life-and-death decisions being increasingly mediated by algorithms raises profound moral questions.

As robotics advance, uncrewed systems may come to dominate land, sea, and air operations. If a nation cannot field large human crews, fleets of autonomous vehicles may become increasingly attractive. If machines can fight at speeds beyond human reaction times, the implications for deterrence, escalation, and geopolitical stability could be profound.

The development of AI-powered cyberattacks, defensive cyber tools, new operational strategies, and even weapons introduces further complexity. If AI proposes tactics or interventions that no human fully understands, armed forces may feel pressure to adopt them simply because they work. That, in turn, raises difficult questions about what "control" means in such an environment, and how adversaries can be prevented from doing the same.

It is too early to say precisely how defence will evolve as AI matures. But the combination of demographic pressures and accelerating technological capability suggests that change will be far-reaching, and that militaries may be transformed as profoundly as the conflicts they seek to deter.

The Price of Progress

While AI offers extraordinary possibilities, it also introduces a number of serious difficulties and challenges. In earlier eras, new technologies transformed society gradually, allowing institutions and cultures the time to adapt. For example, the Industrial Revolution played out over more than a hundred years. AI moves at a different pace. Its reach is wide, its adoption rapid, and its impacts often subtle in how they unfold.

We should not indulge in pessimism, but it is important to anticipate the risks clearly and prepare for them intelligently. The best outcomes are built not on fear, but on foresight. With that in mind, let's enumerate (in no particular order) some of the most pressing areas where care and vigilance will be essential:

Misinformation and deepfakes: AI makes it simple to create convincing fabrications—fake videos, synthetic audio, manipulated images, and entirely invented text—far more rapidly and cheaply than ever before. Deliberate deception becomes easier to produce and harder to detect. This places strain on institutions that rely on verifiable evidence: journalism, the courts, elections, and public health. The challenge is not merely spotting individual falsehoods, but maintaining trust in shared reality when fabrication becomes trivially easy.

Dilution of reliable information: Beyond deliberate falsehood lies a different problem: the sheer volume of machine-generated content now flooding the information ecosystem. When vast quantities of synthetic material—however plausible—bury carefully researched sources, serious inquiry becomes harder. The difficulty is not only distinguishing truth from lies, but finding signal amid overwhelming noise. When people can no longer easily tell what was authored through expertise or verified routes, confidence in evidence itself begins to weaken, and public debate, education, and democratic decision-making all become harder to sustain.

Economic disruption: As with every major technological shift, the benefits of AI will not be distributed evenly. Some industries may undergo rapid transformation, while others experience turbulence or decline. Workers in certain sectors may face displacement unless adequate support, retraining, and new pathways are created. The disruption is not an inevitable catastrophe, but it does require deliberate policy and thoughtful planning to ensure that the burden of change does not fall unfairly on particular groups.

Environmental and resource impact: Training and running large-scale AI systems requires vast amounts of compute, electricity, cooling, water, and physical hardware, all of which carry environmental and geopolitical costs. As adoption grows, these hidden demands may place increasing pressure on energy systems, supply chains, and natural resources. If AI is to contribute meaningfully to a better future, its material footprint will need to be measured carefully and managed responsibly.

Dependency and de-skilling: As AI systems take on more cognitive labour—writing, planning, navigating, researching—there is a risk that people gradually lose proficiency in everyday skills. Dependence on automated help may make life easier in the short term, but over time it can contribute to a broader erosion of skills, weakening the resilience and adaptability that come from active engagement. Learning to find a healthier balance between what machines do and what we continue to do for ourselves will be crucial.

Bias and fairness: AI models inherit patterns from the data on which they are trained. When that data reflects historical inequalities or social prejudices, the resulting outputs can reflect, reproduce, or amplify them. This can show up in subtle ways—from skewed decision-making to uneven performance across demographic groups. Ensuring fairness requires constant monitoring, rigorous evaluation, and a willingness to intervene when the underlying data or model behaviour starts to shift in problematic ways.

Concentration of power: The resources required to build, deploy and, operate cutting-edge AI systems—compute, data, expertise—are increasingly held by a small number of corporations and nation-states. This concentration risks creating imbalances in economic influence, political leverage, and cultural impact. When a handful of entities shape the tools that mediate how we all learn, work, and communicate, questions of accountability and democratic oversight become paramount.

Autonomy and oversight: As AI systems are granted more autonomy to carry out tasks on our behalf, they will inevitably face situations that are ambiguous, poorly defined, and perhaps even high-stakes. Even without science-fiction scenarios, there are real risks that a misinterpreted instruction, a flawed assumption, or an edge case could lead to unintended consequences—whether financial errors, misallocations of resources, or even safety-related incidents. Maintaining appropriate human oversight remains a critical safeguard.

Erosion of human relations and growth: As AI systems become ever more responsive, personalised, and agreeable, many people may find them easier to interact with than other humans. Machines that never criticise, never misunderstand, and never push back can become an appealing refuge, offering companionship without friction. Yet growth often depends on precisely the opposite: being challenged, questioned, and exposed to perspectives that differ from our own. If AI becomes the default channel for interaction, there is a risk that we retreat into worlds shaped entirely around our preferences, losing the discomfort that helps us learn and grow.

None of these challenges is inevitable, and none is insurmountable. What they share is the need for deliberate attention, thoughtful design, and a willingness to adapt as understanding deepens. The risks are real, but so too are the tools and institutions we have to address them. The path forward lies not in avoidance, but in clear-eyed engagement.

Choosing the Future We Want

As AI becomes increasingly embedded in the rhythms of daily life, mindful use will be essential. This is not simply a matter of individual caution, but of recognising that AI is now woven into the systems that inform, guide, and support our choices. The technology offers extraordinary benefits, but only if we remain conscious of how and where it is applied, and alert to the ways it can shape our behaviour and expectations.

Striking the right balance between citizens, governments, and the companies that create these systems will become one of the defining tasks of the coming decade. Mindful use alone, however, is not enough …

We are currently in a phase of international competition, with states and firms racing to secure advantage through AI capability. That is unlikely to disappear, but in time it must give way, at least on core safety questions, to a greater degree of international alignment. In other high-stakes domains such as aviation and nuclear safety, rivalry did not remove the need for shared rules, common protocols, and trusted institutions. AI will require the same. If systems are to be deployed safely across borders, there will need to be growing agreement on standards for transparency, testing, accountability, and the responsible use of intelligent systems.

That will place renewed importance on global institutions. The United Nations, international standards bodies, and similar forums may have an important role in building common guardrails, coordinating responses to cross-border risks, and helping states cooperate even where their wider interests diverge. They may also provide the setting in which shared goals, shared motivations, and shared expectations around safety can be expressed clearly and turned into practical norms.

Crucially, the burden of responsibility cannot rest solely on individuals or public institutions. The companies that build, deploy, and operate AI systems must also be expected to uphold high standards of quality, security, and ethical design. Meaningful oversight, independent auditing, and mechanisms for redress will all play important roles in ensuring that the incentives of the technology industry align with the wellbeing of the societies they serve.

If we approach AI with care, insight, and a willingness to learn from past technological transitions, there is good reason for confidence. The future of AI is shaped by the choices we make today. Used wisely, AI can extend human capability, sharpen our understanding, and help us confront problems that would otherwise overwhelm our institutions and resources.

The path forward lies not in avoidance, but in clear-eyed engagement. All of us need to understand what AI is and what it isn't … what it's good at and what it struggles with … what we want it to do for us and what we want to keep for ourselves. Only then can we engage in debates about application, regulation, and governance with confidence, helping to realise a future where AI plays an important role in our lives for the good of us all.

Index

Note: Page numbers in *italics* refer to figures.